Southern Baptists and Muslims

Southern Baptists and Muslims

A Path to Dialogue through Narrative Empathy

CHARLES W. POWELL

Foreword by Mae Elise Cannon

WIPF & STOCK · Eugene, Oregon

SOUTHERN BAPTISTS AND MUSLIMS
A Path to Dialogue through Narrative Empathy

Copyright © 2024 Charles W. Powell. All rights reserved. Except for brief quotations in critical publications or reviews, no part of this book may be reproduced in any manner without prior written permission from the publisher. Write: Permissions, Wipf and Stock Publishers, 199 W. 8th Ave., Suite 3, Eugene, OR 97401.

Wipf & Stock
An Imprint of Wipf and Stock Publishers
199 W. 8th Ave., Suite 3
Eugene, OR 97401

www.wipfandstock.com

PAPERBACK ISBN: 979-8-3852-1250-7
HARDCOVER ISBN: 979-8-3852-1251-4
EBOOK ISBN: 979-8-3852-1252-1

08/06/24

For my daughters, Scarlett Sophia and Saskia Emilia, and for Emilia.

Contents

Foreword by Mae Elise Cannon | ix

Preface | xiii

Acknowledgments | xv

1. Introduction | 1
2. What Is Going On: Southern Baptists—A Narrative Vacuum | 17
3. Why Is It Going On: The Reality of Anti-Muslim Rhetoric in the Southern Baptist Denomination | 69
4. What Should Be Going On: Returning to the Sources of Islam | 108
5. What Do We Do about It: The Much Needed Reflective Conversation | 158
6. Conclusion | 185

Appendix 1: "I think Islam hates us": A Timeline of Trump's comments about Islam and Muslims | 195

Appendix 2: The Baptist Faith and Message 2000 | 203

Appendix 3: Executive Summary of Open Letter to al-Baghdadi | 213

Bibliography | 215

Foreword

I AM DEEPLY INDEBTED to the Southern Baptists as I came to faith in Christ Jesus at First Baptist Church of Calvert County, Maryland, as an elementary school student. A neighbor had invited me to their weekly AWANA program that taught children the fundamental principles of the Bible and the commandments to love God, love our neighbor, and also love our enemy. To this day, I hold in my heart and mind many of the Bible verses I memorized on summer nights in the basement of that Southern Baptist congregation.

The Gospel clearly teaches us how we need the redemptive power of Jesus and faith in His death on the cross to be forgiven of our sins and to be made whole again through the transforming nature of the Holy Spirit at work within us. The Scriptures say, "All have sinned and fallen short of the glory of God" (Romans 3:23), but as we receive Christ, we are forgiven and "transformed into the same image" that comes from the "Lord who is the Spirit" (1 Corinthians 3:18).

All of us, as members of the body of Christ, have things we believe and ways that we act that are remnants of our sinful nature and not yet fully in accordance with the nature of God. The Apostle Paul speaks about this struggle as he said in Romans 7:23: "I see another law at work in me, waging war against the law of my mind and making me a prisoner of the law of sin at work within me." We must be willing to do the work of "waging war" against the sin that remains within us as people and communities who are a part of the body of Christ.

Dr. Charles W. Powell invites us into this journey of transformation, forgiveness, and healing as he seeks to uncover the Southern Baptist denomination's "preconceived biases and misunderstandings of Islam." Not only for the sake of constructive dialogue and collaboration, but also so that members of the body of Christ can better love and serve like Jesus. The love of God extended to communities outside of the Christian faith, particularly followers of Islam, serves as an invitation for people to know the powerful witness of the disciples of Christ (John 13:35).

Read Powell's quest for narrative empathy with an open heart and mind, praying that God might give eyes to see and ears to hear (Proverbs 20:12) as he does not enter into this endeavor lightly. His commentary and observations often include profound indictments and painful truths. But Powell writes with courage and a prophetic voice—calling the church to be better, to do better, and to follow the commandments of God more holistically rather than through the limited lens clouded by American nationalism and Western biases.

Powell writes about the history and current realities of the Southern Baptist Convention's engagement with Islam with the primary goal of offering an invitation to embrace narrative empathy, better understand Islam and the motivations of practices of Muslims, and create a space for collaboration across Christian and Muslim divides. This book serves as a practical manual seeking to answer the question, "How can we do better?" at not ostracizing Muslims because of a lack of understanding or political fervency. How can we do better to truly live out the Gospel of Christ across the divisions of faith between Christians, particularly Southern Baptists, and Muslims?

I have had the privilege and, at times, challenge of speaking all over the country, mostly at churches, but sometimes at mosques and synagogues, about realities affecting the Christian community in the Middle East. On one of these tours, I was traveling with an Arab Christian and a very well-known leader from an evangelical megachurch. We had an event at a several-thousand-person church in Southern California where one of the pastors attending our presentation asked the question, "How can we be faithful to God and not support the wars against Muslims in the Middle East?" I'm paraphrasing some, but the essential nature of this pastor's question was that God is against Islam. Islam supported 9/11 and the death of Americans. And so, according to his logic, Christians must support US wars in the Middle East for the purpose of "eradicating Islam."

To this day, I will never forget the response of the Christian from Bethlehem who was seated beside me. A Palestinian Christian, he took a deep breath—and the room was silent in anticipation. He put his hand on his heart and, in the most loving tone of comfort and understanding, said, "I hear your anxiety. And I am speaking to myself now as much as I am speaking to you. . ." He paused and then continued, "When I read the Scriptures, and I see the teachings of Jesus, I can't help but come to believe that God wants us to *love* Muslims, not to *kill them*."

I wish I could say after that event that we had "won the day" and that the people in the room were moved by deep empathy and love for Muslims. It was one of the most criticized events where I've ever spoken, and yet I challenge you—and Charles Powell challenges you here—to ask the question, "How would God have us respond to our Muslim neighbors?" This book provides some amazing practical tools to wrestle with practical theology as applied to the relationship between Christians and Muslims. I am grateful for the courage and witness of Dr. Powell in his research and writing of this text. I truly hope it will serve the church and, ultimately, God, with the goal of seeking to become more like Christ and manifesting a living expression of the kingdom of God here on earth.

But when it comes down to it, don't listen to me or Dr. Powell (with all due respect!), but instead listen to God. My hope and prayer: Might God move your hearts—and my heart—together to better live out the Gospel, to exemplify the love of Christ across all divides, and to be motivated by empathy and love as we respond to our Muslim neighbors.

As war rages in parts of the Middle East from Israel to Gaza, to the Houthis in Yemen, to other pockets of violence throughout the Arab world, this message of love and an invitation to collaboration toward a better world has never been more needed. We need all to come to the table, letting go of the sin that hinders us and so easily entangles and instead engaging with perseverance the race that God marked out for us (Hebrews 12:1)—working toward peace, reconciliation, safety, and security, and self-determination and freedom for all.

Rev. Dr. Mae Elise Cannon
Washington, DC
February 15, 2024

Preface

THE SOUTHERN BAPTIST DENOMINATION, founded in 1845, is the largest evangelical Protestant religious group in the United States. Since the terrorist attacks of 9/11 there has been an increase of negative rhetoric among many Southern Baptists towards Muslims. I have discovered a pathway that can promote healthy relationships and cooperation between the two faith traditions. Consequently, I ask to what extent a *lack of* narrative empathy towards Muslims can be altered in the life of the Southern Baptist leader. Such transformation can enable the local pastor, and the denomination, to better understand and communicate the teachings of the Prophet Muhammad. Teachings that I have found embody spiritual discipline and peaceful living—a discipline and way of life that indeed promote the common good. The theoretical framework and in-depth qualitative interviews I set forth in this book provide invaluable insights into the dynamics and use of anti-Islamic rhetoric among Southern Baptists. I propose concrete strategies of action such as strategic personal encounters between Southern Baptists and Muslims. Personal encounters, when combined with a better understanding of Islam can help uncover the Southern Baptist denominations' preconceived biases and misunderstandings of Islam that so often hinder constructive dialogue and collaboration. Moreover, a thorough understanding of Islam can help the Southern Baptist better understand and appreciate his or her own religion. This book has crucial practical implications that can foster a path to dialogue between Southern Baptists and Muslims, which, in my judgment, has not yet received the scholarly attention it deserves.

Acknowledgments

I DEDICATE MY BOOK to the Southern Baptist pastors and teachers of my youth and young adulthood of whom introduced me to the Christian faith. Moreover, instilled within me a passion for communicating the good news of Christ to the world in meaningful and palpable ways. My mother, Rose Daniels and stepfather, Paul Jones who took me to church every Sunday and Wednesday and fostered my personal relationship with Christ. Warm gratitude to my professors at the Florida Baptist Theological College, New Orleans Baptist Theological Seminary, Luther Rice Seminary, and Catholic Theological Union, all of whom significantly shaped my Christian worldview. Lastly, to my wife Emilia and my daughters Scarlett and Saskia: Emilia who encouraged me to stay the course, listened to my thoughts, and provided helpful feedback along every stretch of the journey. Scarlett and Saskia who provided me with laughter and love along the way.

When I was actively pastoring in the Southern Baptist denomination, I had the pleasure of providing pastoral instruction and care to thousands of congregants both in the church and the many people listening to my sermons and inspirational messages on the radio. Sometimes I got it right and sometimes I got it wrong, nonetheless they graciously entrusted me with the privilege and responsibility of preaching and teaching from the Bible. My hope is that this book will inspire my dearly beloved Southern Baptist family and greater evangelical community to engage in inter-religious dialogue with Muslims; a dialogue that can foster good and worthwhile relationships that advance understanding, trust, and collaboration between the two faiths.

1

Introduction

"Men often hate each other because they fear each other; they fear each other because they don't know each other; they don't know each other because they cannot communicate; and they cannot communicate because they are separated."
—Dr. Martin Luther King Jr.

A Specific Concern and Missional Opportunity for Southern Baptists

The Southern Baptist denomination has come under scrutiny for fostering an atmosphere of intolerance towards Islam. This intolerance of Islam is most clearly observed in the sermons preached and literature published by pastors and spiritual leaders throughout the denomination. To take but one example, apologist and author Dr. Alex McFarland has stated:

> Satan is real. And Satan's intent is to destroy the human race. Sin exists, and there are things of this world that are objectively evil. The Muslim world may believe what they live, but in reality, they are bound in sin, evil and Satanic delusion. All of the liberal, politically correct, pluralistic "spin" cannot change the dark nature

of Islam. The longer American pulpits are silent on this—and the longer that U.S. leaders coddle Islam—the more lives will be lost and the greater the likelihood that Islam will continue to undermine American security. Our leaders must recognize the truth about Islam, and preachers need to lead the way in calling their people to know the truth about Islam, pray for world peace and pray for the conversion of Muslims.[1]

I want to explore why there is such intolerance in the Southern Baptist denomination towards Islam and its adherents and reflect upon ways that can foster meaningful dialogue—dialogue that articulates the message of Christ, that bids us to love friend and stranger alike. Charles F. Stanley, former two-term president of the Southern Baptist Convention writes,

> Jesus commanded His followers to love their enemies. He understood that believers would come in direct contact with people who wanted to oppress them and make their lives impossible. . . . Whether you are dealing with non-Christians or backslidden believers, the same is true—they need Jesus and they need you to reveal Him to them. Friend, you cannot change them, but you can control your reaction to them. . . . As Christ's representative, you are responsible for how you respond. Therefore, don't give others a reason to criticize you. Rather, obey Him, do good, and show His love. Because by so doing, you show them the way to eternal life.[2]

According to the Gospel of Luke, Jesus commanded His followers, "Love your enemies, do good to them that hate you" (Luke 6.27). To be a Christian is to follow the teachings of Christ; what is more, it is to try to fulfill both the letter and the spirit of the Law—love. The Synoptic Gospels and John narrate that love and truth emanated from Christ. This love for humanity and truth that came from Christ is the foundation of Christianity. Billions of lives have been transformed by His teachings. As a professor of Muslim-Christian dialogue and multifaith engagement, as well as a former pastor within the Southern Baptist denomination, I have come to view as a significant part of my spiritual formation the need to empathize with "the religious other" while being faithful to my own religious beliefs.

Certainly, there are many social problems in the United States that continue to deserve our attention, such as poverty, systemic racism,

---

1. Creech, "There, I Said It."
2. Stanley, *Every Day in His Presence.*

climate change, immigration, and the healthcare and education systems. But in recent years one concern has risen to the top of the list, the negative perception of Islam and distrust in Muslims by many non-Muslim Americans. Muslims have worked and attended school with non-Muslims for centuries in North America. Moreover, they have peacefully gathered in their houses and places of worship. Muslims came to these shores as early as the sixteenth century, though usually not of their own accord. However, it was not until the terrorist attacks of 9/11 that a majority of non-Muslim Americans gave considerable attention to the influx of Muslims immigrating into the United States from regions of the world such as the Middle East and North Africa. For many non-Muslim Americans, the attacks on 9/11 formed and framed their first impression of Islam and it was not good. Growing up in the rural South, I had never met a Muslim. In college and seminary, I had been introduced to the basic beliefs of Islam, but the major news outlets on 9/11 presented me with information about Islam and graphic images of Muslims attacking and shouting inflammatory words at the United States that really framed my immediate thinking. I had been preconditioned to believe that Muslims were anti-Christ, thus anti-Christian, and the events that unfolded on 9/11 seemed to reinforce that conditioning. I argue throughout this book that the horrific events experienced by thousands and seen by millions of people throughout the United States empowered an unfair bias against Islam and Muslims. When the attacks on 9/11 occurred, Islam was a religion of nearly 1.8 billion world-wide with 2.5 million Muslims living in the United States. As of 2018, there were nearly 3.5 million Muslims living in the United States, still only comprising less than one percent of the population.[3] Current trends suggest that the Muslim population in the United States will double by the year 2050—projected to reach 8.1 million. In the United States, the attacks that occurred on 9/11 forced an unprecedented political and religious conversation, from Main Street to Pennsylvania Avenue, exposing Islam and its adherents to public scrutiny and anger. Consequently, many Christians, myself included, were challenged in extraordinary ways to practice their faith—a faith that generally embodies love for God, family, friends, strangers, and even enemies—towards Muslims. Naturally, the different segments of the Christian population responded differently to these attacks. Responses ranged from Christians shouting inflammatory words of anger at Muslims and tearing hijabs

---

3. Muhamed, "New Estimates Show."

from Muslim women's heads, to providing help and counseling. Some chose, knowingly or not, to feed the anger, fear, and insecurity felt by many non-Muslim Americans by creating an "us against them" mentality, thereby limiting the capacity of many to engage with the perceived enemy in a way that was constructive.

By and large, non-Muslim citizens of the United States became at once the progenitors and the beneficiaries of a biased narrative—a narrative that portrayed Islam in a negative way and fueled the false notion that all Muslims are alike. This narrative quickly defined the perceived enemy, and soon took root among the broader populace. It also exacerbated the "us against them" mentality that has existed off and on between Christians and Muslims since the rise and spread of Islam in the seventh century. In the chaotic aftermath of 9/11, many non-Muslim Americans felt threatened by Islam. Muslims who had been living peaceably in the United States, some with family lineages dating back four hundred years, were thrust into the arena of negative public opinion. Because of their faith, school children were bullied, workers were fired from their jobs, Muslim men were accused of being home-grown terrorists, young men and women were denied job opportunities because of their facial features and skin color, some were denied U.S. citizenship, and families in the United States were unable to unite with relatives living across the ocean. Feelings of fear, anger, and insecurity gripped many non-Muslims throughout the country. This tidal wave of destructive emotional reactions hit the Christian Church fast and hard and put pressure on it to respond. Christian denominations, Catholic and Protestant, within the United States were challenged with the task of offering a reasonable and timely response to the terror witnessed. Consequently, millions of evangelical Christians looked to the largest Protestant denomination in the United States—Southern Baptists—to see how they would respond to the attacks.

To offer a bit of history, since the resurrection of Jesus the Church has by and large embraced the Great Commission given by Him to his disciples to go forth and to make disciples of all nations, baptizing them in the name of the Father, and of the Son, and of the Holy Spirit, and teaching them to obey everything that He commanded.[4] Faithfulness to this commission is evident in the Southern Baptist denomination. Since the formation of the Southern Baptist Convention in 1845, thousands of

---

4. Matthew 28:18–20 (NRSV).

missionaries have been commissioned to evangelize the nations. Many of these missionaries have been appointed to Muslim-majority countries with the intent to evangelize and transform the spiritual lives of individuals, families, and even communities by sharing with them what they believe to be the Christian worldview rooted in both Old and New Testament teachings, teachings that are entrenched in the Great Commission and article XII of the Baptist Faith and Message.[5] Currently, with the influx of Muslims immigrating to America—some to escape religious persecution, famine, and war, or seeking prosperity through education and employment—Southern Baptists have the opportunity to welcome the culturally and ethnically diverse people of Islam to the United States. It is an opportunity for Southern Baptists to partially fulfill their missional goal by being the life of Christ to a religious group that has historically held Jesus, the son of Mary, in high esteem. For example, in the Qur'an, Surah 2:253 states, "We favored some of these messengers above others. God spoke to some; others He raised in rank; We gave Jesus, son of Mary, Our clear signs and strengthened him with the holy spirit."[6]

Like other religious groups within the United States, the Southern Baptist denomination was taken aback by the events of 9/11. The spiritual stamina of the denomination was tested in unprecedented ways. In the aftermath of 9/11, the Southern Baptist Convention, along with many of its partnering churches, was criticized for its use of anti-Muslim rhetoric, coming especially from the denomination's leaders.[7] This has been an alarming trend, inadvertently causing many Christians to deny Muslims entrance into their community circles, only furthering the divide. I purposefully use the word "inadvertently" because most Southern Baptists that I know understand that the teachings of Christ promote wholehearted love of God and love of neighbor. After all, Jesus was a Jew who carried on conversations with non-Jews and social outcasts. Interestingly, from my conversations, interviews, and personal knowledge of the Southern Baptist denomination, I have learned that most Southern Baptists do not personally know a single Muslim. This lack of encounter has created a deficiency of narrative empathy, that is the ability for one to share in and perceive the world from another's point of view. I propose that this lack of narrative empathy is the primary reason behind the anti-Muslim rhetoric and the negative perceptions of Muslims within

5. Hobbs, *Baptist Faith and Message*, 106.
6. The Cow 2:253 (The Qur'an, trans. Abdel Haleem).
7. Hoover, "Is Evangelicalism Itching for a Fight?"

the Southern Baptist denomination. In the next chapter I show that anti-Muslim rhetoric and negative perceptions of Islam are widespread in the Southern Baptist denomination. Indeed, the purpose of my book is to shape an improved, if not *new*, perception of Islam, the Prophet Muhammad, and jihad via the lens of narrative empathy. I elaborate this new perception in chapter 3, where I also define narrative empathy and offer reasons why Southern Baptist leaders should consider it a valid topic. In chapter 4 I set forth some teachings of Islam that are widely accepted by the majority of Muslims, specifically, teachings on the spirituality of the Prophet Muhammad and on jihad, warfare, and marriage. Finally, in chapter 5, I demonstrate that personally knowing a Muslim and having a more thorough understanding of what the majority of Islamic scholars agree upon can promote constructive dialogue and neighborliness. Coincidentally, as Southern Baptist leaders encounter Muslims and develop a better understanding of Islam, narrative empathy will be fostered.

Since the Iran hostage crisis (1979–1981), Islam has received heightened publicity (at least in the United States and Europe)—most of it negative. The emergence of militant Islamic extremist movements in the Middle East (Iraq, Iran, Afghanistan, Syria, etc.) has caused great unrest among Christians and Muslims worldwide. (It should be borne in mind that the majority of Muslims live outside the Middle East, with 62 percent of the global Muslim population inhabiting the Asia-Pacific region.) The terrorist attacks of 9/11 exacerbated the emotions of anger, fear, and insecurity already present within the country. When you combine the emotions of anger, fear, and insecurity with the lack of narrative and knowledge regarding Muslims and Islam, then pandemonium materializes. In that moment, many Southern Baptist pastors, though well educated in theology and the history of Christianity, were not well versed in the Islamic tradition. And yet, despite this lack of knowledge, they sought to address the teachings of Islam and the perceived threat posed by some of its adherents. As a result, some Baptist leaders consciously made it a priority to relieve fears and misunderstandings by speaking knowledgeably about the Muslim faith—perhaps some knowledge already possessed or a quick yet objective study of the basic beliefs. Others, however, still processing their own emotions after the attacks and with little or no knowledge of Islam, inadvertently stirred up negative emotions, preexisting biases, and misunderstandings among their audiences; they fed the Islamophobic industry. This biased narrative was perpetuated and quickly spread throughout the denomination, thus further intensifying the "us against them" mentality. Below I set forth the methodology I use to help alleviate this enormous problem.

Practical Theological Method to Bring about Desired Change

In her seminar "Foundations and Methods for the Study of Spirituality" Catholic Theological Union professor Mary Frohlich has emphasized three primary reasons out of seven why the study of spirituality is important. First, it enables humans to move from being participants and "consumers" of spirituality to being "scholars" of spirituality. Second, and equally important, is the learned ability to discuss issues involved in defining what the term "spirituality" itself means in a variety of contexts. Third, the study of spirituality equips one to analyze spiritual experiences and texts from the points of view of horizon, genre, narrative construction, tradition, and so forth. I agree with Frohlich's emphasis and use these three ideas throughout this book, especially in chapters 4 and 5.

I also make use of the methodology proposed by Princeton Theological Seminary professor Richard Osmer, which I have found to be the most useful method for describing patterns of behavior. Osmer proposes four tasks of practical theology: descriptive-empirical, interpretive-empirical, normative, and pragmatic.[8] I deploy these four tasks to explain why there is such widespread use of anti-Muslim rhetoric within the Southern Baptist denomination. This method also enables me to propose a wholesome interpretation of the life and teachings of Muhammad, as seen in his lived spirituality, and, finally, to propose concrete strategies of action to alleviate much of the anti-Muslim bias within the Southern Baptist denomination. In sum, I employ Osmer's four tasks of practical theological interpretation to make sense of anti-Muslim hostility and to offer practical steps for furthering a dialogue of respect and camaraderie between Southern Baptists and Muslims.

I begin, in chapter 2, with the analysis of a substantive issue-area within Islam: Muhammad's lived spirituality. I explore some misconceptions common among Southern Baptists, which I have gathered over the course of more than twenty years of ministry-related work. I use Osmer's *descriptive-empirical* task to describe "what is going on" within the Southern Baptist denomination with regard to its teachings on the

---

8. Osmer, *Practical Theology*, 4.

Prophet Muhammad and on jihad. I bring together information on these misconceptions to discern "patterns and dynamics in particular episodes, situations, or contexts."[9] For my purposes, these "episodes, situations, and contexts" are the life, teachings, and lived spirituality of the Prophet Muhammad. I provide systematic evidence such as citations from scholarly sources, news articles, and radio programs, as well as sermons of the Southern Baptist leaders (often available on YouTube or churches' official websites). I also rely extensively on insights from in-depth qualitative interviews I conducted with Southern Baptist pastors. The leaders interviewed represent churches ranging in size from one hundred to over three thousand active members and embody intergenerational pastoral leadership styles and experiences. They provide significant insight into why common patterns and dynamics are occurring in the denomination.

In chapter 3, I use Osmer's *interpretive-empirical* task to set forth what I take to be the issues surrounding many misunderstandings Southern Baptists have of Islam. I draw on "theories of the arts and sciences to better understand and explain why these patterns and dynamics are occurring."[10] The theories that I rely on, rooted in sociology and political science, help me explain why there is widespread anti-Muslim rhetoric being communicated throughout the Southern Baptist denomination. As in the preceding chapter, I make use of my interviews with Southern Baptist pastors.

In chapter 4, I focus on "what should be going on." Here I employ Osmer's *normative* task: "to interpret particular episodes, situations, and contexts, constructing ethical norms to guide our responses, and learning from 'good practice.'"[11] Specifically, I return to the sources of Islam in order to obtain a historical critical narrative. I elaborate on the widely accepted view, as understood by Islamic scholars, of the lived spirituality of the Prophet Muhammad, paying special attention to the concept, meaning, and interpretation of jihad. In accordance with the normative task, I put forth an interpretation of Muhammad's character that is grounded in the religious and contemporary ethical norms of Islam, norms that promote respect and cooperation between the world's two largest religions—Christianity and Islam.

Finally, in chapter 5, I employ Osmer's *pragmatic* task to propose concrete strategies of action that, if undertaken by leaders in the Southern

---

9. Osmer, *Practical Theology*, 4.
10. Osmer, *Practical Theology*, 4.
11. Osmer, *Practical Theology*, 4.

Baptist denomination, may increase their knowledge and understanding of Muhammad's life and teachings. I indicate how Southern Baptist leaders can respond to members' concerns about frequently misunderstood tenets of Islam.

In the words of Osmer, "these four tasks constitute the basic structure of practical theological interpretation."[12] The implications of my research are important: the awareness of shared values and beliefs between Muslims and the Southern Baptist denomination in the United States can encourage interreligious dialogue. Incidentally, interreligious dialogue can promote love for neighbor and stranger—a love that eclipses hatred and is at the center of Christian living. This dialogue can build bridges of understanding, trust, and collaboration.

Christianity and Islam are monotheistic religions that share common origins, values, and theological views believed to have been passed down from God through His prophets. An awareness of and appreciation for these commonalities can foster an atmosphere of respect and cooperation between Southern Baptists and Muslims. Such an appreciation promises to reduce religious bigotry and violence in communities throughout the United States. By exploring the lived spirituality of the Prophet Muhammad, I open the possibility of uncovering the biases and misunderstandings that afflict so many Americans, especially those within the Southern Baptist community. I propose that if Southern Baptist leaders will purposefully seek to develop relationships with Muslims, combined with a more thorough knowledge of Islam and the lived spirituality of the Prophet Muhammad, these actions will promote increased neighborliness and cooperation between Southern Baptists and Muslims. To this end, I expect to accomplish the following goals in this book:

1. *Describe* the negative rhetoric, misunderstandings, and misinterpretations of Islam—especially as they relate to the life and teachings of the Prophet Muhammad and the concept of jihad—held by many leaders in the Southern Baptist denomination.

2. *Explain* why the Southern Baptist denomination by and large lacks narrative empathy concerning Muslims and uses inflammatory language towards the Prophet Muhammad and Islam.

---

12. Osmer, *Practical Theology*, 4.

3. *Provide* a more scholarly, hence more objective, rendering of the life and teachings of the Prophet Muhammad and his understanding and reasons for jihad.

4. *Propose* concrete strategies of action that Southern Baptist leaders can take that will foster narrative empathy and improve their understanding of Islam and their prospects for collaboration with Muslims.

Biographical Background

In order to promote neighborliness and cooperation between Southern Baptists and Muslims, I ask: To what extent can a lack of narrative empathy (feelings for people in a different social group, in this case Muslims) be altered in the life of the Southern Baptist leader, thus enabling that leader to understand and communicate the life and the teachings of the Prophet Muhammad and the concept of jihad as embodiments of spiritual discipline and peaceful living? This idea is very radical to many Christians. Consequently, this research has important practical implications.

My personal experiences have largely motivated my research presented in this book. As a young adult, I had no significant comprehension of Islam, and had never encountered a Muslim. The bit of knowledge I had about Islam was taught to me in the Southern Baptist Church. Preachers and teachers alike taught me that Islam was indeed a foreign and diabolical religion that threatened our very core of life—a life which, according to many Southern Baptists, is to be based solely on the tenets of the Bible. My Protestant and deeply religious upbringing greatly influenced my career path. As a young adult in preparation for pastoral ministry, I enrolled at the Florida Baptist Theological College, now Baptist College of Florida, and began my pursuit of studying the transcendent God of my childhood faith.

While attending several Southern Baptist theological institutions and eventually earning my Master of Divinity degree, not once did I hear a positive statement about Islam from professors, pastoral colleagues, family, and friends. I heard from peers, spiritual leaders, and laity how anti-Christ and anti-Christian the Muslims are. Moreover, there was (and still is) a widespread perception that the chief goal of the *umma*, or Muslim community, is world domination, by way of force, e.g., jihad, if need be. My spiritual leaders and colleagues taught that the Prophet Muhammad's message was anti-Christ and that he furthered his cause against non-Muslims through an aggressive measure called jihad. Incidentally, the violence that often erupted between Christians and Muslims in the 10/40 Window did not help to improve my perception of Muslims. I recall hearing stories (some of them horrific) of missionaries from the region called the 10/40 Window speaking to efforts being made to evangelize the Muslims. Incidentally, Professor Melani McAlister, who teaches at George Washington University, has written extensively about the 10/40 Window. McAlister writes, "the 10/40 Window was a map of (missionary) opportunity; in practice, it was also a work of political and moral geography. It claimed to show the 'enslaved' and unreached nations of the world, many of which would be marked as persecutors of Christians."[13] As a pastor, I sat through many pastoral lunches listening to colleagues and prominent spiritual leaders of the Southern Baptist denomination express distrust and even hatred towards Muslims. One evening over dinner, my wife and I engaged in dialogue with a good pastor friend of ours, the associational director for over 130 Southern Baptist churches, regarding the influence and spread of Islam in Western Europe and North America. His words concerned me and horrified my wife, a professor of political science, Islamic law, and international law, when he said, "The Middle East should be nuked, and every Muslim annihilated." Reflecting upon his statement, I pondered whether this pastor's attitude would be different had his daughter married a Muslim or non-Muslim Arab from one of the Middle Eastern countries. What if he had friends living in the Middle East or North Africa? He had no narrative empathy for the people living in the Middle East. Further into my pastoral ministry, I began to feel increasingly uncomfortable associating myself with such negative and hateful rhetoric stemming from a group of people who were supposed to be representatives of Christ to the larger church body. Interestingly enough, to my knowledge none of my colleagues had any substantial relations with a Muslim or was well versed in the religion of Islam—a reality that will be further explored in chapter 2.

Several years later, while pursuing a doctoral degree at Catholic Theological Union in Chicago, I developed an interest in the history of religion, specifically Islam. I began to wonder whether Muslims were indeed a religious group to be feared and excluded from the United States,

---

13. McAlister, *Kingdom of God*, 144–58.

or a people to understand, embrace, partner with, respect, and perhaps—dare I say it—love. My wife, Emilia Justyna Powell, travels extensively in Muslim-majority countries for the purpose of interviewing scholars of Islamic jurisprudence and policymakers with the goal of understanding how Muslim states view international law and diplomacy. She returns from each [visit/trip/sojourn] with a greater appreciation, admiration, understanding, and respect for Islamic jurisprudence and for the Muslim people. This personal journey of hers is partially responsible for prompting my interest and research into the matters of peace and justice in Islam. Emilia's positive experiences, when juxtaposed with my interactions with Southern Baptist leaders, created an important puzzle in my mind—a puzzle that I needed to put together; one that would offer explanations for such open displays of hostility on the part of the leaders. While earning my Doctor of Ministry degree from CTU and in the years since, I have befriended Muslims from around the world. I am honored to be friends with many Muslims who work as imams and professors (many of them scholars of Islam), medical professionals, policymakers, homemakers, and blue-collar workers. I have held two Academic Fellowships at the Oxford Centre for Islamic Studies, University of Oxford, where I have been privileged to converse with very knowledgeable people who spend their whole lives studying Islam. I have engaged in many conversations with my wife regarding Sharia (a topic that she teaches at the University of Notre Dame and has written on extensively) and continue to discuss the Islamic communities with several of my colleagues at the University of Notre Dame. These conversations and experiences have aided and continue to influence my understanding of Islam as well as the many diverse individuals who practice the faith.

My pastoral experience and observation of Southern Baptist pastors is that they incline to be engaged in practical theological matters and pastoral concerns that require most of their time. When I was pastoring, I engaged in at least three primary activities every week—sermon preparation, funerals, and conflict resolution. The overwhelming majority of pastors tend not to engage in the pursuit of abstract theoretical knowledge. For this reason, I refer to Omser's method—practical theological interpretation—which, as Osmer argues, has the ability to inform not only "academic practical theology," but also "interpretative tasks of congregational leaders."[14] Thus, the overarching goal of this book is to

---

14. Osmer, *Practical Theology*, 13.

foster the development of narrative empathy among Southern Baptist leaders. This narrative empathy leads to an improved, if not entirely new, perception of Islam, the Prophet Muhammad, and jihad, a perception that is firmly rooted in scholarly research and personal encounter.

The Audience for This Book

Southern Baptist leaders are my intended audience for this book, though my research extends to the larger fundamental and evangelical Protestant and Catholic communities of faith in the United States, the Global South, and perhaps Europe. I believe these evangelical leaders can put my findings into practice in a way that will foster constructive dialogue and collaboration between evangelical leaders and laity and their Muslim counterparts. The spiritual leaders of the denomination have significant influence over the laity in palpable, meaningful ways. Within the denomination, the laity tend to follow tenets of religious texts as interpreted by their spiritual leaders. It is these leaders, therefore, who have the power to either promote or discredit the notion of shared values and beliefs between Islam and Christianity. Thus, I intend this book to be read by Southern Baptist leaders—primarily pastors—for the purpose of initiating a more informative narrative of the lived spirituality of the Prophet Muhammad and his understanding of jihad. I believe that shifting the narrative in the evangelical church can help its members to reimagine some of the historical bonds between the two faith traditions, which can in turn help to forge a more peaceful and just path forward among Southern Baptists and Muslims in the United States and conceivably the Global South. On a national level, Southern Baptists can promote tolerance, understanding, respect, trust, and love towards Muslims and help deter the current rhetoric of intolerance, antipathy, misunderstanding, disrespect, and hatred that has far too often contributed to religious hate crimes in the United States and abroad. Incidentally, in 2018, Southern Baptist leaders Micah Fries and Keith Whitfield tackled some of the primary concerns Southern Baptists have about Islam in their collection *Islam and North America: Loving our Muslim Neighbors*.[15] The book—which I believe it an important read for pastors—is a series of chapters by different authors addressing concerns and questions asked by leaders and laity alike within evangelical churches. Though the authors raise some pertinent questions,

---

15. Fries and Whitfield, *Islam and North America*.

and indeed elaborate on the importance of loving our Muslim neighbors, the answers provided are almost exclusively evangelical in nature and in my opinion neglect to take into account the lived spirituality of the Prophet Muhamad. Moreover, my perception of the book is that one of the primary concerns of the editors is to show evangelicals that the God of Muhammad is not the father of Jesus. Though there is clearly a time and a place for evangelization, my primary goal in this book is to foster a path to dialogue with Muslims that appreciates shared values and beliefs, thus building bridges of understanding, trust, and cooperation—a theme I have already mentioned and will return to repeatedly throughout.

As the Bible and the Qur'an indicate (if in different ways), Jesus and the Prophet Muhammad both taught that there are two crucial actions that must be lived out in the lives of their followers in order to please God: love God with all your heart, soul, and mind, and love your neighbor as yourself.[16] Furthermore, Jesus said the entire law and all the demands of the prophets are based on these two commandments. These actions—love of God and love of neighbor—are essential if peace and justice are to govern relations between Southern Baptists and Muslims today and in the future. There is reason to think that there will be several waves of intense anti-Muslim sentiment in the United States as the population of Muslims increases and non-Muslims (both conservative and liberal in their political and religious ideas) feel their way of life is threatened. For example, according to a 2017 article in *Christianity Today*, Pew Research found that most white evangelicals do not believe Muslims belong in America.[17] Moreover, the early history of relations between Protestants and Catholics in the United States offers an alarming precedent.

The earliest anti-Catholic movements in the United States occurred during the American Revolution and then in the late nineteenth century as a Protestant-minded religious society confronted a growing Catholic population. US ambassador Francis Rooney writes, "As the country became increasingly Catholic, it continued to become more vocally anti-Catholic. Many native-born working-class Protestants objected to the rapid influx of Catholic (mainly Irish) foreigners, whom they resented not just on religious grounds but as competitors who flooded the labor market and stole jobs."[18] Fast forward to the twenty-first century and some of America is convulsing in hatred yet again, especially as Catholics and

---

16. Matthew 22:37–40 (NLT Study Bible) and Women 4:36 (The Qur'an).
17. Shellnut, "Most White Evangelicals."
18. Rooney, *Global Vatican*, 51.

Protestants respond to the rapid influx of Muslim immigrants, a religious group that many perceive to be a threat to Christian values and doctrine, indeed to Western civilization. The need for ethnic and religious understanding between Muslims and non-Muslims is just as necessary now to help prevent another and perhaps worse episode of civil unrest in the United States.

Before proceeding any further, an important issue warrants attention. I am acutely aware that some spiritual leaders within the Southern Baptist Church, especially the more fundamental branch, will be reluctant to learn and share with their congregations a more historical-critical analysis about the Prophet Muhammad and jihad. I also realize that many Southern Baptists are unwilling and at times unable to hear and understand these scholarly and contextual interpretations because of a cultural environment that has preconditioned them to think and act in certain ways. Indeed, some Southern Baptists (leaders and laity alike) simply lack or even choose to resist narrative empathy towards Muslims and view the reading of the Qur'an as a sin. But any study of a similar nature is bound to be constricted by similar limitations. In no way is it my intention to suggest that the majority of leaders within the Southern Baptist denomination purposefully spread a message of intolerance or are ignorant of Islam. Missionaries living in the 10/40 Window know the power of narrative empathy and understand the importance of being familiar with the teachings of Islam as well as the cultural and ethnic environment they are in. I confess that when I reexamine some of the sermons I have preached on Islam, it is clear I did not know what I was talking about. I was not objective, and I did not apply the same standards of historical criticism to Islam as I did to Christianity. Some Southern Baptist leaders do, however, have a thorough understanding of the Prophet Muhammad, and though they disagree with many of the doctrinal beliefs and conclusions in Islam, they still promote love and respect for the people of Islam—for example, Micah Fries and Keith Whitfield. So, while I wish to avoid sweeping generalizations, my experience as a former pastor within the evangelical church nonetheless suggests that there are patterns of behavior on the leadership level, patterns that often disrupt normal interactions between Christians and Muslims. In some instances, it may even be that spiritual leaders purposefully instill a degree of fear in their followers and their communities to build a sense of "us against them." These feelings hamper the emergence of a spirit of respect and camaraderie between Southern Baptists and Muslims.

This project is not a short-term research agenda. Furthermore, it is not designed to repair all the problems that continue to surface in the context of relations between Southern Baptists and Muslims. However, it can potentially decrease the amount of hatred, intolerance, ignorance, and misperception that many have about the Prophet Muhammad and his lived spirituality and foster constructive dialogue from which might flow enduring friendships and collaboration.

What This Book Is Not Meant to Be

It is essential to be clear about what this book is not meant to be. This book is situated in the practical theology and inter-religious dialogue literatures. My intention is not to examine the rich and diverse history of Muslim-Christian relations. There are many authors who have already tackled this topic and done a superlative job—Hugh Goddard, to take one example.[19] Neither is my goal to speak to all the debates surrounding Muslim-Christian relations found in systematic theology, divinity, missiology, and other Muslim-Christian disciplines. This book is not a textbook on Southern Baptist or Islamic faith and history.

Instead, my work builds on the existing literature that addresses many of the crucial matters and issues connected to these two faith traditions in a contemporary setting. The focus of my research is to glean a more thorough understanding of the social context behind the reluctance of many within the Southern Baptist denomination to engage in dialogue with the larger Muslim community, a dialogue that might foster understanding and collaboration between the two faiths. This book, birthed out of my own personal experience, is intended to be a practical guide for Southern Baptist leaders, enabling them to connect, collaborate, and gracefully pursue common interests with the majority of Muslims in advancing integral human development. While I engage theoretical concepts and constructs, this work is principally practical in nature.

---

19. Goddard, *History of Christian-Muslim Relations*.

2

What Is Going On

Southern Baptists—A Narrative Vacuum

IN THIS CHAPTER, I offer an analysis of a substantive issue-area within Islam, using the first of Osmer's four tasks, the descriptive-empirical task. I begin by exploring some common misperceptions of Islam that I have observed during my nearly twenty years of pastoral ministry, as well as my teaching career, touching on how Southern Baptists view Muhammad's lived spirituality. Next, I describe "what is going on" within the Southern Baptist denomination with regard to the news and scholarship they consume about the Prophet Muhammad and jihad. I then present some information on these misperceptions, drawn from scholarly sources, news articles, and radio programs, as well as sermons of Southern Baptist leaders (in many cases available on YouTube or churches' official websites), to discern "patterns and dynamics in particular episodes, situations, or contexts,"[1] as they relate to the lived spirituality of the Prophet Muhammad. Finally, I share insights from in-depth qualitative interviews I conducted with Southern Baptist pastors.

1. Osmer, *Practical Theology*, 4.

Introduction

The United States is a hodgepodge of ethnicities, ideas, political leanings, and religious beliefs. The American spirit is perhaps best summed up in the words of Patrick Henry in his speech to the Second Virginia Convention on March 23, 1775: "Give me liberty, or give me death!" Historically, people came to these shores for many reasons, but the one overarching reason was, and still is, the promise of religious freedom. Many early Americans, particularly Protestants, believed that if freedom of religion—and perhaps even freedom from religion—could not be achieved, then life was not worth living. The United States was built by immigrants—immigrants from Great Britain, France, Spain, Prussia, and so on. Of course, many came to this country involuntarily, such as the African people who were sold into slavery and then forced to work plantations, build houses, and care for many of the European settlers. People have come to America to escape tyranny, poverty, persecution, and bondage. Some have come in hopes of finding prosperity through education or employment in a country with democratic values and opportunities for self-improvement.

Since the era of European exploration and colonization, issues around immigration have played a major role in shaping the American cultural landscape. The Native Americans (estimated to be nearly ten million during colonization) resisted the influx of European settlers as they began to forcefully confiscate Native American land and resources. Eventually, Eurocentrism and White supremacy led to the genocide of Native Americans (in the twentieth century only 300,000 remained). Many were forced into slave labor, children were forced to learn the White man's way of thinking and living, religious beliefs were outlawed, and most were condemned to a life on a reservation, often deficient in the natural resources needed to flourish. As late as the twentieth century it was not uncommon to hear words like those once spoken by Capt. Richard H. Pratt regarding Native American children receiving an education: "kill the Indian, but save the man."[2] Fast forward several years later and these European settlers, who were immigrants themselves not long ago, would begin to call into question immigrants arriving from countries other than their own. Legal and ethical issues surrounding immigration continued to be part of American politics when the Founders gathered and signed the Declaration of Independence in 1776. Tensions have

---

2. Pratt, "Advantages of Mingling Indians with Whites."

flared throughout the years regarding the migration of Africans, Asians, Irish Catholics, Japanese, Hispanics, and other ethnicities into the United States, Muslims have been immigrating since the days of Colonialism. Though the exact time and place of Muslims arriving in North America is unknown, many historians believe that the earliest Muslims came to North America from a region in Africa called the Senegambian, possibly as early as the fourteenth century. Some even suggest that Christopher Columbus relied in part on the writings of Portuguese Muslims who had navigated their way to the Americas in the twelfth century when he charted his own way to America. In fact, many African Muslims were brought forcibly to the United States in the Euro-American slave trade and then required to convert to Christianity. Between 1878 and 1924 Muslim immigration considerably increased and by 1952 there were over 1,000 mosques scattered throughout the country.[3] Today, it is estimated that one percent of the American population is Muslim.

Prior to the terrorist attacks of September 11, 2001, most Muslim and non-Muslim Americans lived in harmony with each other, or at the very least tolerated each other. Of course, hate crimes did occur, but these hate crimes against Muslims were relatively contained within the framework of the local community. The media coverage of the Iranian hostage crisis and the Gulf War certainly did not help the majority of non-Muslim Americans to construct a positive view of Islam, but these events took place thousands of miles from the United States' shores, hence the perceived threat from Muslims was on a much lower scale than it would later be.[4] After September 11, 2001, national and even worldwide attention was focused on Islam. The religion that heretofore was perceived by many non-Muslim Americans, particularly Jews and Christians, as a mere nuisance became a threat. Outside of large metropolitan cities, most non-Muslim Americans could not identify a Muslim they knew personally, nor could they recount the basic tenets of Islam. Unfortunately for American Muslims and non-Muslims, the much-needed conversation between Christianity and Islam was birthed out of a tragic event. These horrific attacks tainted the perceptions and attitudes of many non-Muslim Americans towards Muslims and the religion of Islam. My research shows that this negative perception of Islam is acute within evangelical Christianity, and in particular among the Southern

3. GhaneaBassini, *History of Islam in America*.

4. For a more comprehensive reading regarding the perception of Islam in America, I recommend Said, *Covering Islam*.

Baptists. In order to understand the causal mechanisms behind this negative perception, it will be useful to paint a panoramic picture of Muslim demographics in the U.S.

Demographics of the Muslim Population in the U.S.

A broad understanding of who American Muslims are can help to correct many of the misperceptions held by non-Muslims. Some helpful questions are: What are the countries of origin for many first-generation American Muslims? What level of education have they received? Where do most Muslims live in the United States? Are they enjoying good health? Briefly sketching these demographic facts will help non-Muslims better understand Muslims in the United States. Indeed, as I demonstrate later, many Southern Baptist leaders are unaware of how diverse American Muslims are, or the everyday challenges many of them face. The Pew Research Center found that "Muslim Americans are a diverse and growing population, currently estimated at 3.45 million people of all ages, including 2.15 million adults. The U.S. Muslim community is made up heavily of immigrants and the children of immigrants from around the world. On average Muslim Americans are considerably younger than the overall U.S. population."[5] The majority of immigrant Muslims migrate from South Asia, Middle East, North Africa, and other Asia/Pacific countries. They are a culturally diverse group and overwhelmingly adhere to either Sunni or Shia Islam. Within Sunni and Shia Islam there are many sub-denominations reflecting distinct interpretations of the Qur'an and cultural identities. It is also interesting to note, as table 2.1 illustrates, as of 2011, almost sixty percent of Muslim adults residing in the U.S. were first-generation Americans (were born outside the U.S.).[6]

---

5. Pew Research Center, "Demographic Portrait of Muslim Americans."
6. Greenwood, "Demographic of Muslim Americans."

Nativity and Immigration

% of U.S. Muslims who are

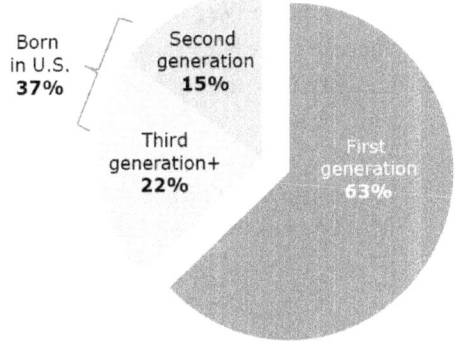

	U.S. Muslims	Foreign born
	%	%
United States	37	--
Middle East/N. Africa	26	41
Pakistan	9	14
Other South Asia	7	12
Iran	3	5
Sub-Saharan Africa	7	11
Europe	5	7
Other	<u>6</u>	<u>10</u>
	100	100
Year of arrival		
2000-2011	25	40
1990-1999	20	31
1980-1989	10	16
1979 and earlier	8	12
Native born	37	--
U.S. Citizen		
Yes	81	70
No	19	30

PEW RESEARCH CENTER 2011 Muslim American Survey. BIRTH, FATHER, MOTHER, Q204, CITIZEN. First generation are immigrants born outside the U.S. Second generation are born in the U.S. but have at least one parent who was born outside the U.S. Third generation are born in the U.S. and both parents were born in the U.S. Figures may not add to 100% because of rounding.

Table 2.1. Demographics of Muslim population in the U.S.[7]

7. Pew Research Center, "Muslim Americans: No Signs of Growth."

Civil unrest, violent conflict, and poverty in several Muslim-majority countries, including Afghanistan, Iran, Iraq, Pakistan, Syria, and Yemen, have caused a massive migration of Muslims to Western Europe and the U.S. Over thirty-two percent of Muslims in the U.S. came in the twenty-first century, compared to twenty percent in the twentieth century. As table 2.2 demonstrates, the large majority of Muslim adults living in the U.S. are citizens, eighty-two percent compared to eighteen percent.

Large majority of U.S. Muslim adults are citizens

	All U.S. Muslims %	Foreign-born U.S. Muslims %
U.S. citizens	82	69
Born in U.S.	42	-
Naturalized	40	69
Not U.S. citizens	18	31
	100	100

Note: Results repercentaged to exclude nonresponse. Figures may not add to 100% or subtotals indicated due to rounding.
Source: Survey conducted Jan. 23-May 2, 2017.
"U.S. Muslims Concerned About Their Place in Society, but Continue to Believe in the American Dream"

PEW RESEARCH CENTER

Table 2.2. Demographics of Muslim population in the U.S.[8]

Moreover, it is difficult to distinguish by race alone who is Muslim and who is not, considering that four in ten Muslims are white, twenty percent are black, twenty-eight percent are Asian, eight percent are Hispanic, and three percent are other or mixed (see table 2.3). As stated before, the American Muslim population is much younger than U.S. adults overall. The median age of adults in the U.S. is 47, whereas among Muslim adults it is 35. Muslims also have a higher fertility rate than the average non-Muslim American (2.4 to 2.1).[9] A recent projection of the Pew

---

8. Pew Research Center, "Demographic Portrait of Muslim Americans."
9. Pew Research Center, "Demographic Portrait of Muslim Americans."

Research Center indicates that the U.S. Muslim population is growing at a very rapid rate and by the year 2040 will be the second-largest religious group in the U.S., after Christians. By 2050, the American-Muslim population is expected to reach 8.1 million people.[10]

Four-in-ten Muslim American adults are white

	White %	Black %	Asian %	Hispanic %	Other/mixed %
All U.S. Muslims	41	20	28	8	3=100
Foreign born	45	11	41	1	1
U.S. born	35	32	10	17	5
Second generation	52	7	22	17	2
Third generation+	23	51	2	18	7
U.S. general public	64	12	6	16	2

Note: Results repercentaged to exclude nonresponse. Figures may not add to 100% due to rounding. White, black, Asian and other races include only those who are not Hispanic. Hispanics are of any race.
Source: Survey conducted Jan. 23-May 2, 2017. U.S. general public data from U.S. Census Bureau's 2016 Current Population Survey Annual Social and Economic Supplement. "U.S. Muslims Concerned About Their Place in Society, but Continue to Believe in the American Dream"

PEW RESEARCH CENTER

Table 2.3. Demographics of Muslim population in the U.S.[11]

Where do the majority of Muslims reside in the United States? Given that they represent about one percent of the U.S. population, it can be a challenge for people in many parts of the country to make the acquaintance of a Muslim, much less see a mosque on the horizon. It is no wonder, therefore, that many Americans lack a narrative encounter with the Muslim population. Furthermore, far fewer Muslims live in the rural areas of the country than live in the larger cities. The largest concentration of Muslims is currently found in the state of New Jersey, where they make up three to four percent of the state's population (see figure 2.1). As I discuss in chapter 3, this reality may very well be a large factor in the widespread lack of empathy among Southern Baptist leaders and laity.

10. Mohamed, "New Estimate."
11. Pew Research Center, "Demographic Portrait of Muslim Americans."

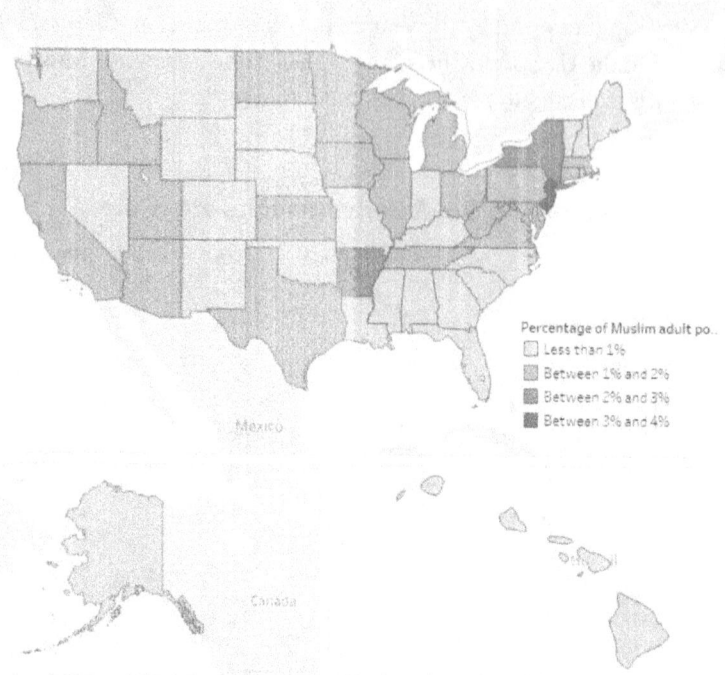

Figure 2.1. Percentage of adult population that's Muslim, by state.[12]

Studies indicate that Muslim America is on par with and surpassing non-Muslim America in its pursuit of an education. As of 2017, twenty-one percent of Muslims were college graduates, compared to nineteen percent of the general public. Tables 2.4 and 2.5 indicate that a good number of Muslim immigrants (38%) have or acquire an advanced degree, and basically the same number (35%) end up earning more than seventy-five thousand dollars.

12. Pew Research Center.

Immigrant Muslims more likely than other Muslims to have college degrees

Educational attainment of U.S. Muslims

	U.S. Muslims			U.S. general public
	Total %	Foreign born %	U.S. born %	%
Less than HS	8	10	7	12
HS graduate	30	27	36	33
Some college	30	25	37	25
College graduate	21	23	16	19
Graduate degree	11	15	5	11
	100	100	100	100

Notes: Results repercentaged to exclude nonresponse. Figures may not add to 100% due to rounding.
Source: Survey conducted Jan. 23-May 2, 2017. U.S. general public data from U.S. Census Bureau's 2016 Current Population Survey Annual Social and Economic Supplement.
"U.S. Muslims Concerned About Their Place in Society, but Continue to Believe in the American Dream"

PEW RESEARCH CENTER

Table 2.4. Immigrant Muslims more likely than other Muslims to have college degrees.[13]

In general, American Muslims experience many of the same health challenges as non-Muslim Americans do. However, as David Hodge shows, discrimination, e.g., offensive name calling or being singled out by law enforcement as a result of being a Muslim, results in greater levels of depression among Muslims.[14] Interestingly, the mitigating factor in this is directly tied to faith: those Muslims who say daily prayers and live out their faith alongside other Muslims seem to be less prone to depression.[15] Furthermore, the general health of Muslims is good, owing to relatively low intakes of alcohol and cigarette smoking. Less than nine percent of the sample group consumed alcohol and less than eleven percent inhaled tobacco. Sadly though, twenty-eight percent of the participants reported clinically significant levels of depressive symptoms.[16] It seems there-

13. Pew Research Center, "Demographic Portrait of Muslim Americans."
14. (odds ratio [OR] = 3.39, 95% confidence interval [CI] = 1.82, 6.32).
15. Hodge et al., "Correlates of Self-Rated Health."
16. Hodge et al., "Correlates of Self-Rated Health," 287.

fore, that with the onslaught of anti-Islam rhetoric in politics and many non-Muslim religious communities, depression is an increasing health concern for Muslim Americans, especially those who have migrated from the Middle East and North Africa. To illustrate, in the summer of 2021 I visited two mosques—Islamic Center of Rochester, New York, and Jami Masjid, in Buffalo, New York—and met with their leadership. I was taken aback by the hospitality they extended to me and my family and what seemed to me a genuine love for their community—both Muslim and non-Muslim. Both centers were engaged in community outreach efforts to feed the hungry, care for the sick, shelter the homeless, and counsel the hurting. Not to mention, they had constructed or purchased facilities to accommodate their own faith community for purposes of prayer, worship of God, education, and fellowship. I witnessed first-hand a thriving community that supported each other. In areas like Rochester and Buffalo, as I mention above, the community is strong, but in other areas where Muslims are few, the stories are not as positive. For instance, when I teach a course on Muslim-Christian dialogue, I intentionally invite a Muslim-American student to my class to share her or his life experience in the United States. In every occasion, the student has expressed feelings of second-class citizenship resulting from both hate speech and physical acts of violence directed towards them. The women in particular are singled out because of their hijab. One of my guests (a Muslim born and raised in California) told of a man stalking her in a Walmart Superstore. He told her to go back to where she came from and eventually walked up to her and ripped her hijab off her head. In most cases the American Muslims who have spoken in my class have lived in smaller Muslim communities where they are seen by non-Muslims as the outsiders.

Muslims as likely to have high incomes, but also more likely than general public to earn less than $30,000 per year

% of U.S. Muslims whose annual household income is ...

	U.S. Muslims			U.S. general public
	Total %	Foreign born %	U.S. born %	%
Less than $30,000	40	37	45	32
$30,000-$49,999	17	17	16	20
$50,000-$74,999	11	11	11	13
$75,000-$99,999	8	6	9	12
$100,000 or more	<u>24</u>	<u>29</u>	<u>18</u>	<u>23</u>
	100	100	100	100

Notes: Results repercentaged to exclude nonresponse. Figures may not add to 100% due to rounding.
Source: Survey conducted Jan. 23-May 2, 2017. U.S. general public data from aggregated Pew Research Center surveys conducted January-April 2017.
"U.S. Muslims Concerned About Their Place in Society, but Continue to Believe in the American Dream"

PEW RESEARCH CENTER

Table 2.5. Muslims as likely to have high incomes, but also more likely than general public to earn less than $30,000 per year.[17]

Muslims immigrate to the United States from unique and distinctive countries bringing with them their own set of values and cultural identity—no two Muslims are identical. Most Muslim leaders I have met with are in many ways conservative. For example, they tend to support traditional marriage and believe in the sanctity of life and freedom of religion. Still, research reveals that the majority of Muslims are registered with the Democratic Party, rather than the more conservative Republican Party. By way of an example, in 2016 the political leanings of most Muslim Americans polled were as follows: Democrat for president, Clinton—forty percent, Sanders—twenty-seven percent, and Republican for president, Trump—four percent.[18] Why is this? It can be argued that one of the leading factors shaping these patterns had to do with the

---

17. Pew Research Center, "Demographic Portrait of Muslim Americans."
18. Wolfe, "Muslim Business Entrepreneurs."

Republican candidate, Donald Trump, vowing to implement a temporary Muslim ban and to deport undocumented Muslim immigrants from specifically named Muslim-majority countries. Furthermore, certain media outlets reported that deportation would be based on religion and country of origin, not illegal actions, though illegal actions within the U.S. would certainly result in deportation.[19] According to Foundation for Ethnic Understanding (FFEU) president Rabbi Marc Schneier, "Evangelical Christian-Muslim relations is today's largest interreligious challenge."[20] A study conducted by FFEU shows there are several U.S. political and geopolitical issues that unite and divide the two faiths:

- *President Trump*—Muslims did not vote for President Trump and three in four express disapproval of his performance in office (58-percent strong disapproval); Evangelicals voted for and continue to support the president.
- *The Travel Ban*—Evangelicals and Muslims do not agree on the travel ban. Evangelicals are more likely to support it (61-percent), while Muslims consider it a "Muslim ban" (70-percent).
- *Migrant Caravan*—Evangelicals and Muslims do not agree on the issue of the migrant caravan—58-percent of Evangelicals see it as a threat, while Muslims do not.
- *Joint Comprehensive Plan of Action (JCPOA)*—Evangelicals (57-percent) tend to approve of President Trump's decision to pull out of the JCPOA and re-impose economic sanctions on Iran, while Muslims are not nearly as supportive.
- *Jamal Khashoggi*—Both Muslims (52-percent) and Evangelicals (55-percent) fault Saudi Arabia for Khashoggi's death, but Muslims are more critical of President Trump's response to the event.
- *Israel and Palestine*
  - Across both religions, over half either blame both Israelis and Palestinians or don't have an opinion, signaling a potential area for common ground.
  - Muslims (58-percent) are more optimistic for a peaceful solution between Israel and Palestine.

---

19. Vitali, "In His Words."
20. Foundation for Ethnic Understanding, "Survey of U.S. Evangelical Christians."

- Evangelicals strongly support U.S. policies towards Israel-including moving the U.S. embassy to Jerusalem—while Muslims do not.

- *Muslim Countries Support for Israel*—Both groups are receptive toward Muslim nations cooperating with and supporting Israel (82-percent of Evangelicals and 72-percent of Muslims). Evangelicals tend to perceive lower levels of support for Israel among Muslim nations.[21]

At this juncture, it would be helpful, perhaps even necessary, to survey the current, widespread use of anti-Islamic rhetoric in U.S. politics. It is reasonable to expect that there is a clear connection between Muslim-American demographics and anti-Islamic rhetoric.

Anti-Islamic Rhetoric in Politics

Two terms need to be defined before I examine anti-Islamic rhetoric in U.S. politics: "Islam" and "Muslim." The word "Islam" originates from the Arabic root *Sal'm*, which means peace, purity, submission, humbling oneself and obeying commands. In the religious sense, Islam means submission to the will of God and obedience to His law.[22] There is no reference to a person or place in the name, as there is in Judaism (Judah) and Christianity (Christ). According to Muslims, Islam is the right path unto God. The term "Muslim" literally means one who submits to God.[23] A Muslim, then, is one who adheres to the religion of Islam, which teaches submission to God. The Muslim is to adhere to the teachings of the Prophet Muhammad as found in the Qur'an and the Sunnah[24] of the Prophet; every thought and action is to be held captive to God's will. In chapter 4, I elaborate on the teachings of the Prophet Muhammad and certain tenets of the faith that have been misunderstood by many non-Muslims, and by some Muslims. For the moment, let us say that Islamic scholars overwhelmingly agree that Islam is a religion of peace

---

21. Foundation for Ethnic Understanding, "Survey of U.S. Evangelical Christians."
22. Saalih al-Munajjid, "Meaning of the Word Islam."
23. www.merriam-webster.com, s.v. "Muslim."
24. Sunnah is a record of sayings, practices, and silences of the Prophet Muhammad.

and justice, and that it has been widely taken advantage of and exploited by the ill-informed both within and outside Islam.[25]

As beautifully illustrated by historian Hugh Goddard, the relationship between Muslims and Christians is complicated and should not be oversimplified. Disagreements have certainly surfaced between Christians and Muslims ever since the rise of Islam. Some disagreements have been political, territorial, and of course religious. In the ninth century in particular, hatred of Islam was on the rise within the Western church. Goddard writes, "One of the most important legacies of the very negative judgement on Islam which emerged in Spain in the ninth century was the subsequent rise, towards the end of the eleventh century, of what has to be called a movement of militant Christianity. The supporters of this movement, the Crusaders, were convinced that that had a religious obligation to take up the cross, literally, in order to recapture the Holy Land—the land in which Jesus had lived and taught—from the infidel Muslim in order to facilitate or expedite the return of Christ."[26] Since the medieval expeditions of the Christian Crusaders (1095–1492) to forcibly take back the Holy Land from the Muslims and to stop the spread of Islam in Europe, there have been uneasy relations between Western and Middle Eastern civilizations. However, not since the sixteenth century (the official ending of the Crusades) have tensions between the West and the Middle East been as severe as they are now, specifically owing to the terrorist attacks of September 11, 2001 in New York City, Washington D.C., and Pennsylvania. On that perilous day, nearly 3,000 people were killed and over 6,000 injured. Many have died in the aftermath of 9/11 as a result of illnesses associated with toxic exposure. In the immediate response to the attacks, news agencies, social media, the government, and even many church leaders reported that America was at war with Islam and there would be hell to pay for the loss of innocent lives. The situation quickly escalated into what many perceived to be a religious war—though this idea is a great oversimplification. In the chaos, many non-Muslim Americans entered unwittingly into the realm of Islamophobia. To understand what Islamophobia is, it is necessary to define what a phobia is. A phobia is an exaggerated, usually inexplicable, and illogical fear of a particular object, class of objects, or situation. It may be hard for the afflicted to adequately determine or communicate the

25. Royal Aal al-Bayt Institute for Islamic Thought, "Common Word."
26. Goddard, *History of Christian-Muslim Relations*, 84.

source of fear, but it exists. Prior to 9/11, the symptoms of Islamophobia existed, but they had never received as much attention, nor caused such anti-Islamic rhetoric, as would occur in the West, particularly the United States, after the attacks. Research conducted by Gallup in 2011 found that "more than 160 Muslim-American terrorist suspects and perpetrators were identified in the decade since the attack of 9/11, just a percentage of the thousands of acts of violence that occur in the United States each year."[27] Owing to the horrific events of 9/11, almost every time a Muslim commits a violent crime in the U.S., it receives national media attention; this in turn creates an atmosphere that fosters phobia. The outcome is an impression among the general populace that Islamic terrorism is more widespread than it really is. For example, Erin M. Kearns writes:

> Terrorist attacks often dominate news coverage as reporters seek to provide the public with information. Yet, not all incidents receive equal attention. Why do some terrorist attacks receive more media coverage than others? [P]erpetrator religion is the largest predictor of news coverage.... [A]ttacks by Muslim perpetrators received, on average, 357% more coverage than other attacks.... The disparities in news coverage of attacks based on the perpetrator's religion may explain why members of the public tend to fear the "Muslim terrorist" while ignoring other threats. More representative coverage could help to bring public perception in line with reality.[28]

Of particular interest is that since the attack of 9/11, "the Muslim-American community has helped security and law enforcement officials prevent nearly two of every five al-Qaeda terrorist plots threatening the United States[29] and that tips from the Muslim-American community are the largest single source of initial information to authorities about these few plots."[30] Because terrorism is carried out in the name of God, it has had the effect of placing upon Islamic scholars and leaders the burden of showing the deviation of such groups. Islamic scholars, religious leaders—not just imams, but rabbis and pastors as well—and the community at large must condemn such acts of terrorism and educate Muslims and non-Muslims alike on the basic tenets of Islam; tenets that the majority of Islamic scholars agree upon as to the lived spirituality of the Prophet

27. Gallup, "Islamophobia."
28. Kearns, "Why Do Some Terrorist Attacks."
29. Beutel, "Data on Post-9/11 Terrorism."
30. Kurzman, "Muslim-American Terrorism since 9/11."

Muhammad. The religion of Islam is susceptible to abuse at the hands of false representatives and bad actors—just as Christianity is: consider the Crusades, the Inquisition, David Koresh, Eric Rudolph, Robert Lewis Dear, Robert Doggart, the Klu Klux Klan, and White Supremacists. Today, most Christian leaders and the Christian majority are quick to differentiate the actions of such people from the faith proper, but are less quick to do the same for terrorist groups acting in the name of Islam. Nearly half of Christians polled say that terrorists acting in the name of Islam are Muslims. The Public Religion Research Institute recently asked the question: Is someone who acts violently in the name of a faith truly a member of that faith? The answer displayed a clear bias: Christians were swift to say that other Christians who acted in a violent manner were not true Christians but failed to provide the same latitude for Muslims.[31] This leads into what may very well be a cause of anti-Muslim rhetoric in the political arena. There are nearly 200 million professing Christians in the United States, compared to roughly three million professing Muslims. With such a difference in the general populace, it is no wonder that there is a bias against Islam. The leanings of any political system have a direct correlation to the commonly held beliefs of the populace. Though identities and motivations are varied, certain voices tend to dominate the conversation and the tone. History is full of political agendas carried out in the name of religion (religion is a powerful tool that politicians often use to unite a community, nation, or country around a political ideology); however, upon close examination it can be determined that some Christians and Muslims alike behave in ways that are incompatible with their faith. This does not mean that a judgment can be made regarding the authenticity of one's faith. A Christian may be acting in a way that he or she believes is consistent with Christianity, all the while failing to grasp the root tenets of the faith. So, in theory, terrorists may indeed believe themselves to be true to their faith, be they Muslim or Christian. Notwithstanding this observation, the media and political representatives rarely use the word "terrorist" when describing the actions of a self-professing Christian even when the act is a clear act of terrorism. Yet will draw attention to a Muslim's faith when an act of terrorism is carried out. European and American history is stained by the blood of many horrific acts that were carried out in the name of Christ.

---

31. Withrow, "Is There a Christian Double Standard?"

The Reformation, and later the Enlightenment, with its emphases on reason, the scientific method, and progress, generally helped to tone down Christian extremism—though some religious groups became more fundamental in their beliefs. Modernity has also played a significant role in normalizing Christian groups—to compete with other, non-Christian, worldviews, Christians had to learn to coexist without dominating them. In a like manner, in response to the violence by religious militant extremists, Islamic scholars around the world are uniting and vehemently denouncing such horrible acts of terrorism carried out in the name of God. This movement is uniting Muslims and clarifying the basic tenets of the Islamic faith—a feat that will take incalculable time, energy, and resources from the scholars of Islam and Muslim leaders worldwide. Yet this monumental effort is underway, and is already yielding positive results. Two major examples are the Amman Message[32] and "A Common Word between Us and You."[33] Non-Muslims and Muslims alike are hearing from Islamic scholars regarding the consensus of what is and is not doctrinally acceptable in Islam. Naturally, there are disagreements about interpretation and application, but the underlying principles that unite Muslims and promote Islam as a religion of peace are receiving a heightened awareness and consensus throughout the non-Muslim world, thus significantly improving relations between the two religions, Christianity and Islam.

The 2016 U.S. presidential race revolved around one particular debate—immigration,[34] specifically immigration from countries whose primary religion is Islam. Though a strenuous 20-step security process, which takes up to two years to complete, had been in place, Republicans challenged the process by demanding more security measures be instituted to slow the pace of Muslim immigration and ultimately prevent any perceived Muslim terrorist from entering the U.S.[35] Though many issues were discussed in the campaign, such as the economy, the environment, health care, and privacy, the Republican Party used the crisis in Syria and the flight of many Muslim refugees to the U.S. as a means of rallying

32. The full manuscript can be viewed on-line at ammanmessage.com.

33. The full manuscript can be viewed on-line at www.acommonword.com.

34. Immigrants are often seen as a threat to culture and a nuisance to cherished local values and traditions. For more information on this topic see Chandler and Tsai, "Social Factors"; Dustmann and Preston, "Racial and Economic Factors"; Hainmueller and Hiscox, "Attitudes toward Immigration"; Ford, "Acceptable and Unacceptable Immigrants; Hainmueller and Hangartner, "Who Gets a Swiss Passport?"; Miller, "Economic Anxiety or Ethnocentrism?"

35. Park and Buchavan, "Refugees Entering the U.S."

their base. As a result, in large part, of their in effect adopting an "us vs. them"[36] strategy, the Republicans succeeded in capturing the White House, with the majority of White, born-again/evangelical Christians voting for Trump (see table 2.6). Suffice it to say, both political parties use ethnocentrism to promote their own agendas when necessary, even at the expense of misrepresenting and alienating a particular demographic group—in this instance, Muslims. As humans we are predisposed to ethnocentrism,[37] and insofar as this predisposition has a direct impact on our views about issues such as war and peace, human rights, the economy, and immigration, it is politically significant.

Presidential vote by religious affiliation and race

	2000		2004		2008		2012		2016		Dem change '12-'16
	Gore	Bush	Kerry	Bush	Obama	McCain	Obama	Romney	Clinton	Trump	
	%	%	%	%	%	%	%	%	%	%	
Protestant/other Christian	42	56	40	59	45	54	42	57	39	58	-3
Catholic	50	47	47	52	54	45	50	48	45	52	-5
White Catholic	45	52	43	56	47	52	40	59	37	60	-3
Hispanic Catholic	65	33	65	33	72	26	75	21	67	26	-8
Jewish	79	19	74	25	78	21	69	30	71	24	+2
Other faiths	62	28	74	23	73	22	74	23	62	29	-12
Religiously unaffiliated	61	30	67	31	75	23	70	26	68	26	-2
White, born-again/evangelical Christian	n/a	n/a	21	78	24	74	21	78	16	81	-5
Mormon	n/a	n/a	19	80	n/a	n/a	21	78	25	61	+4

Note: "Protestant" refers to people who described themselves as "Protestant," "Mormon" or "other Christian" in exit polls; this categorization most closely approximates the exit poll data reported immediately after the election by media sources. The "white, born-again/evangelical Christian" row includes both Protestants and non-Protestants (e.g., Catholics, Mormons, etc.) who self-identify as born-again or evangelical Christians.
Source: Pew Research Center analysis of exit poll data. 2004 Hispanic Catholic estimates come from aggregated state exit polls conducted by the National Election Pool. Other estimates come from Voter News Service/National Election Pool national exit polls. 2012 data come from reports at NBCnews.com and National Public Radio. 2016 data come from reports at NBCnews.com and CNN.com.
PEW RESEARCH CENTER

Table 2.6. Presidential vote by religious affiliation and race.[38]

It became apparent to the Republicans in 2016 that to win the election, they would have to tap into the base and speak on issues that would resonate with White, born-again/evangelical Christians, White Catholics and Mormons. To this end, Republican politicians turned their attention to immigration, terrorism, and crime, vowing to restrict refugees from Syria and build a border wall between Mexico and the U.S. to cut down

36. Kinder and Kam, *Us against Them*.
37. Miller, "Economic Anxiety or Ethnocentrism?"
38. Pew Research Center, "How the Faithful Voted."

on the influx of drugs and violent gangs. Leading up to the election, candidate Donald Trump called for a ban on Muslims entering the United States. One supporter said, "I think that we should definitely disallow any Muslims from coming in. Any of them. The reason is simple: We can't identify what their attitude is."[39] Statements such as this stereotype American Muslims and Muslims in general. Moreover, these sorts of statements generate more fear within non-Muslim communities, thus creating more space for religious hate crimes to occur. Senator Lindsey Graham said on Fox News that America is in a religious war and we need to tighten our immigration vetting process for Muslims migrating from countries where radical Islam flourishes.[40] The word "radical" is often used when describing those who operate outside of the normal parameters within Islam, but is this a fair and unbiased term to use? At what point does a person of faith become radical? Would it be more prudent to remove one's religious affiliation from the word terrorist and simply label the perpetrator as a villain, a criminal, or a terrorist? Most politicians refrain from calling a White Christian male a radical Christian or a Christian terrorist because the two descriptions do not fit the commonly accepted and perceived understanding of the religion. Moreover, it would suggest that all Christians are susceptible and perhaps prone to such acts of violence. To draw these conclusions and use such terminology would result in an outcry of the Christian community condemning such a description. After the January 6 insurrection on the U.S. Capital by many QAnon supporters—some of whom touted their Christianity—Christian leaders need to be vigilant in denouncing such acts of radicalism, lest public opinion be persuaded to turn on American Evangelicalism. In the United States more Americans have been killed by White non-Muslim American males with no known ties to Islam. In spite of this, in 2017 President Donald J. Trump signed an executive order banning Muslims from seven Muslim-majority countries from entering the U.S. He expanded the restrictions to six more countries in 2020. The reason: to protect Americans from radical Islamic terrorists. President Trump would go on to say, "We don't want 'em here."[41] As the political leader of the United States, what the president verbalizes and chooses to remain silent on affects the country by setting a certain tone of tolerance and even intolerance.

39. Yan, "Fierce Backlash."
40. Beinart, "Lindsey Graham's 'Religious War.'"
41. Williams, "White American Men."

When candidate Trump was seeking for the presidency, he consistently campaigned on the notion that should he become president he would decisively implement a stringent plan to vet Muslims seeking entrance into the U.S. and root out the anti-American Muslims, sending them back to their country of origin. He rallied much of his political base around this promise of extreme vetting and deportation, to the shock and dismay of many Americans—Muslim and non-Muslim, Democrat and Republican. As can be found in full in Appendix 1 and partially in the timeline below, Johnson and Hausiohner with the *Washington Post* retroactively pulled anti-Muslim statements made by Trump, both as candidate and later as president.[42] These statements highlight Trump's perceived insensitivity to Muslims in general, his *perceived* lack of empathy for the majority of innocent victims within Islam, his *perceived* political strategy to create an "us against them" mentality within his political base, and his *perceived* inability to clearly articulate the objective facts from subjective resources. None of this would have been possible had his base not supported his political views. Potential presidential candidates and certainly the elected and serving president of the United States have great social and political influence both at home and abroad. No matter the political party he or she belongs to, what he or she says has far reaching implications, be they positive or negative. Therefore, in an effort to bring about a more peaceful and just society, it is essential for the president to speak and act in a wise manner, a manner that embodies the highest elected office in the United States and brings out the best in people, while keeping the country safe from those who wish to do it harm. Muslims represent a fifth of the world's population and they represent many countries, ethnicities, political leanings, and cultures. In the United States they are distinctively diverse, and for this reason I believe it is important for a presidential candidate, and certainly for a sitting president, to understand that there is no such reality as a "Muslim world." The following is an excerpt of the chronological timeline of rhetoric used by candidate and later president Donald Trump. Of great note is the number of times he uses the term "Muslim" or "Muslims" and the implied connotation. Often, the rhetoric used is negative and provocative; moreover, he seems to assume (whether sincerely held it is impossible to know) that most Muslims are somehow plotting together to bring about the demise of Western culture and democracy.

---

42. Johnson and Hauslohner, "'I Think Islam Hates Us.'"

March 30, 2011

For years, Trump publicly questioned then-President Barack Obama's religious beliefs and place of birth. As he debated running for president in the 2012 election, Trump said in a radio interview: "He doesn't have a birth certificate, or if he does, there's something on that certificate that is very bad for him. Now, somebody told me—and I have no idea if this is bad for him or not, but perhaps it would be—that where it says 'religion,' it might have 'Muslim.' And if you're a Muslim, you don't change your religion, by the way." (Obama is a Christian, and state records show he was born in Hawaii.)

Sept. 17, 2015

At a campaign town hall in New Hampshire, a man in the audience shouted out: "We have a problem in this country; it's called Muslims. We know our current president is one." The man mentioned Muslim "training camps" and asked: "When can we get rid of them?" Trump responded: "We're going to be looking at a lot of different things. You know, a lot of people are saying that, and a lot of people are saying that bad things are happening out there. We're going to be looking at that and plenty of other things."

Sept. 30, 2015

At a New Hampshire rally, Trump pledged to kick all Syrian refugees—most of whom are Muslim—out of the country, as they might be a secret army. "They could be ISIS, I don't know. This could be one of the great tactical ploys of all time. A 200,000-man army, maybe," he said. In an interview that aired later, Trump said: "This could make the Trojan horse look like peanuts."

Oct. 21, 2015

On Fox Business, Trump says he would "certainly look at" the idea of closing mosques in the United States.

Nov. 20, 2015

In comments to Yahoo and NBC News, Trump seemed open to the idea of creating a database of all Muslims in the United States. Later, he and his aides would not rule out the idea.

Nov. 21, 2015

At a rally in Alabama, Trump said that on Sept. 11 he "watched when the World Trade Center came tumbling down. And I watched in Jersey City, N.J., where thousands and thousands of people were cheering as that building was coming down."

Dec. 3, 2015

The morning after Syed Rizwan Farook and Tashfeen Malik killed 14 people in San Bernardino, Calif., Trump called into Fox News and said: "The other thing with the terrorists is you have to take out their families, when you get these terrorists, you have to take out their families." (Killing the relatives of suspected terrorists is forbidden by international law.) Later, in a speech to the Republican Jewish Coalition, Trump criticized Obama for not using the phrase "radical Islamic terrorism" and commented: "There's something going on with him that we don't know about."

Dec. 6, 2015

On CBS News, Trump said: "If you have people coming out of mosques with hatred and death in their eyes and on their minds, we're going to have to do something." Trump also said he didn't believe the sister of one of the San Bernardino shooters who said she was crestfallen for the victims, saying: "I would go after a lot of people, and I would find out whether or not they knew. I would be able to find out, because I don't believe the sister."

Dec. 7, 2015

Trump's campaign issued a statement saying: "Donald J. Trump is calling for a total and complete shutdown of Muslims entering the United

States until our country's representatives can figure out what is going on." Trump read this statement aloud at a rally in South Carolina.

Dec. 8, 2015

On CNN, Trump quoted a widely debunked poll by an anti-Islam activist organization that claimed that a quarter of the Muslims living in the United States agreed that violence against Americans is justified as part of the global jihad. "We have people out there that want to do great destruction to our country, whether it's 25 percent or 10 percent or 5 percent, it's too much," Trump said.

March 9, 2016

On CNN, Trump said: "I think Islam hates us. There's something there that—there's a tremendous hatred there. There's a tremendous hatred. We have to get to the bottom of it. There's an unbelievable hatred of us."

March 22, 2016

Soon after three suicide bombings in Brussels tied to a group of French and Belgian Muslims, Trump told Fox Business: "We're having problems with the Muslims, and we're having problems with Muslims coming into the country." Trump called for surveillance of mosques in the United States, saying: "You have to deal with the mosques, whether we like it or not, I mean, you know, these attacks aren't coming out of—they're not done by Swedish people."

On NBC News, Trump added: "This all happened because, frankly, there's no assimilation. They are not assimilating. . . . They want to go by sharia law. They want sharia law. They don't want the laws that we have. They want sharia law."

March 23, 2016

In an interview with Bloomberg TV, Trump said that Muslims "have to respect us. They do not respect us at all. And frankly, they don't respect a lot of the things that are happening throughout not only our country, but they don't respect other things."[43]

The above words and statements used by Donald Trump have been construed by many Americans—Muslim and non-Muslim alike—to be intolerant, mean-spirited, ignorant of context, and lacking in coherent thought. Many of the statements are generalizations about Muslims: for example, on January 12, 2016, at a rally in Iowa, "Trump shared his suspicions about Syrian refugees and then read the lyrics to Al Wilson's 1968 song 'The Snake,' the story of a 'tender woman' who nursed a sickly snake back to health but then was attacked by the snake. Trump often read these lyrics at rallies." (Later, in chapter 4, I counter this story by offering a constructive, historical description of who the Prophet Muhammad was and what he taught regarding acts of violence and intolerance, revealing in the process what the majority of Islamic scholars and Islamic communities think about violence and intolerance.) To highlight an example found in the above timeline of Trumps comments, on March 22, 2016, he said, "Soon after three suicide bombings in Brussels tied to a group of French and Belgian Muslims, Trump told Fox Business, 'We're having problems with the Muslims, and we're having problems with Muslims coming into the country.' Trump called for surveillance of mosques in the United States, saying, 'You have to deal with the mosques, whether we like it or not, I mean, you know, these attacks aren't coming out of— they're not done by Swedish people.' On NBC News, trump added, 'This all happened because, frankly, there's no assimilation. They are not assimilating. . .they want to go by sharia law. They want sharia law. They don't want the laws that we have. They want sharia law." Once again, this is an overgeneralization of Muslims, not only in America but from other countries as well. The language used is seen by many as divisive, non-constructive, and hurtful to the millions of peaceful American Muslims who are good citizens and embrace democracy and freedom of religion. Furthermore, according to Asifa Quraishi-Landes,

> Sharia isn't even "law" in the sense that we in the West understand it. And most devout Muslims who embrace sharia conceptually don't think of it as a substitute for civil law. Sharia is not a book of statutes or judicial precedent imposed by a government, and it's not a set of regulations adjudicated in court. Rather, it is a body of Koran-based guidance that points Muslims toward living an Islamic life. It doesn't come from the state, and

43. Johnson and Hauslohner, "'I Think Islam Hates Us.'"

it doesn't even come in one book or a single collection of rules. Sharia is divine and philosophical. The human interpretation of sharia is called "fiqh," or Islamic rules of right action, created by individual scholars based on the Koran and hadith (stories of the prophet Muhammad's life). Fiqh literally means "understanding"—and its many different schools of thought illustrate that scholars knew they didn't speak for God.[44]

There are many misrepresentations about Islam, and many of them have at their center a misunderstanding of what sharia is. To be clear, sharia means "the correct path" in Arabic and it provides Muslims with instruction on how to live a moral and ethical life. Moreover, it helps them to grow closer to God. Granted in the scholarship as well as non-scholarly discourses there are many definitions and conceptions of sharia.[45] But, in general, sharia denotes "that which Allah ordained in the Qur'an."[46] It is also crucial to note that sharia encompasses a variety of principles and precepts regulating behavior, ethical, moral, and societal norms. These dictates cover a wide range of issues central to human life, including marriage, familial relations, inheritance, contracts, criminal activities, fasting, and so on. The two primary sources for sharia are the Qur'an and the Sunnah. Sharia is not the same as Islamic law, though Islamic law is a large part of sharia; Islamic law is based on interpretations of sharia.

This sort of negative rhetoric and misrepresentation has a profound influence upon its listeners. It forces a conversation throughout the country which in return incites many fierce emotional debates. In particular, it creates an environment in which a previously relatively quiet group of citizens going about their day-to-day routines are thrust into the limelight of public debate and scrutiny. If you are an American Muslim attending a mosque, a female Muslim wearing a hijab, a Muslim saying your daily prayers in public, or have family ties to an Islamic country, you find yourself being misperceived and negatively judged by many within the general public. So much of this misperception is propagated by media bias, religious intolerance, and political rhetoric intended to rally one's political and religious base in support of his or her position. To be clear, according to the most recent research conducted, Democrats are less likely to engage in anti-Islamic rhetoric in comparison to Republicans.

44. Quraishi-Landes, "Five Myths about Sharia."
45. See Abou El Fadl, "Conceptualizing Shari'a."
46. Bassiouni, *Shari'a and Islamic Criminal Justice*, 39.

Why bring attention to this difference? Because most Southern Baptists identify themselves as members of the Republican Party, a party that promotes nationalism, traditional family values, and preserving the Constitution of the United States from progressivism. I often heard my congregants speak of wanting to go back to the "good ole days." Interestingly, every one of them had a different opinion about when that was. But they seem to have in mind a time when America was more homogenous. If the leader of the Grand Old Party engages in anti-Islamic rhetoric it will certainly persuade many within the party to follow suit. Additionally, fringe groups can use such rhetoric to recruit bigots and inflict harm upon innocent bystanders. I argue that the leader of a given political party—Republican or Democrat—will most likely pursue those ideologies that are most present in his or her constituency. Furthermore, if the leader of that party is elected to the highest political office in the world, it reveals that the majority of voters within the United States are in support of or at minimum comfortable with what is being said and acted upon.

Media outlets in the United States, including cable news, newspapers, television and films and video games have directly contributed to the negative perceptions many have regarding the religion of Islam and Muslims. The news tends to broadcast that which shocks and awes the viewers. Disasters, wars, violent disagreements, terrorism, deaths, and the like dominate the news industry. It is no wonder that so many non-Muslim Americans have a negative perception of Islam. Intentionally or not, Muslims are portrayed as violent and aggressive via the news outlets. Fear sells and despite the abundance of knowledge available to U.S. citizens about Islam, many Americans have been preconditioned to associate Islam with an image of "an intolerant religion lacking in gentleness and embracing fanatic followers that strike fear and hostility in the hearts of outsiders."[47] For example, "one study found that reliance on media for information about Muslims was associated with Americans' support for public policies targeting Muslims three months later. These policies included military action against Muslim countries, separate and more thorough airport security lines for Muslim travelers, and revoking the right to vote for American Muslims."[48] On a related note, a personal friend, a highly educated woman and Muslim American, informs me that when she flies the friendly skies over America, she is usually removed

---

47. Haji Adnan, "Mass Media," 63.
48. Saleem, "Spreading Islamophobia."

from the check-in line at the airport and physically searched for weapons. She says that many of the male security guards rub their hands across her breasts and between her legs in a way that violates her body. Because she feels like a second-class citizen and fears repercussion if she speaks out, she remains silent and only reveals her hurt and pain to close friends and family. Furthermore, such news coverage influences how minority groups view themselves and their acceptance within the mainstream society.[49] With the exception of a few well-educated and wealthy Muslims who tend to live in a state of privileged seclusion, most of the Muslim-Americans I have spoken with are aware that many non-Muslim Americans mistrust them and it causes them distress. According to Espiritu, "The point is that Islam has been consistently portrayed by global media as a violence-prone religion that is diametrically opposed to the West."[50] Additionally, Noor argues that, "Muslim identity and the concerns of Muslims are increasingly being defined in terms of an oppositional dialectic that pits Islam and Muslims against the rest of the world, as Islamophobia has become the mainstream media discourse where images of Muslims as murderous fanatics abound in movies, videos and computer games."[51] This onslaught of negative media coverage, film, video and computer games has villainized Muslims, when in reality, as mentioned above, more violent crimes are committed in America by non-Muslim white males than by Muslim Americans. Yet in spite of this, according to the Center for the Study of Hate and Extremism, the number of hate crimes against American Muslims has tripled since the Paris attacks and the mass shooting in San Bernardino, California, at the end of 2015, to 38 per month. Prior to these events, there were 12.6 suspected hate crimes against Muslims per month.[52] Negative rhetoric coming from politicians, non-Muslim religious leaders, the media, filmmaking, video games, and the like has the tendency to further divide the country instead of uniting non-Muslim and Muslim Americans around the central ideas of freedom and democracy. The overwhelming majority of Americans both Muslim and non-Muslim, wants to see personal freedom and democratic values abound in the United States.

49. Saleem, "Spreading Islamophobia."
50. Espiritu, "Negative Media Portrayal of Islam."
51. Moten and Noor, *Terrorism, Democracy*, 261 and 267.
52. Habib, "Islamophobia Is on the Rise."

Islam as Perceived by Southern Baptists—News and Scholarship

Owing in large part to misunderstandings, there is great tension between some Islamic and Western cultures. This tension can be clearly seen at the political level, but what is often overlooked as a cause in America's perception of and indeed systemic mistreatment of Muslims, is religion. Though the Constitution of the United States declares that "Congress shall make no law respecting an establishment of religion, or prohibiting the free exercise thereof," it is reasonable to expect that many policymakers at every level of government are indeed religious, in some cases even vocal in their faith. Can there ever really be a separation of Church and State in practice? Consequently, in practice, precepts of Christian religious thought trickle up to state governance, though the law explicitly orders a separation between the two domains. After all, how can one expect a policy maker to leave his or her religion at the door while entering their place of work? My observation is that devout Christians and Muslims will seek the wisdom and favor of God throughout their daily interactions with people—they don't simply leave their faith at the door. Theologian and businessperson David Miller has explored the question of religious diversity in the workplace and reveals how valuable faith in the workplace is to employees, CEOs, and the general marketplace. Miller writes, "The Faith at Work movement is the desire to live an integrated life, where faith teachings and workplace practices are aligned. Workers of all types, whether data entry clerks or senior executives, are no longer content to leave their souls in the parking lot. Businesspeople today want to find moral meaning and purpose in their work."[53] As a pastor, I used to encourage my congregation not to leave their faith at the door of their workplace. I implored them to take it with them, in the belief that Christian values, morals, and ethics can positively impact the workplace environment by improving personal relationships, the work ethic, and community relations. I have found that people are happier and more productive when they can bring all of themselves to work. Recognizing that there is a contemporary movement to allow for religious diversity in the workplace, it is important for us to note that while the three branches of government in the U.S. in theory draw a sharp dividing line between the secular and the religious, there are nonetheless religious overtones written into the very fabric of our Constitution. Polling shows that

---

53. Miller, *God at Work*, 6.

eighty-three percent of Americans identify as Christian, thirteen percent as nonreligious, and four percent as Buddhists, Muslims, Jews, and a smattering of other religions.[54] Research conducted by Rowatt, Franklin, and Cotton found that evangelical Christians are more likely to be less tolerant towards Muslims.[55] There is a paradox: religions teach tolerance and love for others, and yet they inadvertently create an "us against them" ethos. I will explore this topic much further in the next chapter.

In the case of evangelical Christians (those who are born-again by the Holy Spirit) and members of many mainline Protestant denominations, though they profess love of one's neighbor and of the stranger, they fundamentally believe that there is only one path to everlasting salvation, that path being the belief in Jesus the Christ. Any belief contrary to this can be construed as a threat—specifically a threat to culture and the Christian worldview. In the summer of 2021, at the Religious Liberty Summit at Notre Dame Law School, I heard American-Muslim public intellectual, religious-liberties attorney, and activist Asma T. Uddin speak to the fears that many evangelicals have about Islam. In her book *The Politics of Vulnerability* Uddin locates, with great sensitivity, the root of America's polarization in the Muslim and evangelical Christian divide and suggests how it can be healed. Many conservative Christians believe that traditional Christian values in America are under attack by the Left. Moreover, there is a growing fear that these values are running the risk of being replaced with an Islamized America—a conspiratorial theory, that Uddin says has given rise to an 'evangelical persecution complex,' a politicized vulnerability. Her research shows that Islamophobia and certain aspect of the conservative Christian movement are interrelated.[56] As I listened to Umma share her work, I was struck by her objectivity and sensitivity for both Muslims and evangelical Christians; it was clear to me that her work significantly contributes to the Muslim-Christian conversation on addressing the underlying factors of the politics of vulnerability and healing the divide.

The Christian worldview, more specifically the early Puritans influence on the founding of America, is woven into the political—both domestic and foreign, landscape. Amstutz writes, "From the time the first English migrants established settlements in New England in the early seventeenth century, the Christian religion has played an important

54. Langer, "Poll: Most Americans."
55. Glazier, "For God or Country?"
56. Uddin, *Politics of Vulnerability*.

role in public life, providing spiritual values, religious symbols, and more inspiration for the emerging American nation. The most important early settlers in North America were the Puritans."[57] Additionally, a determinant of American foreign policy can be traced back to the evangelical publication *The Christian Herald*, founded in 1878. *The Christian Herald* urged its readers to give money and time to alleviate hunger, poverty, and suffering at home and abroad. It became a very influential newspaper and arguably had a significant impact on how Americans perceived themselves and their role in world affairs.[58] The influence of the Puritans as well as publications such as *The Christian Herald* gave rise to this idea of American exceptionalism. Many Christians, especial conservative Christians, perceive the growth of Islam in America as a threat to their worldview and is consequently a plausible causal mechanism as to why there is such an alarming rate of anti-Muslim rhetoric in the United States. For instance, two Tennessee Republican state legislators, both belonging to the Methodist denomination, put forward a bill in 2011 that would prohibit recourse to what they call "sharia law." Why? Because, according to Hefner, they believe sharia is "prima facie evidence of an act in support of the overthrow of the United States government . . . by the likely use of imminent criminal violence and terrorism with the aim of imposing sharia on the people of [Tennessee]."[59] Though this bill was struck down, other legislation and statues have sought, and continue to seek, to prevent the "onset of 'other' legal traditions from threatening the ongoing existence of the American spirit as found in its legal tradition."[60] Quraishi-Landes notes, "at least nine states have passed 'foreign law' statutes banning sharia in American courts—even though no U.S. court has ever ruled based on sharia."[61] The sheer number of Southern Baptists in the United States has serious implications for local, state, and federal government. In 2016, there were 32 Southern Baptists elected to the U.S. Congress.[62] In 2019, there were 31.[63] Southern Baptists are the largest Evangelical denomination in the United States and have some of the most influential lobbying

---

57. Amstutz, *Evangelicals and American Foreign Policy*, 16.
58. For more on this topic see Curtis, *Holy Humanitarians*.
59. Hefner, *Shari'a Law*, 41.
60. Hefner, *Shari'a Law*, 41.
61. Quraishi-Landes, "Five Myths about Sharia."
62. Weaver, "Baptist in the 111th Congress."
63. Strode, "Protestants Remain Majority Group."

groups—For example, the Ethics and Religious Liberty Commission,[64] which speaks to issues in the public square. Southern Baptists and the greater Evangelical association of churches have a profound impact on United States policy both at home and abroad.

With a membership of nearly 14 million and over 47,000 clergy in the pulpit every Sunday preaching their interpretation of the Bible, it is paramount to explore what many of the leading preachers are saying about the religion of Islam and its founder, the Prophet Muhammad. Franklin Graham, the son of the late Southern Baptist evangelist Billy Graham said, "We're not attacking Islam, but Islam has attacked us. The God of Islam is not the same God. . . . It's a different God, and I believe it is a very evil and wicked religion."[65] Graham is the CEO of the Billy Graham Evangelistic Association and Samaritan's Purse, he is a multimedia evangelist, and has authored numerous books; he has a following of millions around the world. What he says carries significant weight in the evangelical community, comprising the family, the academy, the local church, and the Southern Baptist denomination.

In a 2002 interview with CNN's Paula Zahn, another well-known Baptist, Pat Robertson, said of Islam: "I have taken issue with our esteemed president (Bush 43) in regard to a stand in saying Islam is a peaceful religion. It is just not, and the Qur'an makes it very clear if you see an infidel, you are to kill him. . . . Islam is not a peaceful religion that wants to coexist. They want to coexist until they can control, dominate, and then if need be destroy."[66] Robertson is a media mogul, former Southern Baptist Minister, CEO of Regent University, and chairman of the Christian Broadcasting Network (CBN). *The 700 Club*, the longest-running syndicated program of Robertson, is viewed by at least a million people every day.

Dr. Jerry Vines, former president of the Southern Baptist Convention and long-time pastor of the megachurch First Baptist in Jacksonville, Florida, said at the Southern Baptist Convention in 2002, "They would have us believe that Islam is just as good as Christianity. Christianity was founded by the virgin-born son of God, Jesus Christ. Islam was founded by Muhammad, a demon-possessed pedophile who had 12 wives, the last one of which was a 9-year-old girl. . . . And I will tell you Allah is

---

64. Ethics and Religious Liberty Commission of the Southern Baptist Convention, erlc.com.
65. Hoover, "Is Evangelicalism Itching for a Fight?," 11.
66. Hoover, "Is Evangelicalism Itching for a Fight?," 11.

not Jehovah, either. Jehovah's not going to turn you into a terrorist."[67] In the aftermath of 9/11 another prominent figure in Southern Baptist life, the late Jerry Falwell, said, "I think Mohammed was a terrorist. I've read enough of the history of his life written by both Muslims and non-Muslims, that he was a violent man, a man of war."[68] The remarks by these leaders and similar remarks by other leaders not mentioned here, have led to the widespread belief within the evangelical Christian church that Islam is a wicked religion, and to the political repercussions that this belief has had upon the Muslim community in the United States.[69]

At the annual Southern Baptist Convention (SBC) held in 2016, many SBC leaders voiced concern, frustration, anger, fear, and opposition over allowing Muslim refugees from Syria into the United States and the building of mosques throughout the country. These concerns stem from various sources: perceived danger for homeland security, the threat of Islamic growth, conflicts of interest related to building mosques, and so forth. One of the most vocal pastors at the convention in 2016 was Carl Gallups, pastor of the Hickory Hammock Baptist Church in Milton, Florida. He fiercely voiced opposition to allowing more Syrian refugees into the U.S. and characterized Southern Baptists helping Muslims to build mosques as cooperating with evil. He said, "Has the SBC forgotten the Ottoman Empire? Have they forgotten the Barbary Wars, or 9/11? Has the SBC forgotten that the FBI says they are now tracking ISIS cells in all 50 states of the U.S.? Are you not aware of the fact that several Islamic mosques in America have been officially identified as nothing more than Islamic terrorist recruiting centers?"[70] He went on to call mosques Islamic brainwashing centers. Ethics and Religious Liberty Commission (ERLC) president Russell Moore argued that the government must not have the power to decide, on the basis of a religious group's doctrines, whether that group may erect a house of worship, since otherwise Southern Baptist churches might be prohibited from being built in parts of the country.[71] In other words, what is good for the goose is good for the gander. Further support for this idea is provided by Robert A. Dowd's comment, "In religiously diverse settings, religious leaders are more likely to come to learn that it would be in the best interest of their religious

67. Hoover, "Is Evangelicalism Itching for a Fight?," 11.
68. Hoover, "Is Evangelicalism Itching for a Fight?," 12.
69. Sachs, "Baptist Pastor Attacks Islam."
70. "Pastor to Southern Baptist Convention."
71. McCammon, "Southern Baptists Split."

communities if they would work to ensure that no religious institution has a privileged relationship with the state, rather than to persist in their efforts to maintain or achieve a privileged position for their religious communities over all others."[72]

There is great tension within the Southern Baptist denomination as to how best to respond to the religion of Islam and Muslims, especially post 9/11. The denomination is a complex organism, comprising millions of faithful people from all walks of life. A few interact with Muslims daily, while the vast majority have never spoken to a Muslim, much less seen a mosque. The evangelical church goes to great lengths every year to educate and provide the membership with the necessary knowledge and tools to engage in one-on-one evangelism. The denomination articulates its beliefs and practices in the Baptist Faith & Message 2000[73]—a document that provides the framework within which the denomination interprets the Holy Scripture. Southern Baptists believe that the repenting of one's sinful nature, the turning away from sin and self and the turning to Jesus the Christ and then (if able) following through with baptism by immersion is the only path to everlasting salvation in Heaven. The controversy regarding Islam is not whether it is a legitimate path unto God (according to Baptist doctrine it is not), but whether Southern Baptists should support legislators and legislation that seek to legitimize Islam and give equal religious rights to its followers in the U.S. As noted above, many Baptist leaders view Islam as a threat to the historical American culture and to civil peace. This sentiment was very clearly articulated by Arkansas pastor John Wofford at the 2016 Convention: "why should a Southern Baptist support the right of Muslims living in the United States to build mosques, when these people threaten our very way of existence as Christians and Americans?"[74] Wofford went further: "They (Muslims) are murdering Christians, beheading Christians, imprisoning Christians all over the world."[75] He also put forth a motion calling for the removal from office of SBC leaders who supported the right of Muslims to build mosques. Research reveals that this type of speech and action is common, especially when a person or group feels a certain level of threat to their way of life. Dowd writes, "They [religious leaders] may also negatively

72. Dowd, *Christianity, Islam, and Liberal Democracy*, 8.
73. For the text of the Baptist Faith and Message see http://www.sbc.net/bfm2000/bfm2000.asp.
74. McCammon, "Southern Baptists Split."
75. Mattingly, "Wait a Minute!"

portray other religious faith traditions in order to discourage conversions to these rival religions. We might even expect leaders of historically dominant faith traditions to use the legislative process and the courts to limit the freedoms of new or different religious faith traditions and communities. In fact, this is often what happens in religiously diverse settings until religious leaders realize that such efforts are futile and immensely costly for the religious institutions they lead."[76]

Some Baptist leaders are warning—not so fast! Russell Moore, president of the SBC's Ethics and Religious Liberty Commission, at a panel discussion in Washington D.C., urged Christians to consider the repercussions of turning away Syrian refugees and demonizing Muslims, arguing that the political tides could turn against Christians in the future, and that Federal policies implemented today could come to haunt another religious faith's freedom. In a response to then presidential candidate Donald Trump's and evangelical leader Franklin Graham's hard stance against Muslim immigration, Moore stated, "Demonization of Islam is not only wrong, but could lead to some very difficult situations in terms of security. If we are going to confront radical Islam, we're going to have to have Muslim and Arab partners."[77] One of the panelists, Afshin Ziafat, pastor of Providence Church in Frisco, Texas, was not always a devout Christian. He was born into a devout Muslim family in Iran in 1972 and fled during the Islamic revolution. His family endured great hardship while immigrating into the U.S. From his family's car tires being slashed, rocks thrown into the windows of their house, and BB guns being fired at them, on top of all the verbal insults, they found themselves being re-victimized. It wasn't until a Christian tutor took interest in him and loved him unto God that he became a Christian. Ziafat said, "I'm thankful that one lady looked at our family and particularly looked at me and didn't see a threat, but saw an opportunity."[78] As a Christian pastor, he urged those attending the panel to keep a "gospel-oriented" point of view on the Syrian refugee crisis and to remember that "the goal of a Christian shouldn't just be to preserve my life but to expend my life for the gospel."[79]

The annual Southern Baptist Convention consists of an appointed group of people who seek to understand and faithfully execute a worldview that they believe is in harmony with the Holy Bible, their local

76. Dowd, *Christianity, Islam, and Liberal Democracy*, 8.
77. Derrick, "ERLC Panel."
78. Derrick, "ERLC Panel."
79. Derrick, "ERLC Panel."

church, and denomination. I believe this is a lofty and admirable goal—one that requires rigorous theological debate, consensus of the majority, political aptitude, and sociocultural awareness, especially as it relates to Muslims. The denomination has very vivacious and healthy educational programs and institutes which inform and guide its membership on personal growth and public involvement. Though the Baptist Faith and Message provides a systematic theological structure of norms that guide local churches and congregants regarding matters of life, by and large, Southern Baptists resist spiritual hierarchy within church government. However, the influence of elected leaders and seminaries can and indeed do have powerful sway over pastors and churchgoers.

Numerous Southern Baptist scholars have effectively communicated the denomination's stance on Islam and how to relate to the people of Islam. One of the more widely accepted views of Islam within the denomination can be found in renowned authors John Ankerberg and John Weldon in their short book *The Facts on Islam*.[80] Over two million copies of this work have been sold and it is widely used by Southern Baptist ministers to educate their people about Islam and the prescribed response to it. Ankerberg and Weldon introduce their book by raising the question, "Why is Islam important?" They identify several causes relating to the growth, spread, and influence of Islam. These "facts," as they put it, can cause great angst within a predominantly evangelical audience. Without a proper grounding in how best to confront the upsurge of feelings these "facts" produce, one may find oneself giving way to misdirected anger and frustration targeting American Muslims. The list below breaks down some of the key reasons offered by Ankerberg and Weldon as to why Christians might well be concerned about Islam.

1. There are more than one billion followers of Islam in the world.
2. The collective power of Islam is able to dramatically influence the world economy through OPEC
3. The growing religious influence of Islam outside Islamic nations is unmistakable.
4. Islam has the ability to play a key role in the social stability or instability of dozens of governments around the world.
5. A principal goal of Islam is to bring Islamic law to every nation.

---

80. Ankerberg and Weldon, *Facts on Islam*.

6. Islam has the power to change the destinies of hundreds of millions of people—and perhaps the West itself.
7. Arab nationalism and the Muslim religion have become the single most crucial issue in the volatile Middle East.
8. Islam is the fastest growing religion in the world.
9. Islam dominates more than 40 countries on three continents.
10. Over 30 countries now have populations that are at least 87% Muslim. It has become the second largest religion in Europe and the third largest in the U.S.
11. The ideological influence of Islam expands to other nations on a daily basis, and Islamic fundamentalism is increasingly aggressive.
12. World Watch Persecution Index, published by Open Doors, revealed that, apart from North Korea and China, Islamic-dominated countries occupied every single spot on the top ten list of countries where persecution of Christians is most severe.

When I was actively pastoring, I can assure you that these facts were very concerning to me as an evangelical Christian and preacher. I felt as though it was my duty to share this information with my congregation and then provide them with informational tools to effectively witness to Muslims. My rhetoric and tone needed to be one of love, otherwise it might unintentionally incite feelings of anger among the congregation, possibly resulting in varying degrees of religious hate crimes against Muslims—crimes that would work against our belief that God loves all people and that, consequently, we are instructed to love all people as well. My understanding of Islam greatly affected my congregation's perception of Islam and the character of their dialogue with Muslims. Hence, I argue, it is crucial to take into account the local minister's perception of Islam as it will directly affect people within his sphere of influence, some of which are policymakers in the United States government. Owing to this realism, during the fall of 2017 and winter of 2018, I set out on a journey to interview pastors and spiritual leaders within the denomination regarding their understanding of Islam and Muslims. Below are my findings.

Islam as Perceived by Southern Baptists— Insights from In-Depth Interviews

At this point, I have identified the demographics of the Muslim population in the United States and uncovered some of the anti-Islamic rhetoric in politics as well as identified some of the official beliefs of Southern Baptists. I purposefully began rather broadly and will now narrow the descriptive-empirical task down to gathering information from grass roots Southern Baptist leaders. In this connection, I believe it is essential to note that religious people will most often choose religious leaders who share and seek to promote their beliefs, which in return fosters a greater sense of belonging, community, security, and power. A Southern Baptist example of this is seen in the conservative resurgence of the late 1970s and 1980s, by which conservative leaders gained control of the denomination in order to stop the liberal trajectory. The changes implemented during that resurgence are present within the denomination today. Southern Baptist leaders remain in power so long as the people they represent are content with the message being spoken. Therefore, to appreciate the general perception of Islam and the degree of influence the Southern Baptist denomination has in the United States, it is important to hear from their spiritual leaders. To hear from the leaders is to hear from the masses of people they represent. The nineteenth-century sociologist Max Weber argued in his *Sociology of Religion* that people pursue their own interests and find religious leaders and structures that will aid them in supporting their goals.[81] Furthermore, religion is a tool that offers both stability and social change. Weber identified several processes by which this change has occurred: magicians, gods, priesthood, and prophets—the latter being the primary tool of change in modern times. Sociologist Jeremy Townsley further explains this point of Weber's:

> Similar to magicians, they [prophets] are empowered by the community because of their gift of charisma. However, the difference is that the purpose of the prophet is to disseminate a new doctrine or ethical standard not to perform magic. So when cultural changes produced various injustices, a prophet would arise to reveal a new doctrine to supplant the old system, thus correcting these injustices.
>
> It is at this point that the structure is laid for the larger pattern of society. First, members of a community have material

---

81. Weber, *Sociology of Religion*.

interests, be they food, shelter or protection from enemies. Magicians at one time helped them with these needs, but as society stabilized into better developed political systems and as population density grew, the random practices of magicians were systematized by priests through a process of rationalization, which developed into structures to support standardized community practice for efficient control, placation and supplication of the gods. These systems developed into bureaucracies, a concept that is foundational to Weber's view of social stabilization, the maintenance of cultural symbols and the distribution of goods and services to the modern state. He carries over the concept of the prophet, pointing to individuals who, because of charismatic ideas, produce changes in the direction of society. For example, Luther and Calvin evolved religious ideas that developed into an asceticism that allowed capitalism to establish itself and become the dominant social and economic structure in the West. The ideas of a prophet, once they become established and rationalized, then become bureaucratized and wait for the next prophet to come along and start the cycle again.[82]

In this vein, it is helpful to hear what community pastors and leaders within Southern Baptist congregations are saying about the religion of Islam, the Prophet Muhammad, and jihad. In order to hear from the pastors, I met and interviewed fifteen licensed and ordained pastors of the Southern Baptist denomination, all of whom have earned advanced degrees in theology. These men have pastored small, medium, and large congregations with memberships ranging from 300 to 3,000 people. These pastors constitute what I believe to be a sufficient sampling of representatives from the denomination, thus offering me insights into the generalized view of Southern Baptists regarding their perceptions of Islam and the Prophet Muhammad. Some of these men I know personally, while others were recommended to me by former colleagues and friends. To protect their identity, I withhold their names and the names of their churches, referring to them only by the state they preach in. I asked the following questions:

- Can you share with me what you know about the founder of Islam?
- What is your perception of Islam and what factors have contributed to your perception?

---

82. Townsley, "Marx, Weber and Durkheim on Religion."

- Do you have a personal relationship with any Muslim in the workplace, the community, and/or in an ecumenical setting, and if so, what is your relationship with them?
- What is one word or phrase you would use to describe Muslims and why?
- Are there any passages from the Qur'an that you are familiar with or have heard the media speak of and how do they make you feel?
- How would you describe the religion of Islam?
- In a word or a brief statement, what comes to your mind when I say "Qur'an" and why?
- In a word or a brief statement, what comes to your mind when I say "Muhammad" and why?
- On a scale of 1 to 5, do you think Islam is a peaceful religion (5 being extremely peaceful, 1 being not peaceful at all) and can you share with me why you feel this way?
- Do you perceive Islam as being a threat to your way of life, why or why not? What is your greatest fear of Islam and why?

It is interesting to note that, as can be seen in table 2.7, the answers were remarkably similar across interviewees; it made no difference where the pastor was from, be it Alabama, Florida, Georgia, Mississippi, North Carolina, or Tennessee, his age, or the college or seminary that he graduated from.

Prior to conducting the interviews, I contacted each participant by phone or by email requesting that he participate in a research study that seeks to better understand the perception of Southern Baptists toward world religions. I was careful not to disclose too much information up front for fear that some participants would research the topic more thoroughly prior to the interview, thus skewing their existing perception of Islam. The participants, though eager to be part of my research efforts, were none the less concerned about not knowing the specific topic ahead of time. The day for each interview arrived and without exception the pastors who agreed to be interviewed were very welcoming. After the greetings and small talk, I introduced them to the subject of my research and in every situation the pastors were eager to disclose the knowledge and perceptions they had of Islam, the Prophet Muhammad, and jihad. The average interview time spent with each pastor was one hour. In each conversation, the pastor or spiritual leader began with a disclosure that went something like this: "I don't know a lot about Islam nor do I know many, if any Muslims, but I'll answer your questions the best I can." Then with a slight grin and a gesture of the hand by the pastor, the interview would commence.

During the interview sessions, I asked the eleven questions listed above, emphasizing that there were no right or wrong answers; I only wanted their perceptions to be disclosed in that moment. I requested they liken the questions and their responses to an informal conversation held with one of their church members after Sunday evening worship. After reassuring them that I was not seeking a specific answer, only their immediate replies to the questions, they offered responses that, unbeknownst to them, shed light on some of the causal mechanisms that underlie anti-Muslim beliefs in the United States—causal mechanisms that I will explore in the next chapters. Below I list the interview questions and provide some excerpts of the responses offered by the pastors.

Q. Can you share with me what you know about the founder of Islam?

Not a whole lot | He came from a shady background | He was a pedophile | He received a vision and was told to recite | He had multiple wives | Not a good guy | He killed a lot of Jews | Lived during the fifth century

Q. What is your perception of Islam?

U.S. Muslims are peaceful people | Some Muslims are terrorists | Not all Muslims are evil, some are peaceful | Muslims are often easier to get along with than Jews | Extremist religion | A religion of false assumptions | The Qur'an is questionable | One is born into Islam and dies as a Muslim or departs as an infidel | No guarantee of Heaven unless you die in jihad | Willing to kill children

Q. What factors have contributed to your perception?

News Media | Personal encounter | Religious course in seminary | Baptist press | Social media | Conversations with colleagues

Q. Do you have a personal relationship with any Muslims in the workplace, the community, and/or in an ecumenical setting? If so, what is your relationship with them?

No | Once | Very little | I don't know any Muslims | My doctor is Muslim | A Muslim family attended our fall festival | There are no mosques in our community | I don't know any Imams | Yes, my professor in college was Muslim and converted to Christianity

Q. *What is one word or phrase you would use to describe Muslims and why?*

Dedicated but uninformed | Misdirected | Very religious | Lost | Salvation is works based | Direct contradiction to the Bible | Good hearts | Different | Low view of women | The way they exercise their religion tends to be a lot more extreme than Western civilization | Speak differently | Somewhat difficult to comprehend | Culturally and religiously different | Sincerely misguided | They do not trust in Christ as their savior

Q. *Are there any passages from the Qur'an that you are familiar with or have heard the media speak of*

Not particularly | I don't put a lot of stock in the Qur'an | My views trump what the media tells me about Muslims | I've never read the Qur'an | I've never heard the media quote any part of the Qur'an | I remember reading a verse that those who follow other religions should be eliminated | Jihad by the sword | Kill the infidels

Q. *How did the passages make you feel?*

I don't have any particular feelings about the Qur'an | I don't encounter Muslims often and I don't study it much | I ignore the media, I know what I know about Islam and the media isn't going to change it | Surprised to hear the call to kill infidels | I check the facts when I hear some disturbing news about Islam in the media | Upset that Islam takes away from the person of Christ

Q. *How would you describe the religion of Islam?*

Lots of rules | Stated time of prayer, fasting, etc. | Rules about how women should dress, very different from our religion | Works based | A religion that demands a stringent adherence to their laws and belief system | Islamic women are controlled by their husbands | A father can kill his daughter when there is a moral violation | I'm sure not all Islamic countries are extreme | A religion of obedience | Misguided

Q. In a word or a brief statement, what comes to mind when I say "Qur'an," and why?

I think of Muslims | I can't think of anything—honestly | A sham | An unholy book, not authored by God | A book of religious persuasion | A religious cookbook | A recipe for living | I've not studied the Qur'an | Man-made teaching

Q. On a scale of 1 to 5, do you think Islam is a peaceful religion (5 being extremely peaceful, 1 being not peaceful at all) and can you share with me why you feel this way?

2—acts of terrorism plagues the religion | 3—everyday Muslims seem peaceful enough, but can be radicalized | 3—there are a lot of incidents in the world where jihadist and followers of Islam have committed horrible acts of violence in the name of their religion | I have not read the Qur'an and cannot say whether it is a peaceful religion or not | Between a 2 and a 3—there are peaceful people within the religion, but there are also many who are violent | 2—some teachings call for the slaughter of non-Muslims | 4.5—5—most Muslims in the United States are peaceful people, but Muslims who adhere to sharia are not peaceful at all, they believe in killing the infidels

Q: Do you perceive Islam as being a threat to your way of life? Why or why not?

Yes | I see them as a threat | Militant type Muslims are trying to take over the world | They are having a lot of children, more so than Christians | Yes and no, no religion is a threat to my way of life, to live is Christ, but to die is gain | Sharia law is a threat to our democracy | I don't see Islam as a threat, but as an opportunity | I can't say, I really don't understand that much about Islam | Eventually there will be more of them in the world than us | A potential threat, I do not see it as a threat at this time | If sharia law is allowed in parts of America it will be a definite threat | Any religions that does not preach Jesus Christ is a threat

Q: What is your greatest fear of Islam and why?

False salvation | I fear that they seem to be very militant | I'm concerned that they are willing to kill others to promote their belief | I fear we will not take Islam seriously and not be prepared to be an effective witness | It is a false foundation that leads people in the wrong direction | I don't fear Islam | I fear more and more people will go down that path

| They are reaching people we should be reaching | God has everything in control, I don't fear Islam | I'm not worried about it, God is in control

The interview questions and the responses provide great insight into the way Southern Baptist leaders view Islam, the Prophet Muhammad, and jihad. All three topics are of considerable interest in my research, especially since I have observed anti-Islamic rhetoric within Southern Baptist conversations, particularly with respect to these three topics. Below I describe the main insights to be gleaned from the interviews. To the credit of most of the leaders interviewed, they have embarked upon some learning of Islam, though it is rudimentary at best. Islam is as diverse as it is large and understanding Islam, if one can use such a general statement, requires personal encounters with Muslims and a thorough education in Islam, which most non-Muslims are not afforded. Suffice it to say at this juncture that it is crucial that non-Muslims, including Southern Baptist leaders, not over-generalize Muslims and the religion of Islam. After the death of the Prophet Muhammad, Islam splintered into many distinctive sects, and within each sect one has to calculate the varying degrees of influence exercised by the State, by ethnicity, and by culture.

The life and spirituality of the Prophet Muhammad are demonstrably unknown to Southern Baptist leaders. When asked to share with me what is known about the founder of Islam, a few struggled to recall Muhammad's name, some were proud to rattle off the dates in which he lived; the majority interviewed said he was a false prophet and a pedophile. One pastor in northwest Florida said, "I know he killed a lot of Jews and Islam was rooted in a lot of violence. Muhammad had multiple wives, I know the youngest was age six and he consummated the marriage at the age of nine. Overall not a good guy, a guy who did not adhere to his own beliefs."[83] Another pastor, from North Carolina said, "He came from a rather shady background and had some things in his life that were not on the up and up. I understand he was a pedophile. As best as I can recall, he wasn't sure of the revelation he received, was it from God or the devil. His wife convinced him it was of God."[84] Time and again, my interviewees conveyed similar messages regarding their knowledge of the founder of Islam. Eleven of those interviewed had very little knowledge of the founder of Islam, three demonstrated knowledge of what century

---

83. Interview by author, tape recording, Florida, 4 Jan. 2018.
84. Interview by author, tape recording, Tennessee, 18 Feb. 2018.

he lived in, and one knew enough to engage in a historical conversation regarding Muhammad's young adult life, revelation experiences, and personal journey. Few were able to name the two primary branches of Islam (Sunni and Shia) or identify the five pillars of Islam (faith, prayer, charity, fasting, pilgrimage to Mecca). Though the questions were not an official test of their knowledge, they did reveal that most were lacking general familiarity of Islam and consequently a bit uncomfortable having their responses recorded. Historically, Islam has not received widespread objective and comprehensive consideration in Southern Baptist seminaries. I was first introduced to Islam at the New Orleans Baptist Theological Seminary by Dr. Steve Lemke in the course *Introduction to Philosophy of Religion*. Reflecting back, I think he was objective when introducing the class to Islam, but unfortunately and due to the nature of the course, very little time was allotted to learning about this religion of nearly 2 billion adherents. Beyond this course, I can only think of one other course that required me to read a few pages on Islam—a reading I talk about later in this chapter. As my interviews suggest and I have personally experienced, there is a pronounced shortage of knowledge among Southern Baptists at it relates to Islam. I do see some trends within the denomination, especially after 9/11, that this lack of knowledge is diminishing.

As I expected, one's perception of Islam and the factors behind its formation varied. Perceptions were determined by such factors as the political party the respondent belonged to, what they heard in the media, where they had traveled for work or vacation, who they knew, and to what extent their knowledge derived from religious education. With regard to political party affiliation, most Southern Baptists are registered and vote Republican (see table 2.7) and most Republicans watch Fox News as their primary source of world news.[85] According to research conducted by Dr. Christine Ogan, Fox news is more critical of Islam and Muslims than similar news outlets such as CNN and MSNBC.[86]

---

85. Pew Research Center, "Demographics and Political Views."
86. Ogan, "Rise of Anti-Muslim Prejudice."

Political ideology among members of the Southern Baptist Convention by political party (2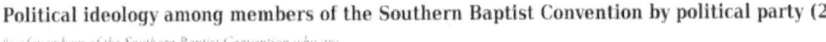
% of members of the Southern Baptist Convention who are...

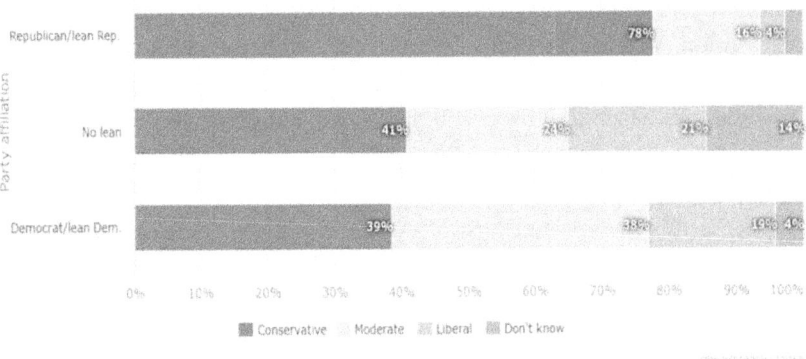

Table 2.7. Political ideology among members of the SBC.[87]

Of the pastors interviewed, only five percent had traveled to the Middle East and in most cases, it was Israel (more specifically Jerusalem)—a country where seventy-four percent of its population is Jewish. Jerusalem is a sacred city to Jews, Christians, and Muslims. King David formed a kingdom in the tenth century B.C.E., Jesus was a first century Jewish preacher and teacher who was crucified for statements made and would later become the anointed one of God for Christians, and finally, it was where the Prophet Muhammad ascended into heaven and met Abraham, Moses, Jesus, and God. For over a thousand years Jewish, Christian, and Muslim rulers have fought over land and holy sites they each deem valuable to their own religious narrative.[88] In 1948, in the aftermath of World War II, Israel was granted statehood and the Palestinians were forced out. Consequently, tensions escalated between Jews and Muslims, and civil as well as political unrest has become a feature of everyday life. When Southern Baptist pastors and leaders visit Israel, this on-going conflict is present to them. They often observe the Israeli army in the streets and along the borders securing the safety of Jews—Palestinian Muslims are viewed as a threat to security. Today, many, if not most, Southern Baptists promote "Christian Zionism"—a movement that arose among Protestants, especially the Puritans, in the sixteenth and seventeenth centuries—that stems in large part from Christian apocalyptic literature. In essence, this is the

87. Pew Research Center, "Political Ideology among Members."
88. For a detailed history of the city of Jerusalem see Montefiore, *Jerusalem*.

belief that the gathering of Jews in Israel is a prerequisite to the second coming of Christ and therefore any group that opposes this movement is frowned upon.[89] Hence, many leave with a negative impression of Islam (since most Palestinians are Muslims), reinforcing any previously existing perception. When a pastor or leader did encounter an amicable Muslim in Israel, it was viewed more as an anomaly than as the norm. One of my interviewees told of his encounter with a taxicab driver in Jerusalem, commenting—as though it was something odd—that the cab driver was Muslim and very friendly. He was at once pleased and yet somehow surprised at this unexpected turn of events. Owing to the denomination's Judeo-Christian roots, Israel, and in particular Jerusalem, is viewed as a sacred place to many Southern Baptists. From the time most Southern Baptists are born until the time they depart this world, they have been taught that Israel is the "chosen" nation of God. In Sunday school, I, along with most Southern Baptists I have spoken with, remember our teachers telling us to pray for Israel. In the call of Abraham God said, "I will make of you a great nation, and I will bless you, and make your name great, so that you will be a blessing. I will bless those who bless you, and the one who curses you I will curse; and in you all the families of the earth shall be blessed."[90] This and other verses throughout the Bible set a certain perception of how one is to feel and act towards Israel. Hence, in the event that this perception is threatened, it can cause a multitude of negative emotions to abound. For example, Jerry Falwell (d. 2007), Southern Baptist, evangelical, founder of the Moral Majority, said, "To stand against Israel, is to stand against God."[91]

In most cases, leaders within the denomination have not visited Israel, and outside of what they have read and been taught, they lack a thorough understanding of the culture, language, and history of Jewish-Muslim relations. In brief, leaders are speaking of a culture and ethnic group that they have very limited understanding of and encounter with. This limitation is exacerbated by geographic separation. As one pastor from Tennessee said, "I do not have many opportunities to encounter Muslims."[92] The majority of pastors live and breathe within their denominational circles and can rarely afford the time to seek out their Muslim counterparts and engage in dialogue, much less discover Muslims living

---

89. Amstutz, *Evangelicals and American Foreign Policy*, 119–42.
90. Genesis 12:1–3 (NRSV).
91. Amayreh, "Against Israel against God."
92. Interview by author, North Carolina, 18 February 2018.

within their community. This is not a judgment, only an observation from personal experience and communication with fellow Baptist pastors—this must change!

As I alluded to above, most of the denominational leaders I interviewed acknowledged that prior to 9/11 they had not been challenged to study Islam. To the extent they had, it was usually incorporated into a broader study of "other religions" while in seminary. For example, when I was in seminary, I was further introduced to Islam by reading the book *Missiology: An Introduction to the Foundations, History, and Strategies of World Missions*.[93] A total of thirteen pages introduced me to the second largest religion in the world, one that, within one hundred years of its founder's death, had become one of the largest and most successful empires in history. Though the authors of the book present Islam in an unbiased way, my case illustrates how little time the average Southern Baptist minister spends while in college and seminary studying Islam and developing a thorough understanding of its tenets and multi-cultural dynamics. With the growth of interest in Islam in this century, some seminaries are now offering degrees with a concentration in Islamic Studies (e.g., New Orleans Baptist Theological Seminary and Southern Baptist Theological Seminary). The pastors I interviewed had completed their studies before the acts of terrorism on 9/11 and the Syrian refugee crisis of 2016, at a time when the seminaries had not yet come to embrace a more thorough education in Islamic studies. For most of the pastors and leaders I interviewed, their seminary education provided them with a general overview of the Prophet Muhammad and a brief introduction to the basic tenets of Islam. More often than not, the purpose of their instruction was to discredit the religion of Islam through quotations of the Bible and other Christian literature. Besides this introduction, some pastors had engaged in a quick study of their own to answer questions from their congregants as well as to have a better understanding of Islam themselves. Most of the sources they consulted, be it in seminary or in the pastorate, were written by authors whose primary purpose was to discredit Islam and promote Christianity. Christian apologetics is a dynamic and useful tool when the pastor is seeking to offer evidence and reasoning behind his Christian beliefs, especially when seeking to unite and strengthen his Christian base; but I believe it is necessary to consult scholarly work on Islam and its founder where the primary intent is not to discredit but to explain the

---

93. Terry, Smith, and Anderson, *Missiology*, 379–92.

history and reasoning behind the religion. Though a seminary education and personal study are good and worthwhile endeavors, the interviews I conducted revealed it was a personal relationship with a Muslim or group of Muslims that significantly altered one's perception of Islam. In most cases, the leaders had positive experiences with Muslims and came to appreciate them as good people—people who were not hell bent on killing Jews and Christians. A pastor of one of the larger churches in northwest Florida told me he was educated under the tutelage of Professor Caner (who is now the president of Truett McConnell University). He said, "I think the contributing factors to my perception of Islam, have been what I have studied and who I have studied under."[94] Prior to becoming a professor, Caner had grown up in a Sunni Muslim family whose father was a leader. Caner led this pastor and others in the class on a journey of understanding Islam through his own experiences. This learning experience by the pastor contributed to his understanding of the humanness of Muslims. He went on to say that while some paint a rather broad picture of Muslims as being evil, he knows some very agreeable Muslims; some of whom are very kind and peaceful in their approach to life. Another of my interviewees, who views Islam as a sham and clearly does not appreciate the salvific-works message it puts forth or the views of its adherents, did state that an infrequent conversation with a fellow co-worker helped him to see that not all Muslims are alike; this particular Muslim was kind and peaceable.[95]

Though I did not specifically ask a question concerning jihad, each conversationalist volunteered their understanding of jihad and why it was of concern to them. The exploration of their perceptions of jihad surfaced on average at least two times during each interview and derived from the following questions: "On a scale of 1 to 5, do you think Islam is a peaceful religion and can you share with me why you feel this way?" and "Do you perceive Islam as being a threat to your way of life? Why or why not?"

The first question revealed a perception among many Southern Baptist leaders that the religion of Islam—not the individual person—calls for violence, which is carried out in the form of jihad. Pastors and leaders answered this question with the following statements: the teachings of Islam are undeniably not peaceful; some teachings call for the

---

94. Interview by author, Florida, 4 January 2018.
95. Interview by author, Florida, 5 January 2018.

slaughter of non-Muslims; horrible acts of violence have been committed in the name of their religion; Sharia Muslims are not peaceful at all—they believe in killing the infidels. In the cases where a pastor knew a Muslim, there was a positive perception of that Muslim, but a negative perception emerged when speaking of Muslims in a larger context. As one Florida pastor commented, "I know some peaceful Muslims, the ones I know are extremely kind and peaceful."[96] In every interview conducted, with the exception of those who did not know a Muslim, denominational leaders spoke well of the Muslim or Muslims they knew. A pastor from North Carolina went as far to say that U.S. Muslims are peaceful people and they want to be good citizens.[97]

The second question revealed a reluctance on the part of most of the Baptist leaders to admit that they felt threatened by Islam. There was usually a pause revealing that the pastor was seeking to carefully gather his thoughts so as to offer a comment that was true to his faith and to his personal perception of the religion of Islam. One pastor said, "I do fear the fact that they seem to be more militant than we are, especially the jihadist. I think they don't mind losing their lives for what they believe. I think they count it a privilege of losing their lives for what they believe."[98] Another pastor responded to the question by saying, "In a sense yes and in a sense no. No religion is a threat to my way of life. . . . I don't perceive Islam as being a threat. On the other hand, I can see how people feel threatened by Sharia Law."[99] Furthermore, the pastor drew a reference to the 2011 comments of Justice Ruth Bader Ginsburg that the U.S. Supreme Court should be open to the understandings and rulings of International Law in its decisions. According to findings published by the Center for Security Policy, at least 50 significant cases of Shariah law were found in U.S. state courts[100]—a finding that has many conservative Southern Baptist leaders raising concerns and demanding answers.

Asked whether Islam is a threat to his way of life, one of my interviewees stated, "I can't say, because once again, I don't really understand that much about Islam. I know their population is expanding faster than any other population in the world and eventually there will be more of

96. Interview by author, Florida, 4 January 2018.
97. Interview by author, North Carolina, 18 February 2018.
98. Interview by author, Mississippi, 3 January 2018.
99. Interview by author, Florida, 4 January 2018.
100. Center for Security Policy, "Shariah Law."

them than anyone else in the world."[101] This response is characteristic on the question whether Islam is a threat. All of my interviewees referred, directly or indirectly, to the growth of the Muslim population and the uncertainty surrounding the impact on the U.S. and the world.

To summarize the results of the interviews, there were 6 prevailing ideas:

1. Most of those interviewed admitted to knowing very little about Islam.
2. Most admitted to having no personal encounter with a Muslim.
3. Consistently voiced that Muhammad was a pedophile and a polygamist.
4. Unfailingly said that Muhammad's message was one of intolerance and violence.
5. Though only one could quote the verse, all interviewees referred to the "sword verses"[102] and the notion that for Muslims killing the infidels was an honor.
6. All stated in various ways that Islam is a lie from the Devil.

Well-known and respected pastor Robert Jeffress of First Baptist Church of Dallas cut straight to the heart of the matter in a sermon broadcasted on August 23, 2010. He captured the general view of Muslims and Islam among Southern Baptist leaders when he said:

> That [the comparison of the Christian Crusades of the Middle Ages to jihad] is something that is often thrown at Christians, and it's true, Christians have done some horrible things throughout history in the name of Christ. . . . These things that Christians have done, they have done in opposition to the teaching of the New Testament. You cannot find a verse anywhere in the New Testament that commands violence against unbelievers. . . . But Muslims, when they commit violence they're acting in accordance with what the Qur'an teaches. There are a least 35 so-called sword verses that explicitly call for violence against infidels, and they are acting in accordance to what their book is telling them to do. And while I'm on that topic, I think we need to be very clear about this, especially in relation to this building of a Mosque in Ground Zero. The only argument that makes

---

101. Interview by author, Mississippi, 3 January 2018.
102. Repentance 9:5; 9:29 (Qur'an).

sense against building the Mosque is to tell the truth about Islam, and that is, that Islam is an oppressive religion. If you don't believe that, just look at the way it treats women around the world, requiring that there be four witnesses for the rape to be reported, beating women who committed adultery, but letting the men go free. It is an oppressive treater of women, it is a religion—and here is a deep, dark, dirty secret of Islam—it is a religion that promotes pedophilia, sex with children, their so-called prophet Muhammad raped a 9 year old girl, had sex with her. . . . It is an evil religion, it is an oppressive religion, it is a violent religion that is inside the attacks against the world and against our country, and for Christians, the worst thing about Islam is that it is a false religion that leads people away from God and to spend an eternity in hell, and I believe, as Christians and conservatives, it's time to take off the gloves and stand up and tell the truth about this evil, evil religion.[103]

This sermon, broadcasted on television and easily viewed on the internet, is a testament to how outspoken and adamant many Southern Baptists are regarding their beliefs about Islam—beliefs that it is an evil and violent religion founded by a pedophile and warmonger. When SBC leaders, who pilot these large mega-churches, speak such rhetoric, it incites the religious base against Islam.

Conclusion

At this juncture, we can see, at least in part, what is going on within the Southern Baptist denomination and to some extent non-Muslim American culture more broadly. The interviews conducted revealed a bias against Islam, leavened, however, by the observation that all of the Muslims personally known to the denomination's leaders were kind and peaceable people. Although as a group Muslims are still viewed as intolerant and violent, those Southern Baptist leaders who personally knew a Muslim expressed their belief that the Muslim is sincerely misguided or wholly wrong in his or her belief in salvation but was indeed a kind and often generous person. Those denominational leaders who had no personal encounter with a Muslim outside of a proselytizing activity (often cloaked in interreligious dialogue) clearly saw them as a threat to American culture—at their perception of American culture. In most cases, the

---

103. Jeffress, Sermon, First Baptist Church.

perception of Muslims was derived from news outlets, teachings of the church, and personal encounters. In chapter 4, I offer ways of improving one's perception of Islam and promoting a cultural environment that allows for authentic transformation of the heart and mind towards the religious other. This transformation can allow for meaningful dialogue—dialogue that can greatly benefit the Southern Baptist leader seeking to share the gospel with non-Christians.

In this chapter I raised the question, "What is going on?"—particularly, what is going on within the Southern Baptist denomination and its leaders regarding their perceptions of Islam and the Prophet Muhammad. I employed the descriptive empirical task to explore this question; a question of utmost importance as tensions between Muslims and non-Muslims continue to flare in the United States. I identified three reasons for the anti-Muslim rhetoric in the U.S. First, I gave a demographic sketch of the U.S. Muslim population showing that only one percent of the general population is American-Muslim and that most of them live in metropolitan cities. Second, via newspaper articles, journals, YouTube videos, and scholarly works, I revealed how Muslims are negatively portrayed, and thus perceived by many within the Southern Baptist denomination. Lastly, via personal interviews, I heard from grassroots religious leaders how they perceived Islam, the Prophet Muhammad, and jihad. Having set forth *what is going on*, I now turn my attention to the second step in discerning the problematic behavior—the interpretive task of practical theology.

3

Why Is It Going On

The Reality of Anti-Muslim Rhetoric in the Southern Baptist Denomination

Introduction

WHY IS THERE SUCH anti-Islamic rhetoric in the Southern Baptist denomination? Using the descriptive-empirical task, in the previous chapter I gathered information to help us formulate this pressing question of why. In this chapter, I give attention to some theories that will help us to gain a more thorough understanding of the anti-Muslim rhetoric that occurs in the denomination and in the United States writ large. To begin with, I emphasize what Osmer calls *wise judgment*. He writes of it, "This is crucial to good leadership. It is the capacity to interpret episodes, situations, and contexts in three interrelated ways: (1) recognition of the relevant particulars of specific events and circumstances; (2) discernment of the moral ends at stake; (3) determination of the most effective means to achieve these ends in light of the constraints and possibilities of a particular time and place."[1] This conception of wise judgment derives from moral philosophy and theology, primarily as they developed in Western Christianity under the influence of Aristotle. Aristotle's concept

---

1. Osmer, *Practical Theology*, 84.

of *phronesis* can be rendered as both "practical wisdom" and "prudence." It is an important concept for the leader to understand, if he is to display discernment and action when addressing an issue of concern.[2] In the New Testament, Jesus is referred to as the wisdom of God (I Corinthians 1:18—2:16). According to many Christian theologians, He is all-knowing and thus able to discern the whys and wherefores of a situation and judge on the basis of all his knowledge. In this vein, all Southern Baptist leaders I know state their desire to promote the truth of God to the best of their ability. But we are all susceptible to the pitfalls of human nature and of our culture, and it requires incredible discipline to consistently scrutinize oneself so as to navigate these pitfalls and to ensure what one believes to be truth is in fact truth.

In this chapter, I rely on concepts fundamental to the study of human and group psychology. I set forth some of the causal mechanisms that can produce emotions of anger, fear, and insecurity, which often contribute to the root causes of defamation, more specifically slander. I found the expression of these three emotions to be common among the leaders of the Southern Baptist church, both in my interviews and in on-line postings, sermons, and articles. To understand these emotions, I have consulted a large body of scholarly literature that describes the fundamental reasons behind such feelings. For example, below I identify attitudinal and behavioral clusters found within the Southern Baptist denomination, such as Right-wing Authoritarianism, which can help explain some of the reasons behind the negative rhetoric used by Southern Baptists towards Islam. Getting to the origin of these emotions can significantly aid the pastor and church leader in being a better conduit of some of God's attributes to a world in need. I argue that a lack of knowledge and education about Islam often produces anger, fear, and insecurity in the non-Muslim psyche. These three emotions tend to stem from a lack of personal encounters with Muslims—a narrative vacuum, leading ultimately to the negative rhetoric. In the next section I show how narrative empathy can significantly improve Southern Baptist leaders' perception and knowledge of Islam and Muslims.

---

2. Osmer, *Practical Theology*, 84.

Narrative Empathy Defined

We can see why Southern Baptist leaders should consider narrative empathy a valid topic by addressing two questions: What is narrative empathy? Did Jesus have anything to say regarding the display of such empathy?

What is narrative empathy? A leading scholar of the subject, Suzanne Keen, defines it as follows:

> Narrative empathy is the sharing of feeling and perspective-taking induced by reading, viewing, hearing, or imagining narratives of another's situation and condition. Narrative empathy plays a role in the aesthetics of production when authors experience it, in mental simulation during reading, in the aesthetics of reception when readers experience it, and in the narrative poetics of texts when formal strategies invite it. Narrative empathy overarches narratological categories, involving actants, narrative situation, matters of pace and duration, and storyworld features such as settings. The diversity of the narratological concepts involved suggests that narrative empathy should not simply be equated with character identification nor exclusively verified by readers' reports of identification. Empathetic effects of narrative have been theorized by literary critics, philosophers, and psychologists, and they have been evaluated by means of experiments in discourse processing, empirical approaches to narrative impact, and through introspection.[3]

Most importantly, narrative empathy can help to bring about a change in attitudes, improved motives, and better care and justice.[4] Narrative empathy is a tool that can help humans to be more compassionate.[5] It goes beyond a mere supportive emotion; it allows a person to cognitively feel the pain or joy of the other person. Studies show that narrative empathy can be produced via the reader's encounters with characters both fictional and non-fictional.[6] Keen notes that "specific narrative techniques of fiction and film narrative have been associated

---

3. Keen, "Theory of Narrative Empathy," 208.
4. Keen, "Theory of Narrative Empathy," 208.
5. In this context, it is also important to add that while reading an autobiography, memoir, or history of a certain person, place, or time can improve one's ability to empathize, it should not be assumed that in all cases such narrative alone can produce an altruistic response in the real world.
6. Keen, "Theory of Narrative Empathy."

with empathetic effects."[7] When the reader is introduced to fictional characters, studies show that these characters have the power to channel perspective,[8] change a point of view,[9] and paratexts of fictionality.[10] Furthermore, such encounters can lead to immersion or transportation of the readers into that world.[11] Thus fictional drama, film, and literature can play a significant role in altering one's perception of "the other." Acknowledging that fictional narrative can create constructive empathy and alter the reader or viewer's perception of person, place, or time, I want to once again highlight that non-fictional narrative, that includes a personal encounter, can play a significant role in shaping one's perception and attitude as well. Moreover, I believe that real-life encounters are more effective in creating narrative empathy. Thus I propose that at the core of successful Muslim-Christian dialogue are strategic personal encounters between Southern Baptists and Muslims. The importance of carefully planned strategy in the context of such encounters cannot be overstated. I elaborate more on this topic later in this chapter and in the next.

Certainly, the biblical Jesus is widely considered a perfect example of empathy. As Lori Freeland writes, "He didn't come to earth to save us as God, detached and gazing down in sympathy and pity. He came as a man, born into the trenches, to live and suffer as a human. His empathy makes Him the perfect sacrifice. The perfect bridge between God and us."[12] Keen distinguishes empathy and sympathy by emphasizing that while sympathy entails feelings of compassion or sorrow, at the core of empathy is feeling what the other person feels. Furthermore, she points out that though these examples emphasize negative emotions—pain and pity—empathy also occurs for positive feelings of happiness, satisfaction, elation, and triumph.[13] Psychologists employ a variety of ways to measure empathetic responses among people. Keen explains: "Psychologists measure changes in heart rate and skin conductance (palm sweat). They collect data on perceptible and imperceptible facial reactions, the latter captured by EMG (electromyographic) procedures. They ask subjects how they feel or how they would act in certain situations, gathering

---

7. Keen, "Theory of Narrative Empathy."
8. Schneider, "Toward a Cognitive Theory."
9. Andringa et al., "Point of View and Viewer Empathy."
10. Nell, *Lost in a Book*.
11. Keen, *Empathy and the Novel*, 88–89.
12. Freeland, "Why Christians Should Show."
13. Keen, "Theory of Narrative Empathy."

responses through self-reports during or immediately after experiments and through surveys. Specialized surveys known as 'empathy scales' are used to assess subjects' strength of empathetic feeling. Recently, Functional Magnetic Resonance Imaging (fMRI) has had a profound impact on brain science, including the study of empathy."[14] Empathy—and more specifically, for our purposes, narrative empathy—is an effective tool to employ when seeking to promote solidarity and peace-building between two religious faiths such as Christianity and Islam.

Many Christians believe that Jesus did not simply feel *for* us; He felt *with* us. This understanding is a powerful tool by which people from diverse backgrounds, be it political, social, cultural, or religious, can feel the human connection. This connection is a pathway that can lead to a more thorough understanding of the other, creating a space for objectivity and respectful truth speaking. Christians believe that the Bible is a compilation of stories that illustrate God's love and plan for humanity. Each story is uniquely communicated in a manner that permits the reader to feel the moment. Many of these stories expose a moral or ethical problem to which a solution is needed and given. Many theologians argue that the underlying principle of each story transcends any particular time and place. Since the dawn of humanity, we have always faced challenges—challenges related to sexual scandal, war, greed, pain, frustration, sorrow, poverty, exile, confusion, and so on. Because of this reality, though the stories in the Bible are set in antiquity, we can still empathize with the characters. Empathy crosses many barriers that can divide us, such as region, culture, ethnicity, time, language, legal system, and religion. This is possible because at the core of humanity are common values and needs.

Narrative Empathy Fostered Via Shared Values and Emotions

Shared needs, values, and emotions are the bedrock of human solidarity. When we can tie a familiar face or story to a certain location or event, it significantly improves our ability to empathize and make more humanitarian decisions. Research by psychologist Martin Hoffman has revealed that humans are basically similar to one another, with a limited range of variations, and that our physiological and cognitive response system

---

14. Keen, "Theory of Narrative Empathy."

causes similar feelings to be evoked by similar events.[15] Hoffman notes that similarity itself is not enough to guarantee an empathic response; the complementary research of Singer and her colleagues shows that "our survival depends on effective functioning in social contexts, and that feeling what others feel, empathizing, contributes to that success."[16] Coincidentally, pastors play a significant role in storytelling and cultural immersion both of which can provide a pathway for congregants to empathize with Muslims and develop a productive relationship that can lead to lasting and meaningful interactions. To illustrate this, Keen notes that "Neuroscientists have already declared that people scoring high on empathy tests have especially busy mirror neuron systems in their brains."[17] For example, fiction writers are likely to be among those who experience high levels of empathy. Furthermore, people who are gifted in storytelling can significantly aid the reader and/or listener in increasing their ability to empathize with the other. In the hope of creating and fostering narrative empathy in the denomination towards Muslims, I believe that pastoral leaders in their local church can promote an empathetic environment that can lead to improved relations with Muslim-Americans.

To further illustrate the significance of shared values, we may use the work of Shalom H. Schwartz. Schwartz identifies ten core values recognized in cultures around the world. He writes,

> These ten values cover the distinct content categories found in earlier values theories, in value questionnaires from different cultures, and in religious and philosophical discussions of values. It is possible to classify virtually all the items found in lists of specific values from different cultures, into one of these ten motivationally distinct basic values:
> 1. Self-Direction. Independent thought and action; choosing, creating, exploring.
> 2. Stimulation. Excitement, novelty, and challenge in life.
> 3. Hedonism. Pleasure and sensuous gratification for oneself.
> 4. Achievement. Personal success through demonstrating competence according to social standards.
> 5. Power. Social status and prestige, control or dominance over people and resources.
> 6. Security. Safety, harmony, and stability of society, of relationships, and of self.

---

15. Hoffman, *Empathy and Moral Development*, 62.
16. Singer et al., "Empathy for Pain."
17. Blakeslee, "Cells That Read Minds."

7. Conformity. Restraint of actions, inclinations, and impulses likely to upset or harm others and violate social expectations or norms.
8. Tradition. Respect, commitment, and acceptance of the customs and ideas that traditional culture or religion provide the self.
9. Benevolence. Preserving and enhancing the welfare of those with whom one is in frequent personal contact (the 'in-group').
10. Universalism. Understanding, appreciation, tolerance, and protection for the welfare of all people and for nature.[18]

Arguably, these shared values form the basis on which all the emotionally coherent can empathize with each other. Hence, cognitive acts of narrative empathy have the power to impact one's worldview. These core values are found in the teachings of Christianity and Islam. Furthermore, Jesus and Muhammad emphasized the importance of resisting behaviors such as selfishness and pride and embracing the behaviors of neighborliness and humility. Rokeach said, "The value concept is able to unify the apparently diverse interests of all the sciences concerned with human behavior."[19] Plausibly, if two religions share a common origin, stories, prophets, and worldview, the adherents of each can experience a deeper empathy for the other. Christianity and Islam represent the two largest religions in the world. Both are monotheistic and share some common values and beliefs—for instance, the sanctity of life, justice, peace, mercy, and neighborliness. Moreover, Christianity and Islam maintain that each person is accountable to God. Accordingly, I seek to shape an improved, if not entirely new, perception of Islam, the Prophet Muhammad, and jihad among Southern Baptist leaders via narrative empathy. My research findings suggest that knowledge and education do not on their own rule out the use of anti-Islamic rhetoric. My findings are displayed in the three diagrams below. Diagram 1 illustrates what is going on in most situations; diagram 2 shows what is going on in some circumstances; and diagram 3 shows what I believe should be going on in every situation, especially among the leaders of the Southern Baptist denomination, i.e., pastors and educational teachers.

---

18. Schwartz, "Basic Human Values."
19. Rokeach, *Nature of Human Values*, 3.

Diagram 1:

| Lack of Knowledge and Education | + | Emotion of Anger, Fear, Insecurity | + | Lack of Narrative | = | Negative Rhetoric |

Diagram 2:

| Some Knowledge and Education | + | Some Contextual Emotion | + | Some Narrative | = | Less Negative Rhetoric |

Diagram 3:

| Basic Knowledge and Education | + | Narrative Empathy via Relationship | + | Contextual Emotions | = | Truthful Rhetoric |

The emotions of anger, fear, and insecurity are widespread throughout the Southern Baptist community with respect to Islam and Muslims. These are emotions that I address and contextualize below. Anger, fear, and insecurity trigger negative rhetoric within the United States and more precisely the Southern Baptist denomination towards Islam. A more thorough understanding of these three emotions can help illuminate the real crux of the problem as it pertains to anti-Islamic rhetoric and offer ways of confronting said emotions to bring about positive change. In the years following the attack of 9/11, as a pastor, I heard not just one or two, but the majority of my congregants voiced deeply felt emotions of anger, fear, and insecurity in relation to Islam and Muslims. Some wanted legislation limiting Muslim immigration. Others were proponents of a war in the Levant that would dismantle Islamic States and kill perceived Muslim terrorists. Men and women alike voiced their opposition to Muslim women wearing the hijab in public, and many said they believed that Islam is a direct threat and enemy of Christianity and Western democracy. I do not recall a single conversation with any of my congregants in which feelings of sympathy or empathy with Muslims were expressed. More recently, most of my conversations and interviews with Christians—Protestant and Catholic—suggest that the primary motivation behind an encounter with a Muslim is to see that Muslim convert to Christianity. In chapter 4, I articulate the differences between proselytizing, evangelizing, and interreligious dialogue and show that evangelization and interreligious dialogue can significantly complement each other. But if the only goal of the encounter is to convert the Muslim, then interreligious dialogue and evangelization will suffer greatly. Imam Dr. A Rashied Omar illustrates my point by raising the following questions: "Does one engage interreligious solidarity in order to convert the other to your faith? Can one get involved in interreligious solidarity with a clear conscience? Is the interreligious encounter legitimated by or compromising our deep-seated beliefs and theologies?"[20] Furthermore Rashied writes, "Unless they [the above questions] are clearly and unequivocally answered, we run the risk of having an outwardly agreeable dialogue that does not dispose of the mistrust and suspicion and in the end is superficial and does not lead us to the goal of peacebuilding."[21]

The Political and Sociological Larger Context

To understand why the feelings of anger, fear, and insecurity are commonplace among Southern Baptists, it is helpful to recognize some of the political and social dynamics of the church. Southern Baptists have no doctrinal creed, yet there is remarkable unity among their churches, not only in the United States but elsewhere in the world. On June 14, 2000, at the Southern Baptist Convention, under the direction of Dr. Adrian Rogers, the convention adopted a revised summary outlining the tenets of the Baptist Faith and Message. A total of 18 articles of faith were presented to the body and approved. These 18 articles of faith sum up the majority of beliefs of Southern Baptists and form the basis for the weekly preaching, teaching, and execution of God's Holy Word. Having pastored in several Southern Baptist churches, I can tell you with great confidence that if one of these articles is not observed by the local Southern Baptist church, the pastor will most likely be called in and questioned by his local congregational leadership or regional association. Local pastors and churches adhering to these statements of faith provide the bedrock for the success of the Southern Baptist denomination and subculture that many Baptists enjoy. A brief account of each of these articles will significantly

20. Omar, *Islam beyond Violent Extremism*, 90.
21. Omar, *Islam beyond Violent Extremism*, 90.

aid in understanding the Baptist worldview and why the emotions of anger, fear, and insecurity often result in defamation of other religious faiths and inadvertently create a prejudice against Islam and Muslims.

Based on my research in chapter 2 and personal experiences within the denomination, I believe that the majority of Southern Baptists can be identified as Right-wing Authoritarians (RWA). RWA is commonly defined as a confluence of three attitudinal clusters: authoritarian submission, authoritarian aggression, and conventionalism.[22] RWA is a personality and ideological variable studied in political, social, and personality psychology. In Table 3.1 Bob Altemeyer identifies the attitudinal and behavioral clusters.[23]

Table 3.1. Attitudinal and behavioral clusters which correlate together[24]

Authoritarian Submission	A high degree of submissiveness to the authorities who are perceived to be established and legitimate in the society in which one lives.
Authoritarian Aggression	A general aggressiveness directed against deviants, outgroups and other people that are perceived to be targets according to established authorities.
Conventionalism	A high degree of adherence to the traditions and social norms that are perceived to be endorsed by society and its established authorities and a belief that others in one's society should also be required to adhere to these norms.

These attitudinal and behavioral clusters help us understand the distinctive organization of the local churches that provide the formation of the Southern Baptist denomination. Furthermore, they are helpful in generally understanding how The Baptist Faith and Message[25] is received and executed among Southern Baptists.

To be in a good relationship with the Southern Baptist denomination, local churches will by and large adhere to these statements of faith. These statements of belief create an ebb and flow of daily life for the many organizations of the Southern Baptist denomination, from the seminaries to the mission field. Through these statements of faith, the denomination seeks to amalgamate the Baptist community as well as its social interactions so as to increase uniformity and minimize diversity of beliefs. To this effort, the attitudes and behaviors of the denomination and its

22. Altemeyer, *Right-Wing Authoritarianism*.
23. Altemeyer, *Right-Wing Authoritarianism*, 27.
24. *Source*: Altemeyer, *Right-Wing Authoritarianism*, 27.
25. See Appendix 2.

churches are closely related to the definition above regarding Right-wing Authoritarianism.

Historically, those in leadership will adhere to and promote the beliefs that have been decided upon by the majority, as stated in the Baptist Faith and Message 2000. Some position statements have been issued by the Convention since adopting the Baptist Faith and Message 2000. Some examples are the following. Sanctity of life: Procreation is a gift from God, a precious trust reserved for marriage. At the moment of conception, a new being enters the universe, a human being, a being created in God's image. This human being deserves our protection, whatever the circumstances of conception. Sexuality: We affirm God's plan for marriage and sexual intimacy—one man, and one woman, for life. Homosexuality is not a "valid alternative lifestyle." The Bible condemns it as sin. It is not, however, unforgivable sin. The same redemption available to all sinners is available to homosexuals. They, too, may become new creations in Christ. Ordination of women: Women participate equally with men in the priesthood of all believers. Their role is crucial, their wisdom, grace and commitment exemplary. Women are an integral part of our Southern Baptist boards, faculties, mission teams, writer pools, and professional staffs. We affirm and celebrate their Great Commission impact.[26] Additionally, well respected leaders will preach and teach *Sola scriptura* (Latin: by Scripture alone). They will teach that everlasting salvation comes "solely" by way of acknowledging sins, repenting of sins, verbally inviting Jesus into one's life, and then following through with believers' baptism, more precisely baptism by immersion. Each congregation, in accordance with article VI in the Baptist Faith and Message, will "operate under the Lordship of Christ through democratic processes. In such a congregation each member is responsible and accountable to Christ as Lord. Its scriptural officers are pastors and deacons." In theory, the pastors are held to high moral standards and expected to be advocates of the SBC. So long as the congregation believes the pastor to be supporting their ideas, they will usually extend to him more power and trust. If the pastor and congregation deviate from the Baptist Faith and Message and Position Statements, the local association of Baptist churches might decide to break fellowship with the dissenting church. For example, moderates within the SBC broke away and formed the Cooperative Baptist Fellowship (CBF) in 1991 (of which 1900 churches belong), due to the SBC's unwillingness to

---

26. Position Statements of the Southern Baptist Convention can be found at www.sbc.net.

accept some of their views, such as women serving in the pastorate. The doctrinal views expressed by CBF were, naturally, criticized by the SBC's leaders and the membership. More often than not, the dissenters' actions were characterized as coming short in fulfilling the true mission of the Southern Baptist denomination—a denomination that had recently experienced a conservative resurgence. Arguably, since many Baptists believe that SBC promotes and executes the true practice of the Christian faith, the Cooperate Baptist Fellowship is frequently depicted as ungodly in some of its decisions. Within SBC life, The Baptist Faith and Message provides the norms by which the congregant, pastor, and other leaders operate and find approval.

Authoritarian aggression can be used and often is used when congregants, pastors, or other leaders consistently act in ways that do not conform to doctrinal norms of Southern Baptist life. For example, if a pastor preaches a message other than creation—such as evolution—he will be brought before the church, questioned, and if unrepentant, told to leave the pastorate. Another example would be a Sunday school teacher teaching that all good people will go to heaven and that a personal belief in Christ is not mandatory to everlasting salvation. Such acts of speech can create an atmosphere of doubt and confusion and unless immediately addressed by the pastor, can lead to disunity. Theological disunity within the local church is generally not accepted by the community of believers. Consequently, many SBC churches require those interested in church membership to enroll in a 'new members class' to ensure they are more or less in agreement with the Baptist Faith and Message 2000.

To be fair, the characteristics of RWA are not peculiar to the SBC; the great majority of organizations, religions, societies, and so forth operate along these same lines. RWA can bring a sense of calm in a consistently changing world. However, with respect to interreligious dialogue, it can be a hindrance in what I call transformational evangelization. That is, evangelization that leads to a life-altering path, consisting of faith and reason, not simply a verbal acknowledgment or agreement with what has been said. Verbal acknowledgment or agreement may very well be a start, but it can be short lived unless faith and reason are present. For a real understanding of the "religious other" to take place, one must be willing to be uncomfortable with his or her own beliefs from time to time. This discomfort will either deepen one's faith or help one to see the fallacies of his or her faith. In the case of a Southern Baptist engaging in dialogue with a Muslim, it seems most helpful to come to terms with shared values and beliefs, to have an authentic respect for the Muslim and his or her religion, and to silently embrace the proverbial phrase, "There but for the grace of God go I." In other words, the practice of humility and respect can benefit efforts towards evangelization.

On the one hand, a statement of faith can unite the group, thus providing a foundation and framework for the work that the group believes needs to be accomplished. On the other hand, RWAs (especially those who seek to follow in the footsteps of Christ) must be heedful to keep an open mind and heart to those who are seeking to do right and honor God, though they may and do come from a different cultural, ethnic, and religious background. A personal and friendly relationship with a Muslim and some knowledge of the tenets of Islam can significantly and positively impact one's perception of Islam. As stated in chapter 2, the emotions of anger, fear, and insecurity often stem from a preventable fear of Islam—a fear that many have coined Islamophobia.

Islamophobia is a relatively new term and the first source to posit a firm definition of Islamophobia came from the Runnymede report in 1997. It defined Islamophobia as the "shorthand way of referring to dread or hatred of Islam—and, therefore, to fear or dislike all or most Muslims."[27] Since that definition was put forward by the British report, other countries such as Belgium and Holland have also attempted to define what Islamophobia is and is not. Chris Allen Associate Professor in Hate Studies in the Department of Criminology at the University of Leicester, UK, has investigated the term and offers the following six points for further consideration as states attempt to understand and define Islamophobia:

- Islamophobia is not a monolithic concept, but instead consists of a multiplicity of varied meanings and can denote a variety of behaviors.
- Because of the fuzzy conceptual boundaries, Islamophobia as a concept can and does frequently overlap with other concepts used in scholarship and in popular discourse.
- There are a variety of ways through which Islamophobia manifests itself. These ways are context dependent. Different actions are considered Islamophobic in different geographic, sociological, cultural, and political locations and conditions.

27. Runnymede Trust, *Islamophobia*, 37.

- It is important to consider the historical rootedness of Islamophobia, since the author admits that "would appear to have the possibility of having a historical legacy from which it draws information, relevance, understanding, and meaning."[28]
- In every context, whether political, cultural, or sociological, there must be a specific and unique process of identification of what it means to be Muslim or Islamic.
- The degree to which the concept of Islamophobia has embedded itself in the society varies significantly; thus the concept lacks clarity in many settings.

In naming the phenomenon a "phobia" to some degree it becomes pathologized; that is, it can be viewed as a disease or an illness. To say that it is a disease or an illness is to open up the possibility that one can be cured of it. Allen writes, "When named as 'Islamophobia', the phenomenon fails to become the fault of the perpetrator but a condition of them, neither founded nor unfounded but biological and natural."[29] In this vein, I believe the negative rhetoric emanating from Southern Baptist leaders does not derive from hatred against the person, as such, but from a lack of narrative and understanding of the religion and the culturally diverse people who subscribe to Islam. This lack of understanding, narrative, and encounter often produces the emotions of anger, fear, and insecurity that feed negative perceptions of Islam and Muslims. To be clear, my interviews and research findings suggest that Southern Baptists are not prejudiced against Arabs, or more precisely Muslims, per se, but against the religious ideologies of certain Muslims, which many perceive to be representative of all Muslims.

Theories That Help Explain the Negative Rhetoric

My research shows that many leaders, and consequently many laities, within the Southern Baptist denomination are greatly hindered in their ability to form an objective narrative of Islam. Primarily since the attacks of 9/11, anger, fear, and insecurity are common emotions found throughout the Southern Baptist denomination towards Islam. To better understand some of the causes of these emotions of anger, fear, and insecurity,

28. Allen, *Islamophobia*, 134.
29. Allen, *Islamophobia*, 136.

in this section I not only define these emotions but provide a framework for understanding how it is that these negative emotions have permeated the perceptions of many within the Southern Baptist denomination.

Anger

What is anger? What are some primal causes of anger? Can anger be useful in fighting negative perceptions of Islam? The American Psychological Association offers this adaptation of the definition of anger from the Encyclopedia of Psychology: "Anger is an emotion characterized by antagonism toward someone or something you feel has deliberately done you wrong. Anger can be a good thing. It can give you a way to express negative feelings, for example, or motivate you to find solutions to problems. But excessive anger causes problems. Increased blood pressure and other physical changes associated with anger make it difficult to think straight and harm your physical and mental health."[30] Behavioral psychologists debate whether anger is a primary or secondary emotion, but suffice it to say, anger is present, to some degree, in all of our lives. If not tamed, this emotion of anger can explode at the wrong time and do a significant amount of harm to ourselves and those around us. In the Bible, anger was first revealed in the account of two brothers, Cain and Abel.[31] In the biblical narrative, God rejected Cain's offering and accepted Abel's. Cain became angry and acted upon his feeling of anger by killing his brother. In this case, anger was a secondary emotion to jealousy. Cain was jealous of his brother and angry that God had accepted Abel's offering. Cain gave in to his jealousy and allowed his anger to swell up within himself to the point of no return. In essence, Cain turned to the dark side of anger. Psychologist Steven A. Diamond writes, "Anger, like anxiety, is a reaction to something threatening to the physical and/or psychological, spiritual, or existential integrity of the individual."[32] In this biblical narrative, Cain felt psychologically and spiritually threatened by God's acceptance of Abel's offering over his own. Rather than exploring the primordial reasons for such anger and addressing the underlying issues, Cain reacted in perhaps a natural, yet an irrational way that resulted in innocent blood being shed and his expulsion from the family.

30. American Psychological Association, "Anger."
31. Genesis 4 (HCSB)
32. Stosny, "Primacy of Anger Problems."

Stepping back and reflecting upon the primordial emotion can be helpful. As clinical psychologist Leon R. Seltzer points out, "In my own clinical experience, anger is almost never a primary emotion in that even when anger seems like an instantaneous, knee-jerk reaction to provocation, there's always some other feeling that gave rise to it. And this particular feeling is precisely what the anger has contrived to camouflage or control."[33] Anger is perhaps the most seductive and addictive of human emotions; if understood and appropriately dealt with, it can be used to benefit self and society.

Seltzer writes, "Anger can act as a sort of 'psychological salve.' One of the hormones the brain secretes during anger arousal is norepinephrine, experienced by the organism as an analgesic. In effect, whether individuals are confronted with physical or psychological pain (or the threat of such pain), the internal activation of the anger response will precipitate the release of a chemical expressly designed to numb it. This is why I've long viewed anger as a double-edged sword: terribly detrimental to relationships but nonetheless crucial in enabling many vulnerable people to emotionally survive in them."[34] Furthermore, the brain produces the hormone amphetamine,[35] which produces a surge of energy throughout our body—an adrenaline rush! When combined these two hormones produce a chemical reaction, that as Seltzer says, can make us feel powerful. He calls it the "magic elixir" and writes it can be every bit as much a drug as alcohol or cocaine. In essence, it can control us. On the more constructive side, anger can be used as a tool. For example, anger can help us be more self-aware and also motivate us to stand up against social injustice.

Particularly since the conservative resurgence, Southern Baptists have felt and experienced attacks against many of the values they believe to be essential to a peaceful and just world, as well as doctrines that promote Christ as the only path to everlasting salvation in Heaven with God. The attacks on 9/11, viewed by the world, immediately penetrated the peaceful bubble that much of the United States and Europe was experiencing. People entered a state of emotional shock. During and in the hours and days following the attacks, the United States entered a state of fear and confusion. Despite their own feelings and emotions, political and spiritual leaders rushed to the microphones and attempted to address

33. Seltzer, "What Your Anger."
34. Seltzer, "What Your Anger."
35. More information on this hormone can be found at www.psychologytoday.com.

the attack and offer words of hope and strength to their constituents and congregations. On this day and in the weeks that followed there was great resolve within the U.S. to bring those responsible for the attacks on our people and our soil to justice. In the Southern Baptist Church, her leaders voiced anger—anger that so many lives were destroyed; anger that this attack occurred on U.S. soil; anger that such attacks were carried out by those claiming allegiance to the Prophet Muhammad; and angry that the United States Citizenship and Immigration Services had allowed so many Muslims to immigrate to the United States. Most Southern Baptist leaders viewed this as a Muslim attack on Christianity and accordingly took to the pulpits and condemned not just the actions but the people who subscribed to a religion that they believed gave birth to such evil. Preachers used their pulpits to voice their own anger as well as the anger of their congregants. Anger fed anger and for a while helped people within the pews find strength to carry on. It created a non-Muslim solidarity—an "us against them" mentality; a mentality that is ethnocentric. This mentality, in many cases, led to an immediate sense of comfort, healing, nationalism, and even church growth. However, left unrestrained, anger can become an enemy of the heart, and consequently hinder effective dialogue between people and groups experiencing conflict. Clearly ethnocentricity has two sides; according to leading scholars Donald R. Kinder and Cindy D. Kam, "Ethnocentrism plays an important part in American opinion in distinctly different domains: the war on terrorism, humanitarian assistance to foreign lands, immigration and citizenship, the sanctity of marriage, Social Security and welfare reform, and school desegregation and affirmative action." Furthermore, they discovered, "each group nourishes its own pride and vanity, boasts itself superior, exalts its own divinities, and looks with contempt on outsiders. Each group thinks its own folkways the only right ones, and if it observes that other groups have other folkways, these excite its scorn."[36]

The raw anger felt on 9/11 and post-9/11 was real; elements of it were justified and even necessary in order for the healing process to begin. Unfortunately, the majority of Southern Baptist leaders and congregations lacked the familiarity with Islam and the personal relationship with a Muslim that would have supplied a more contextual and humane response to the anger. This allowed a certain degree of misguided teaching and anger towards Islam and the Muslims to go unchecked for several years. It

---

36. Kinder and Kam, *Us against Them*.

has been over twenty years since the attacks and this lack of understanding and narrative that continues to be preached Sunday after Sunday has raised a generation of Americans to dislike a demographic group they know very little about. In my interviews with two prominent First Baptist church pastors in Florida, both confessed they knew very little of Islam and the Prophet Muhammad; nor did they personally know any Muslims in their area of ministry. They were not inclined to spend a lot of time studying and learning the spirituality of the Prophet Muhammad and the basic tenets of the religion. They did admit that if more Muslims lived in their area and if their congregations were interested, they would spend more of their time seeking to understand the religion. As it was, both had preconceived ideas of Islam and Muslims and had taken to the pulpit on several occasions to speak what they believed to be the vices of Islam.

Fear

Fear has at least two sides. One side is a useful tool; one is a weapon of destruction. Fear can protect us from harm; it can also cripple our ability to trust and thus be rational in our thoughts, behaviors, and actions. Unlike the rational brain, fear is an emotion that triggers instinctual behaviors and attitudes. Fear acts instantly! The general consensus in the field of psychology is that this act of instantaneous combustion can inhibit conscious thinking and set off involuntary pursuits for escape routes, while preparing the body to freeze, flee, or to defend itself.[37] Fear is a survival mechanism and as it relates to the topic of my research, it can both hinder and stimulate the Christian evangelization of Muslims. There are at least two major events in the last 40 years that have shaped most of the perceptions Americans have of Islam: the Iran hostage crisis and the attacks on 9/11. The older generation recalls the standoff between Iran and the United States that lasted for 444 days; the younger generations recall the images of planes crashing into the World Trade Center on September 11, 2001. The hostage crisis certainly angered many Americans and endangered the lives of a few, but the attacks on 9/11 didn't just anger Americans, it thrust fear into the hearts of Americans. The locations of the attacks, the way they were carried out, and the sheer number of innocent lives lost on that day drove home the point that no one is safe from such acts of terrorism. SBC pastors felt that fear. Members of their congregations felt that fear.

37. "What Causes Fear?"

The reality of this widespread emotion created an opening for SBC leaders to speak to that fear—the fear of terrorism as well as the fear of the unknown. As we saw in chapter 1, many leaders fell short in addressing this fear in a constructive, non-judgmental way. There are reasons behind such shortcomings and failures in speech. Baylor University psychologist Wade Rowatt's research reveals that religious intolerance stems from the human brain registering a different group as threatening; that person in the out group then becomes manifested in a defensive worldview and becomes materialized in offensive-like actions. FBI data collected from 2000 to 2013 shows that hate crimes against Muslims sharply increased over pre-2000 levels.[38] The theory of religious intolerance states that non-Muslims view Muslims as a threat, hence they are more likely to act aggressively towards a different group. In this vein, religion creates an in-group and an out-group. Oddly enough, this act of religious intolerance theory seems inconsistent with the teachings of the Abrahamic faith traditions.[39] In Judaism, Christianity, and Islam there is some variation of caring for one's neighbor. Furthermore, taking up the question of the psychological reasons behind religious intolerance and prejudice and how these feelings originate and develop, Rowatt argues that "like other forms of intolerance and prejudice, religious intolerance and prejudice are likely byproducts of how human brains process perceived threats, subsequent emotional reactions, worldview defense and self-regulation ability. For example, human minds very quickly categorize individuals into social groups, some of which evoke unjustified fears or disgust reactions. Both religion and prejudices can increase security and comfort in a natural and social world full of imagined or real threats and dangers."[40]

In general, fear can overwhelm the human psyche and cause us to make irrational choices. It can affect our ability to think coherently and carry out our daily activities in a constructive manner. SBC pastor, teacher, and author Charles Stanley offers five side effects of fear:

1. Fear stifles thoughts and actions. It creates indecisiveness that results in stagnation.
2. Fear can be a roadblock to God's plan for His children. When we're dominated by negative emotions, we cannot achieve the goals He has in mind for us.

---

38. American Psychological Association, "Social Psychology of Religion."
39. Denney, "Relationships between Religion and Prejudice."
40. American Psychological Association, "Social Psychology of Religion."

3. Fear can lead to destructive habits. To numb the pain of overbearing distress and foreboding, some turn to things like drugs and alcohol for artificial relief.

4. Fear steals peace and contentment. When we're regularly afraid, our life becomes centered on pessimism and gloom.

5. Fear creates doubt. God promises abundant life, but if we surrender instead to the chains of fear, we most likely won't live in the abundance He offers.[41]

All of humanity can empathize with fear—we have all experienced it. As we have seen, fear can stifle spiritual growth and cause physical and mental hurt to our bodies. What occurred on 9/11 was out of our control—no one anticipated such an event happening. In that moment, people felt scared and helpless. Since that attack, there have been other attempted attacks and attacks made on innocent people in the name of Islam. More often than not, media zeroes in on such acts of violence, quickly ties it to Islam, and then sensationalizes it in such a way that it exacerbates a predisposition already present within the American psyche. Unfortunately, fear sells. ABC, CBS, NBC, CNN, FOX, MSNBC, etc. are all media companies competing against one another and seeking more viewership. John Stossel with ABC News put it bluntly: "We at ABC are as guilty as any other media outlet of rushing out to cover every new threat that arises. And the reason we scare people is simple. . . . For broadcast media, eyeballs equal ratings. For politicians, eyeballs equal votes. For activists, eyeballs equal support for the causes. For corporations, eyeballs equal sales. The bottom line: Worry and fear sell."[42] In their book *Selling Fear: Counterterrorism, the Media, and Public Opinion*, authors Brigitte Nacos, Yaeli Block-Elkon, and Robert Shapiro expose how the news media, public officials, and corporations consistently withhold information from the public to make breaking news situations seem more drastic and ominous than they really are, thereby generating higher ratings and promoting agendas that are often hidden from public view.[43] The reality is, we are often pawns in the hands of political, corporate, and religious ideologies that vie for our attention and allegiance. This is not necessarily

---

41. Stanley, "Side Effects of Fear."
42. Stossel and Jaquez, "The 'Fear Industrial Complex.'"
43. Nacos, Block-Elkon, and Shapiro, *Selling Fear*.

bad, but it is crucial for spiritual leaders and congregants to be aware of this often hidden agenda, especially within the institution of the church.

Oddly enough, religious bigotry can boost attendance, financial giving, and a sense of real community, but at what expense to the gospel and to the lives of the religious "others," especially Muslims? Dr. Rowatt says there are a variety of factors that allow for religious bigotry to develop and grow in a person, "including biological processes, maturation, socialization experiences, group identity and cultural learning styles. Curbing intolerant feelings requires a certain degree of emotional awareness and social intelligence."[44] More often than not, spiritual leaders are just like the rest of us, susceptible to the pressures and demands of society that impress upon us to think and act within the norms of a cultural environment or movement. These norms can be and often are tainted with preconceived perceptions passed down to us since birth. Moreover, while "people with an internal motivation to respond without prejudice are fairly skilled at overriding initial incorrect automatic evaluations and responding with kindness, compassion and civility . . . not everyone is motivated to respond without prejudice."[45] If indeed Islamophobia is a phobia that can be cured or set right, the SBC has the tools necessary to rightly embrace truth (not fear) and engage with the Muslim community that results in understanding, trust, and collaboration between the two faiths. This type of engagement will certainly help the Christian and Muslim better communicate their faith traditions to each other.

At present, fear is still deeply embedded in the minds of many within the SBC. As seen in my interviews, there is fear of another terrorist attack, there is the fear of what they call "Sharia Law" being incorporated into our legal system, and there is fear of Islam growing and Muslims converting non-Muslims to Islam. These fears represent real and present concerns for Christians within the SBC. In chapter 4, I discuss ways of overcoming such fears, but for now let's consider some more casual mechanisms that feed fear in our lives. Dr. Theo Tsaousides offers seven facts that people need to know about fear: fear is healthy, fear comes in many shades, fear is not as automatic as you may think, you don't need to be in danger to be scared, the more scared you feel, the scarier things will seem, fear dictates the actions you take, and the more real the threat, the more heroic your actions. Table 3.2 below shows his findings.

44. American Psychological Association, "Social Psychology of Religion."
45. American Psychological Association, "Social Psychology of Religion."

Table 3.2. Seven things you need to know about fear[46]

Fear is healthy	Fear is hardwired in your brain, and for good reason: Neuroscientists have identified distinct networks that run from the depths of the limbic system all the way to the prefrontal cortex and back. When these networks are electrically or chemically stimulated, they produce fear, even in the absence of a fearful stimulus. Feeling fear is neither abnormal nor a sign of weakness: The capacity to be afraid is part of normal brain function. In fact, a *lack* of fear may be a sign of serious brain damage.
Fear comes in many shades	Fear is an inherently unpleasant experience that can range from mild to paralyzing—from anticipating the results of a medical checkup, to hearing news of a deadly terrorist attack. Horrifying events can leave a permanent mark on your brain circuitry, which may require professional help. However, chronic stress, the low-intensity variety of fear expressed as free-floating anxiety, constant worry, and daily insecurity, can quietly but seriously harm your physical and mental health over time.
Fear is not as automatic as you think	Fear is part instinct, part learned, part taught. Some fears are instinctive: Pain, for example, causes fear instinctively because of its implications for survival. Other fears are learned: We learn to be afraid of certain people, places, or situations because of negative associations and past experiences. A near-drowning incident, for example, may cause fear each time you get close to a body of water. Other fears are taught: Cultural norms often dictate whether something should be feared or not. Think, for example, about how certain social groups are feared and persecuted because of a societally-created impression that they are dangerous.
You don't need to be in danger to be scared	Fear is also part imagined, and so it can arise in the absence of something scary. In fact, because our brains are so efficient, we begin to fear a range of stimuli that are not scary (*conditioned fear*) or not even present (*anticipatory anxiety*). We get scared because of what we imagine could happen. Some neuroscientists claim that humans are the most fearful creatures on the planet because of our ability to learn, think, and create fear in our minds. But this low-grade, objectless fear can turn into chronic anxiety about nothing specific, and become debilitating.
The more scared you feel, the scarier things will seem	Through a process called *potentiation*, your fear response is amplified if you are already in a state of fear. When you are primed for fear, even harmless events seem scary. If you are watching a documentary about venomous spiders, a tickle on your neck (caused by, say, a loose thread in your sweater) will startle you and make you jump out of your seat in terror. If you are afraid of flying, even the slightest turbulence will push your blood pressure through the roof of the plane. And the more worried you are about your job security, the more you will sweat it when your boss calls you in for even an uneventful meeting.

46. *Source:* Theo Tsaousides, "7 Things You Need to Know about Fear."

Fear dictates the actions you take	Actions motivated by fear fall into four types—freeze, fight, flight, or fright. *Freeze* means you stop what you are doing and focus on the fearful stimulus to decide what to do next (e.g., you read a memo that your company will be laying off people). Next, you choose either *fight* or *flight*.
	You decide whether to deal with the threat directly (tell your boss why you shouldn't be laid off) or work around it (start looking for another job). When the fear is overwhelming, you experience *fright*: You neither fight nor flee; in fact, you do nothing—well, you obsess about the layoffs, ruminate, complain, but you take no action. Being continuously in fright mode can lead to hopelessness and depression.
The more real the threat, the more heroic your actions	We react differently to real and imagined threats. Imagined threats cause paralysis. Being scared about all the bad things that may or may not happen in the future makes you worry a lot but take little action. You are stuck in a state of fear, overwhelmed but not knowing what to do. Real threats, on the other hand, cause frenzy. When the threat is imminent and identifiable, you jump to action immediately and without flinching. This is why people are much more likely to change their eating habits after a serious health scare (e.g., a heart attack) than after just reading statistics about the deleterious effect of a diet based on fried foods. If you want to mobilize your troops, you have to put yourself in danger.

Dr. Tsaousides concludes his thoughts by saying that fear can be as much an ally as an enemy. Wisdom dictates that fear be used as an ally and not an enemy. As my research and interviews disclose, many within the SBC are giving in to fear, thus unintentionally becoming one with the enemy (fear) and living in a state of freeze, flight, and fright. This living condition cultivates a lack of empathy for Muslims that issues in negative rhetoric, and a spiritual stagnation within the life of the spiritual leader and his followers. Anger and fear are crippling both to the individual and to the greater society.

The next of the most salient negative emotions I perceived among those I interviewed was insecurity. They feel insecure; that is, they experience a great amount of anxiety and uncertainty with respect to the religious and political changes occurring in the United States.

Insecurity

Thomas Friedman wrote, "In today's globalized world, if you don't visit a bad neighborhood, it will visit you."[47] Evil can be likened to a cancer cell within the body: unless the cancer is surgically removed or treatments implemented to keep the cancer at bay, it will continue to invade every part within the body until it has quenched the light of life. Evil and the spread thereof is a legitimate concern that needs to be addressed both on a world-wide and individual scale. The root cause or causes of the present evil troubling and terrorizing much of the world needs to be identified and then appropriately dealt with—dealt with in a constructive way that lends itself to human solidarity and not more human divisions. Of course, one particularly clear and present evil that the world is fighting to eliminate is militant Islamic extremism, an extremism that goes well beyond the norms of Islam and often uses what I term "vulnerable people" to carry out political and theological agendas. These "vulnerable people" often come from poverty-stricken villages within Syria, Yemen, and Afghanistan to name a few, where educational resources are limited, law and order is wanting and where creature needs and comforts such as food, water, shelter, electricity, and financial wherewithal are often limited. These people often live in a state of subsistence; hence, when a perceived leader—who may very well be wealthy and educated—steps forth and makes promises that appeal to their basic psychological needs, they are quick to join the movement and are often easily indoctrinated simply because they know no better. In these regions, the lack of law and order, worldly knowledge and, natural resources are three significant contributing factors to these victimized people who are experiencing anger, fear, and insecurity every day of their lives. In many cases these people have been convinced that the United States is their enemy and that all or at least the majority of its citizens are living and promoting ungodliness and, furthermore, hate Islam. Without humanitarian aid or the prospect of effective government and better leadership, they will continue to follow the leader they have and, in time, evil will produce evil, even at the expense of the innocent. So, is there good reason for Southern Baptists to feel insecure about the world they are living in? The answer is yes and no. It is complicated. On the one hand, militant Islamic extremists do have the upper hand in some remote villages and even cities, recruiting, training, and sending out terrorists. On the other hand, Muslim and

---

47. Friedman, "Thinking about Iraq."

non-Muslim allies are working together to put an end to such abuse. For example, in the aftermath of 9/11 two very influential documents were drafted and published—A Common Word Between Us and You[48] and The Amman Message[49]—by leading figures in the Islamic community denouncing violent acts of terrorism and promoting a dialogue of understanding, trust, and collaboration between religious and political actors throughout the world. Moreover, both of these documents declared what Islam is and what Islam is not. As powerful as these two documents are, many in the West are not aware that such efforts have been made by the Islamic community to reject all words of hate and acts of violence.

Southern Baptists are right to feel a degree of uncertainty and anxiety about their future—a future that many leaders within the Southern Baptist church view as imperiled in light of Islamic growth around the world and especially within the United States. To give an example, prior to the signing of the Declaration of Independence in 1776, Protestantism was the favored faith of the New America, even Catholics were shunned both in law and society. Even the fair-minded Founder John Adams scorned Catholics as "poor wretches fingering their beads," as he wrote home to his wife Abigail after attending a mass in Philadelphia.[50] In that era, many Christians were revolting against political and spiritual monarchy, yet in the blustering heat of the debate, a certain bit of divine providence shone through and 56 Americans signed the Declaration of Independence and endorsed the words: "We hold these truths to be self-evident, that all men are created equal, that they are endowed by their Creator with certain unalienable Rights, that among these are Life, Liberty, and the pursuit of Happiness." As the only Catholic signer of the Declaration of Independence, "Charles Carrol could not endorse that passage without understanding very personally what these unalienable rights entailed: freedom to worship as he saw fit."[51] Consequently, many of the other signers, who interpreted Scripture differently, would not have signed unless they too understood that the freedom to worship the Creator was a personal choice every person should be endowed with.

Today, 240 years later, it is apparent to most historians that America was founded on many of the "principles" of Christianity. It is estimated that there are 150 million Protestants and over 70 million Catholics in

48. Abdullah II, "Common Word."
49. Abdullah II, "Amman Message."
50. Rooney, *Global Vatican*, 9.
51. Rooney, *Global Vatican*, 11.

the United States, in contrast to just over 3 million Muslims.⁵² Thus, any perceived threat to the religious norms of the United States is not overly welcomed by the Christian majority. To this day, Protestants and Catholics continue a type of "cold war" mentality towards each other. Though no physical weapons are used, there is still a lingering negative tone and rhetoric between the two. Yet, many adherents within both denominations converge on the idea that Islam threatens certain coveted social norms which feeds feelings of insecurity and further gives rise to an us-against-them mentality. To a degree, they are right. Muslim Americans contribute to the very fabric of American history and the reality is, the Declaration of Independence—as it is interpreted today—gives all people desiring to immigrate into this country the same unalienable rights bestowed to those who have been here for generations. Islam isn't coming to America, Islam is in America and it is expected to represent nearly two percent of the U.S. population by 2050.

Of particular concern to the post-9/11 Western consciousness is that "Islam poses a threat to our way of life: to freedom of speech, to the role of women, to the security of the state, to secularism, to community cohesion, [and] to the imagined 'Western' way of life."⁵³ Chris Allen argues, however, that "Islamophobia does not need to rest on an entirely imagined perilous 'other,' but is formed from an amalgam of accurate perceptions as well as stereotypes, exaggerations and misrepresentations. It is the perception of threat that gives cogency to the phobia part of Islamophobia."⁵⁴ To this point, most leaders within the Southern Baptist denomination have never traveled to a Muslim majority country and have never critically studied the Qur'an and the Sunnah of the Prophet in a way that provides for a more comprehensive understanding of this "religious other;" an understanding that can help foster neighborliness and trust between the two religions. The knowledge and understanding that most Southern Baptist leaders have regarding Islam comes from a select few leaders who have traveled to a Muslim majority country and/or from those who have some in depth knowledge of Islam due to educational training and/or personal encounters with Muslim leaders. Beyond this, most SBC leaders gather their information about Islam from conservative

---

52. Religious demographics can be found at http://www.pewforum.org/religious-landscape-study/.

53. Pratt and Woodlock, *Fear of Muslims?*, 4.

54. Pratt and Woodlock, *Fear of Muslims?*, 4. More of Allen's arguments can be found in Allen, *Islamophobia*.

news agencies, social media, or Christian publications that usually have the agenda of promoting Western ideas and Christianity. My conversations with many SBC leaders as well as my own experience suggest that rarely do Southern Baptists leaders explore Islam to understand it, rather to discredit it. In large part, due to a lack of knowledge, understanding, and Muslim narrative, Islam is seen as a problem to the non-Muslim Western world and more specifically to the Southern Baptists' faith and doctrine. Allen writes, "the ideological meanings of 'Islam' and 'Muslims', upon which Islamophobia rests, are drawn from a mix of accurate and inaccurate, reflective and constructed, representations and misrepresentations. The ever-present ubiquitous media is one conduit for expression of Islamophobia, helping to make Islamophobia views seem natural and normative in Western societies."[55] My primary goal is to demonstrate to Southern Baptist leaders the value of creating and cultivating relationships with American Muslims to better understand the tenets of Islam, build trust between the two people groups, and foster collaboration on matters of peace and justice. Relationships that bud out of a genuine wish to know and love the other person can significantly curtail much of the Islamophobia found within the Baptist denomination and open up new opportunities for Baptists to share what they believe to be the authentic teachings of Christ with Muslims in America and abroad.

Many of the insecure feelings stem from some horrible acts of violence that have been executed by militant Islamic extremists. These extremists use the religion of Islam as a weapon of destruction and their followers as the ammunition. The extremists are committing vile acts of evil that are rejected not only by the Qur'an but also by scholars of Islam the world-over. Tables 3.3 and 3.4 indicate that Muslims overwhelmingly reject the Islamic militant groups' ideology; furthermore, when polled, American Muslims express abhorrence for the actions of the extremists. They even view acts of terrorism for a specific cause even less favorably than do non-Muslim Americans.

55. Pratt and Woodlock, *Fear of Muslims?*, 3. A more though definition can be found in Allen, *Islamophobia*.

Q12n. ISIS			
	Favorable	Unfavorable	Don't know
Lebanon	0	100	1
Israel	1	97	2
Jordan	3	94	4
Palest. ter.	6	84	10
Indonesia	4	79	18
Turkey	8	73	19
Nigeria	14	66	20
Burkina Faso	8	64	28
Malaysia	11	64	25
Senegal	11	60	29
Pakistan	9	28	62

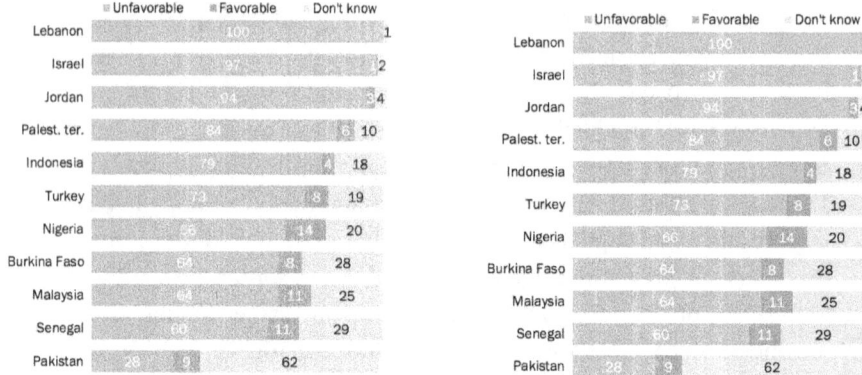

Table 3.3. Views of ISIS overwhelmingly negative.[56]

It is written in the Qur'an, "whoever kills a single soul, except for murder or causing corruption on land, it is as though he has killed the whole of mankind, and whoever saves one life it is as though he has saved all mankind."[57] When this law is violated, it impacts all of those involved. When terrorist attacks occur in the United States, it shoots feelings of anxiety and uncertainty into the lives of non-Muslims and Muslims alike. In times such as these, both parties feel insecure and need to be comforted. Insecurity is a real feeling experienced by many Southern Baptist leaders, not just because of their fear of Islamic doctrine being spread, but also because of the reports of terrorism. But in fact, the FBI revealed that

56. Pew Research Center, "In Nations with Significant Muslim Populations."
57. The Feast 5:32 (The Qur'an).

acts of terrorism carried out by radical Islamic extremists in the United States only accounted for six percent of all terrorist attacks carried out on American soil between the years of 1980 and 2005; 94 percent of terrorist attacks are carried out by non-Muslims.[58] To offer some perspective on the matter, one is more likely to be struck by lightning in his or her lifetime than to personally experience any form of terrorism by an extremist hijacking Islam and using it as a platform for doing evil. Furthermore, I find it thought-provoking that 42 percent of all Nobel Peace Prize winners have been Muslims.

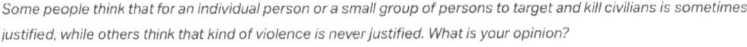

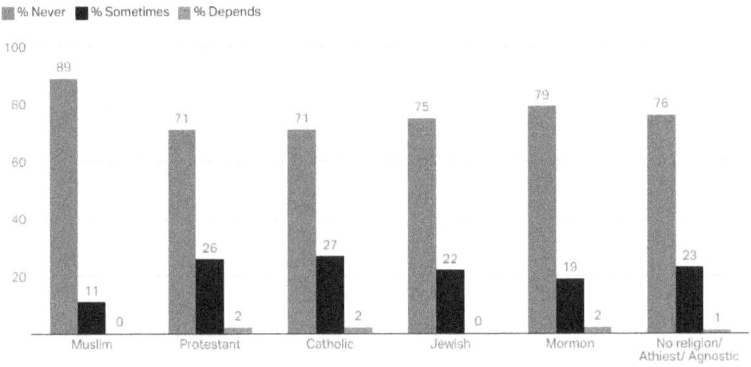

Table 3.4. Is terrorism sometimes justified.[59]

For the Southern Baptist leaders that I interviewed, there were two main reasons for their feelings of insecurity regarding Islam in America. First, Islam is growing rapidly in America, and there is a fear that Islamic law will influence common law. Second, their perception is that "most" Muslims are not seeking to assimilate but to fundamentally alter American culture and values to reflect their faith, moreover, some added the phrase—"by force if necessary." My many conversations and observations of American-Muslims and Muslims abroad do not support this perceived threat of a Muslim uprising in America. This means that much of the perceived insecurity can be relieved if more context can be offered and

---

58. Information can be found at www.fbi.gov/.
59. Gallup, "Most Muslim Americans."

a personal relationship with a Muslim can be created in the life of the leader. Muslim-American Omar Alnatour writes,

> Every time an act of terror or shooting occurs, Muslims closely watch the news with extreme trepidation praying that the suspect is not Muslim. This is not because these terrorists are likely to be Muslim but rather because in the instances where they happen to be, we see amplified mass media coverage and extreme unjustified hatred towards Muslims. As a Muslim, I am tired of condemning terrorist attacks being carried out by inherently violent people who hijack my religion. I am tired of condemning these attacks to people who are calm and apathetic when Muslims are killed by these same radicalized terrorists. I am tired of hearing the word "terrorist" not being used when the suspect in a terrorist attack is a non-Muslim. I am tired of the "mentally disabled" excuse being recycled when the suspect in a terrorist attack is a Caucasian. I am tired of seeing hundreds of terrorist attacks carried out by non-Muslims not get the same coverage of even a single terrorist attack where the suspect happens to be Muslim. Above it all, I am tired of having to repeatedly say that Muslims are not terrorists. It is time we silence this Islamophobia with facts.[60]

The Southern Baptist leaders I spoke with feel threatened by the spread of Islam. They believe the growth of Islam will significantly alter the cultural landscape of America, which is perceived by many to have deep Christian roots. As Muslims continue to immigrate to the U.S., the reality is that more mosques will be built, there will be more interactions with Muslims, and the traditional American culture will evolve to the religious and political ideologies of the new demographics. This unknown reality causes many Southern Baptist leaders to feel anxious and uncertain and thus, at times, whether knowingly or not, to use negative rhetoric when speaking of Muslims. Research shows that when a person or group feels insecure, the primordial instinct is to discredit and villainize the other to make oneself or the group have a better, albeit often misguided, perception of self.

History informs us that churches can often be used a breeding ground for anger, fear, and insecurity. American historian Kenneth Davis writes, "From the earliest arrival of Europeans on America's shores, religion has often been a cudgel, used to discriminate, suppress and even kill the foreign, the 'heretic' and the 'unbeliever'—including the 'heathen'

---

60. Alnatour, "Muslims Are Not Terrorists."

natives already here. Moreover, while it is true that the vast majority of early-generation Americans were professing Christians, the pitched battles between various Protestant sects and, more explosively, between Protestants and Catholics, present an unavoidable contradiction to the widely held notion that America is a 'Christian nation.'"[61] Today, the United States represents a modern, democratic, and law abiding country; hence, it is difficult, though not impossible, for hate groups to carry out violent crimes upon others whom they perceive to be a threat. Countries with governments that have been compromised or perhaps are still in the process of forming a robust and cohesive rule of law are more susceptible to hate groups rising and creating havoc (witness the militant groups in Syria).

In Colonial times, Protestant preachers often spoke hatefully of American Catholics. Most of the colonies had laws preventing Catholics from publicly participating in Mass, churches were burned to the ground, and Catholics were often victimized by the Protestant majority. Kenneth Davis writes,

> While some of America's early leaders were models of virtuous tolerance, American attitudes were slow to change. The anti-Catholicism of America's Calvinist past found new voice in the 19th century. The belief widely held and preached by some of the most prominent ministers in America was that Catholics would, if permitted, turn America over to the pope. Anti-Catholic venom was part of the typical American school day, along with Bible readings. In Massachusetts, a convent—coincidentally near the site of the Bunker Hill Monument— was burned to the ground in 1834 by an anti-Catholic mob incited by reports that young women were being abused in the convent school. In Philadelphia, the City of Brotherly Love, anti-Catholic sentiment, combined with the country's anti-immigrant mood, fueled the Bible Riots of 1844, in which houses were torched, two Catholic churches were destroyed and at least 20 people were killed.[62]

In large part, the Catholic Church in America survived due to its enduring theology and diplomacy. Like the Catholic church of the eighteenth and nineteenth centuries, perhaps the Southern Baptist denomination can find security in its theology, determination, and willingness to engage in diplomacy with the American-Muslims. To do this,

---

61. Davis, "America's True History."
62. Davis, "America's True History."

I propose that Southern Baptist leaders must intentionally engage with Islamic leaders so that the Muslim and Islamic narrative can be contextually understood and then explained to the congregation. To have a more thorough knowledge and understanding of the religious other, is to have a more thorough knowledge and understanding of one's own religion.

At the core of many articles and news segments regarding Muslims and their faith is an underlying Islamic stereotype, which paints Muslims as intrinsically violent "radical insurgents bent on waging jihad" against the West.[63] According to a study conducted by the Quaker organization American Friends Service Committee, 90 percent of news articles and television segments covering violent extremism in 2015 mentioned Islam at least once. While some reports covered topics related to Muslim victims of terrorism or Muslim leaders denouncing extremism, the vast majority of these stories were centered on extremists with "alleged or implied ties to Islam."[64] While the media is responsible for much of the negative rhetoric and subsequently negative perceptions of Islam, the Prophet Muhammad, and jihad, held by many within the denomination, it is a weak excuse for SBC leaders to continue to allow such stereotypes to shape their perceptions of Islam. Due to the apparent perplexity of Islam by many Southern Baptists, as well as, the proximity of Islam in Ameirca, I believe it is necessary for Southern Baptist leaders to venture beyond surface rhetoric and uncover the rich history of Islam—past and present.[65] This action will enable the leader to formulate a more contextual perception above and beyond that which is being circulated in much of Western media and conservative religious news outlets.

The act of "negative" rhetoric is an outward sign of an inner symptom or symptoms that need to be constructively dealt with. To begin with, what is negative rhetoric and why do we use it? Rhetoric is a neutral term that is neither good nor bad, light nor dark. Historically, rhetoric is the art of using language effectively to persuade others. According to Professor of English Ann Curzan, "It's an art form for those who can speak well and persuade others with conviction. However, more and more this former art has been viewed in a more negative light. By the seventeenth century, we start to see some use where people are using 'rhetoric' to talk about sort of overblown speech, speech that is big words, but maybe not

---

63. "Media Portrayals of Religion: Islam."
64. Hallowell, "Mixed Media," 14.
65. Ludwig von Mises has written an informative article on how to write and understand history, which can be found at mises.org.

backed up ... from there it gets more and more negative, and I think now you'll hear people use it to talk about words that seem empty to them."[66] In political and religious circles today it is known that people will usually not remember the content of your speech, but they will remember the particular language used and the extent to which it was used in a taboo way. In this vein, many religious leaders are very persuasive in their rhetoric—they know it, and they use it to their advantage. To give one such example, in 2016 at the Southern Baptist Convention, Pastor Carl Gallups of Hickory Hammock Baptist Church voiced his opposition to the denomination helping to build a mosque at Ground Zero. He said, "I think the Ethics and Religious Liberties Commission would be hard pressed to find anywhere in the scriptures, or elsewhere, where the early church was aligning itself with government entities and 'interfaith coalitions' to assist in the construction of more pagan temples, shrines and altars to Emperor worship in the Roman Empire—in the name of 'religious liberty.' That would not have crossed their minds. There certainly is no scripture to support the idea. Rather the scripture supports having nothing to do with 'darkness,' and being 'separate' from those who align themselves with systems that deny the Jesus Christ of God's salvation."[67] On the same occasion Gallups asked, "has the SBC forgotten the Ottoman Empire? Have they forgotten the Barbary Wars, or 9/11? Has the SBC forgotten that the FBI says that they are now tracking ISIS cells in all 50 states of the U.S.? Are you not aware of the fact that several Islamic mosques in America have been officially identified as nothing more than Islamic terrorist recruiting centers?"[68] Appealing to the senses, nationalism, and religious preeminence, Gallop makes a persuasive appeal to his audience to deny Muslims their constitutional right to build a mosque, and furthermore characterizes any Christian who seeks to help them in their endeavor as an Islamic sympathizer aligning him- or herself with the darkness. Jerry Vines, a former SBC president and pastor, stirred interfaith tumult when he chose to describe Muhammad as a "demon-possessed pedophile." In that same speech given during the Southern Baptist Pastors Conference, he said, "Allah is not Jehovah. Jehovah is not going to turn you into a terrorist that'll try to bomb people and take the lives of thousands of people." In response to this language, Hodan Hassan, a spokeswoman for the Washington-based Council for American-Islamic

66. Curzan, "Rhetoric: Positive, Negative, or Both?"
67. Gallups, Southern Baptist Convention speech.
68. Gallups, Southern Baptist Convention speech.

Relations, said Vines's comments were "divisive and inaccurate."[69] As noted above, rhetoric is neither good nor bad, it is the content of the matter that determines the character of the speech. The person who is well versed in speaking possess the ability to conjure up certain feelings in the audience and then create a pathway forward in response to the content of the speech. The question that every leader needs to ask of him- or herself is, "what is my purpose in this speech?" It also behooves the receiver of the speech to consider the motives of the speaker.

Some Contributing Factors That Can Animate the Use of Negative Rhetoric

The point of any speech is to persuade the person or audience to respond positively to the content of the message. Politicians employ speechwriters that understand what their political base wants their elected leader to champion and then hear proclaimed. In a similar way, most religious leaders are elected by a majority of people who believe that he or she will champion what they believe to be important. In the Southern Baptist denomination, though it is generally believed that the pastor is ultimately chosen and ordained by God to preach and teach, it is the local church that determines whether or not to issue a call of employment to that pastor. Then, for that pastor to remain in a continuous state of favor with the church, he must learn to balance his personal convictions and calling from God and simultaneously entertain and defend the essential beliefs and actions deemed important to the congregation. As a former Southern Baptist pastor, I can tell you this was not an easy feat. As a matter of convenience, political and religious leaders will typically place themselves inside the circle of trust (a circle created by their political party or religious denomination), surround themselves with like-minded people and in time reflexively deliver what the majority of the base wants to hear. By so doing they will reap the rewards of emotional and financial security. As illustrated earlier in my research, the overwhelming majority of Southern Baptists belong to the Republican Party and by and large the Republican Party is nationalistic and is led by many Right-wing Authoritarians. Hence, there is often a spiritual as well as national appeal to solidarity within the group when the preacher is delivering the sermon.

---

69. Jones, "Baptist Pastor's Words."

Each pastor within the denomination consciously or unconsciously chooses his method of sermonic delivery. He can choose to educate his audience, all the while remaining true to the denomination's doctrinal beliefs, or he can choose to indoctrinate his audience with circular reasoning and rhetoric that builds a base that is lacking the knowledge necessary to construct meaningful inter-faith as well as intra-faith dialogue. The benefit of the first can be a deeper appreciation of one's faith and ability to see the world more globally. The benefit of the latter can be a greater sense of belonging to the group. It seems that many within the denomination have chosen the latter and have found it to be a very effective tool in inner-church growth, nationalism, and personal success. I argue that the optimal pathway forward that can lead to deeper faith in God and create a greater open-mindedness to the love and truth of God often found in the "religious other," more specifically American-Muslims, is the desire and capability of the minister to educate his audience in a way that entails contextual truth-telling and dialogue with Muslims. Muslims are not a disease, they are a people of divergent faith, ethnicity, and culture, who are created and loved by God. A people that Christ died for and has commissioned his followers to seek out, to love, and to reveal truth in a manner that reflects the heart and mind of Christ. My interviews with the pastors, and the writings of such pastors as Jerry Vines, Jack Graham, Jerry Falwell, Franklin Graham, and many others, reflect an inner yearning to appropriately interpret and express the truth of God in love to a world-wide audience. However, in times of distress, like the days, months, and years following the terrorist attacks of 9/11, it became commonplace to demonize the religion of Islam and by so doing, in many situations, though seemingly unintentionally, Muslims more generally.

In the fury of responding to the attacks, pastors entertained certain descriptive language and processes of thought that resonated with the denomination. Anger, fear, and insecurity seemingly required a moment in time when it was crucial to quickly define the enemy and create an us-against-them framework. In a way, and at first, it was very unifying for the denomination as well as the country. Unfortunately, it ignored and alienated at least one percent of the population—Muslim-Americans who were already embracing the American dream of life, liberty, and the pursuit of happiness, via democracy. Their ethnicity was different, their cultural upbringings unique to their heritage, and to many non-Muslim Americans, their religion taboo. Nonetheless, these Muslims were citizens of the United States and they were cast under the discriminatory eyes of their non-Muslim American neighbors. In this moment and in the years that followed, Southern Baptists have been trying to determine the best way forward in engaging with this 'religious other'—a 'religious other' that many within the denomination deem to be the "great evil" of the world, one they construe as being in direct opposition to Christianity.

In times of feeling threatened, human nature primarily responds in at least two ways: fight or flight. The Southern Baptist denomination chose to fight. Pastors across the denomination rallied their congregations around the belief that Islam is intrinsically evil and must be stopped. In the words of Franklin Graham, son of late evangelist Billy Graham, "we're not attacking Islam, but Islam has attacked us. The God of Islam is not the same God . . . it's a different God, and I believe it is a very evil and wicked religion."[70] Since 2011, the Syrian civil war has forced many Muslims to seek refuge in Europe and the United States. Consequently, a political and humanitarian debate ensued in the U.S.—should Syrian refugees be allowed in the United States? Pastor John Wofford voiced opposition to Southern Baptists taking in refugees, arguing that "these people threaten our very way of existence as Christians and Americans."[71] One can deduce from this verbiage that Wofford and many others within the denomination perceive Islam as being a direct threat to Christianity, consequently pushing many evangelical Christians into a "fight for survival" mode. Such rhetoric often lends itself to the applause and support of the base and tends to be likened to a balm of soothing oil to the sore. Many of the horrible crimes against humanity, including ethnic cleansings, have arisen from such perceptions of the "other." In 1290, Edward I of England expelled all Jews and had hundreds of Jewish elders executed. On May 26, 1830, President Andrew Jackson of the United States signed the Indian Removal Act which resulted in the Trail of Tears and more or less 15,000 deaths. I consulted with University of Notre Dame professor Ashlee Bird, a Native American, regarding whether or not she thought negative rhetoric led to the massacre of Natives in the United States. According to Bird,

> I think negative rhetoric certainly contributed to the Indian removal act, but there was a lot of other stuff going on there to motivate that atrocity, like the desire for Native land and Jackson even using excuses that it would be for the betterment of

---

70. Hoover, "Is Evangelicalism Itching for a Fight?," 11.
71. McCammon, "Southern Baptists Split."

Indigenous people themselves as they were like children who needed guidance and wouldn't adjust to White society. Another and perhaps better example might be the fact that Custer is valorized for making a last stand against the "savages" that killed him, when really, he had no business being in charge (only because the regiment leader was sick I believe) and he was largely seeking a desire for glory and chose to attack a meeting of Indigenous peoples who were not attacking them knowing they were outnumbered about 3–1 and therefore got himself and most of his men killed. However, it is attributed to the savagery of Natives that he attacked them and that they succeeded. After this attack, the very angry remaining members of his regiment went to Wounded Knee and committed the massacre there and were awarded with medals of honor from the government that still have not been revoked.[72]

During the Russo-Turkish War some 300,000 Bulgarian civilians were slaughtered. From 1894 to 1896 Sultan Abdul Hamid II ordered the killing of ethnic Armenians (along with a Christian minority); estimated death toll: over 300,000. During the Balkan Wars ethnic cleansing took place, resulting in the deaths of hundreds of thousands, and during World War II Hitler's Nazi army killed over six million Jews. These and other horrible crimes against humanity did not come about overnight—the social atmosphere of each country wittingly or unwittingly provided a space for such ideology to be cultivated and executed. These injustices were carried out by people who felt that their way of life was being threatened or was superior to the other. Such emotions are commonplace throughout the world and to a degree at least, some wage a cold war and at times a violent war against those that threaten their ideology. It often begins with the proliferation of negative rhetoric used to solidify the base and define the enemy, then when the political atmosphere lends itself to the cause, action takes place—at best discrimination, at worst ethnic cleansing.

Conclusion

The Southern Baptist denomination is a powerful force for good in the United States and around the world. Southern Baptists are known for evangelical zeal and humanitarian relief efforts. They represent the most influential Protestant denomination in the United States. From a political

---

72. Ashlee Bird, personal email, November 15, 2022.

standpoint, they are very influential. From a religious standpoint, they have had a great impact on moral standards in the U.S. When the leaders of the Southern Baptist Convention speak, many citizens, including political and religious leaders, within the United States listen. Therefore, I argue that it is necessary for Southern Baptist leaders to engage with Muslim-Americans to understand their religion, their values, and their distinct interests and preferences more thoroughly as citizens of the United States. This dialogue, consisting of telling one's story, can lend itself to creating a more contextual understanding and perception of Islam. Psychologist Jeanne Christie says, "The value of the narrative grounds us in the reality of the present and illuminates the reality of the past."[73] In other words, it helps us to understand the context of the other person's thoughts and actions. Though Jewish, Christian, and Muslim historical accounts of the Old Testament diverge at times and there are clear doctrinal differences, could it be that our expectations for peace, justice, mercy, and morality are not incomprehensible to each other? At this juncture, I turn to the sources of Islam—the Qur'an and the Sunnah of the Prophet—to set forth a narrative that seeks to bridge Christian and Islamic thought as it pertains to a proper respect for one another and a common interest in making the world a more godly, peaceful, and just place to live.

Earlier, I raised the question, What is going on? in order to discover some of the casual mechanisms that seem to incentivize anti-Islamic rhetoric, particularly within the Southern Baptist denomination and more generally within the United States. Islam is growing within the United States and it is predicted that Muslims will have doubled in population by the year 2050. Islam is not coming to the U.S.; Islam is in the U.S. and has many faithful practitioners. I concluded in my interviews that many Southern Baptist pastors are concerned that the growth of Islam will negatively influence U.S. democracy by introducing what they called "Sharia law" and that the lived spirituality of Muslims within the U.S. will in effect evangelize non-Muslims causing some, perhaps many, to convert. There is also heightened fear among some pastors that Muslims are discreetly seeking to infiltrate this democracy and conquer Christianity and, moreover, that for Muslims to achieve their goals of infiltration and conquest some will engage in militaristic jihad. However, without exception, every pastor I interviewed who had a personal encounter with a Muslim or Muslims found them to be very peaceable, kind, generous, educated, and

---

73. Christie, "Value of the Narrative."

good citizens. The greatest concerns among my interviewees were that Islam is a false religion that distracts people from knowing, trusting, and loving Christ and, that it is a violent religion. I found that their perceptions of Islam stemmed primarily from a lack of personal encounter and relationship, and from a media that tends to portray Islam in a negative manner. In the next chapter, by returning to the sources of Islam, I reflect upon the lived spirituality of the Prophet Muhammad and Islam—a man and a religion that have been historically misunderstood and feared by Western civilization, particularly many within Christendom.

4

What Should Be Going On

Returning to the Sources of Islam

Introduction

My academic research, my conversations and friendships with Muslims both in the United States and abroad, and my personal travels to Arab countries have significantly altered my initial perception of Islam. These experiences introduced me to an Islamic milieu that is often at odds with the caricature I had found in the newspapers, social media, and personal conversations with colleagues, friends, and family. I have concluded that Islam is both a religion and a culture that encompass a great deal of diversity. Islam comprises a world-wide community of people who are very distinctive yet mysteriously linked to each other. Cemil Aydin writes, "Roughly a fifth of people now living are Muslims. Their societies, located in every corner of the globe, vary in language, ethnicity, political ideology, nationality, culture, and wealth."[1] Though the societies, persons, ideas, and practices that claim a connection with Islam vary greatly, Islam is also a community of shared stories—a history of oppression, defeat, conquest, and values that transcend time and

---

1. Aydin, *Idea of the Muslim World*, 1.

place.² One political scientist has calculated that there are at least three hundred ethnic groups around the globe today that are partly or wholly Muslim.³ Collectively, these various groups within Islam can be traced back to three sects of Islam that emerged in the first century after the Prophet's death: Sunni, Shia, and Kharijites. Proponents of each claim to be the rightful succession from the Prophet Muhammad.

Though there are many sectoral distinctions within Islam, it seems to me that the lived spirituality of the Prophet Muhammad is the glue that bonds the general Muslim population together. And it is the Prophet Muhammad and his lived spirituality that can spur meaningful and constructive intra-religious dialogue among Muslims and inter-religious dialogue between Southern Baptists and Muslims. In this chapter, employing Osmer's third step in practical theology, the normative task, I ask the question, "What ought to be going on?"⁴ with a particular focus on how the Southern Baptist leader can better appreciate, understand, and improve his or her perception of Islam. Our answers to this question can significantly improve Southern Baptist relationships with Muslims, especially American Muslims. To accomplish my goal in developing narrative empathy among Southern Baptists toward Muslims, my arguments in this chapter are developed as follows. In the first section, I elaborate on Osmer's normative task—the method that enables me to explain how narrative empathy can foster Southern Baptists' openness to Islam. Then, drawing theological concepts from Islam, I expound on the lived spirituality of the Prophet Muhammad by examining three different issues. First, I provide an overview of the cultural and religious environment which constituted the context of Muhammad's life. Second, I examine the life of the Prophet, both pre- and post-revelations. Third, I turn my focus to jihad—a concept largely misunderstood by the Southern Baptist community. Finally, I present insights from my personal experiences in developing a narrative empathy for Muslims. Misinterpretations and false narratives surrounding these three issues constitute the most important obstacle to fostering narrative empathy towards Muslims among Southern Baptists.

---

2. Ahmed, *What Is Islam?*, 6.
3. Siddique, "Conceptualizing Patterns and Civilizing Processes," 395.
4. Osmer, *Practical Theology*, 4.

Methodology

A more accurate and objective rendering of Islam through a critical historical analysis can nurture interreligious dialogue between Muslims and Christians. The Christian-Muslim relationship has a long history. At times it has been violent and at times peaceful. Professor Hugh Goddard, in his work *A History of Christian-Muslim Relations*, writes at considerable length about this relationship and argues that a better understanding of this past can significantly improve current relations, especially on matters religious, political, and economic. I believe his historical analysis, spanning the medieval and modern periods, can help the pastor interpret the present state of the relationship and thus foster healing and collaboration between Christians and Muslims of good will.[5] According to Osmer, the normative task can guide the pastor into "interpreting particular episodes, situations, or contexts, constructing ethical norms to guide our responses and learning from 'good practice.'"[6] With my own goals in mind, the normative task enables me to explain crucial concepts of Islam to foster a better understanding of the religion in the Southern Baptist denomination. Significantly, theological and ethical interpretation, as the most formal dimension of the normative task, helps us to discern how fundamental concepts of Islam—in particular the lived spirityalty of the Prophet Muhammad—can be understood in an ethical manner. As Osmer explains, "theological interpretation focuses on the interpretation of present episodes, situations, and contexts with theological concepts."[7] I believe that a much better perception of Islam can be obtained by having a more contextual understanding of the Prophet's lived spirituality. Importantly, this understanding can create a degree of narrative empathy that promotes constructive discussions of Islam. In providing accurate interpretations of the three issues associated with Muhammad's lived spirituality—his cultural and religious environment, his life before and after revelation, and jihad—I am guided by the historical method. The historical method is a tool that helps gain access to authentic spiritual experiences by way of an examination of texts which recount the spiritual experiences of those who have gone before us.[8]

---

5. Goddard, *History of Christian-Muslim Relations*.
6. Osmer, *Practical Theology*, 4.
7. Osmer, *Practical Theology*, 139.
8. Downey, *Understanding Christian Spirituality*, 126.

The historical method also enables me to accurately examine, and develop a better understanding of, the Prophet's experiences. I refer to the religious sources of Islam (Qur'an, Sunnah) as well as scholarly resources recognized by Muslim and non-Muslim scholars as rendering an objective historical account of the Prophet and his times. In so doing, I identify the Prophet Muhammad as a very spiritual and religious person who felt the calling of God upon his life to promote a monotheist belief free from what he believed to be theological contaminants, and who pursued this work via jihad. One weakness of the historical method is the inability to recreate a precise moment in history. Indeed, though the historical method provides the analytical backing of the normative task, I am limited in my ability to flawlessly reimagine the Prophet's life. However, via textual analysis of reliable sources, a written and verbal account of the Prophet's experiences can be accurately documented. Though stories of the Prophet vary ever so slightly at times (similar to the accounts of Christ in the Synoptic Gospels), owing primarily to the writer's perception of the event and or purpose for writing, there is a common thread interwoven throughout the narrative.

Islam's foundational sources—Qur'an and Sunnah—speak of Muhammad's character. He was a man of peace, justice, tolerance, high moral character, wisdom, and mercy. The Qur'an, according to Muslims, is the direct revelation of God, by way of the Angel Gabriel to Muhammad, which he then recited to his Companions. "Sunnah" is a "term of pre-Islamic origin for established custom, the approved practice handed down from the past. In Islam, sunna came to mean the practice of the Prophet, whose example all Muslims should follow: in effect, Islamic law."[9] The hadith, which is found in the Sunnah, "is a report of the words and deeds of the Prophet Muhammad. These reports include commands or legal edicts given by the Prophet, descriptions of his behavior, actions that took place in his presence and of which he implicitly approved, and his predictions of future events."[10] Hadith provide the primary framework by which Muslims seek to better understand the Qur'anic material as it relates to legal, dogmatic, ethical, and political norms and issues dealt with in Islamic thought, but may not be explicit in the Qur'an.[11] M. M. Azami formally defines hadith as follows:

9. *The Princeton Encyclopedia of Islamic Political Thought*, s.v. "sunna."
10. *The Princeton Encyclopedia of Islamic Political Thought*, s.v. "Hadith."
11. *The Princeton Encyclopedia of Islamic Political Thought*, s.v. "Hadith."

According to *Muhaddithin* [scholars of hadith] it stands for "what was transmitted on the authority of the Prophet, his deeds, saying, tacit approval, or description of his *sifat* (features)" meaning his physical appearance. However, physical appearance of the Prophet is not included in the definition used by the jurists. Thus *hadith* literature means the literature which consists of the narrations of the life of the Prophet and the things approved by him. However, the term was used sometimes in much broader sense to cover the narrations about the Companions [of the Prophet] and Successors [to the Companions] as well.[12]

In addition to the Qur'an and Sunnah, I use secondary sources that elaborate on the nature and meaning of Islam's foundational sources. In sum, by drawing insights from Islam's sources, the Qur'an and Sunnah, and reliable scholarly sources such as *The Princeton Encyclopedia of Islamic Political Thought*, I am able to provide an accurate historical account of the Prophet's lived spirituality.

My own personal experience has taught me that to engage in constructive dialogue with Muslims, there must be a feeling of mutual respect among interlocutors. It also helps greatly to have a conversational familiarity with some of their religious customs and history of their beloved Prophet, as well as their affirmation of many Christian beliefs. But it is of the utmost importance that one's knowledge of Islam—however basic—comes from reliable historical and scholarly sources. In sum, to perform the normative task of practical theology I examine classical and modern literature, emphasizing what I have learned about the Prophet and his family, his revelatory experiences, and his understanding and application of jihad. Through this normative task my own narrative empathy for the Prophet Muhammad and Muslims, as have my own perception and understanding of Islam. I believe what I have gleaned from reading much of the Qur'an and Sunnah of the Prophet, as well as scholarly literature on the Prophet Muhammad, can likewise foster a narrative empathy among Southern Baptist leaders and indeed shape a new perception of Islam, one that is more objective and hence more constructive to interreligious dialogue and peace building.

In Christianity, the greatest commandment in the Holy Bible is to love God and the second is to love one's neighbor. Genuine love for neighbor, in this case Muslims, can create and cultivate a narrative that is positive and enduring. To be sure, the default attitude among Christians towards

---

12. Azami, *Hadith Methodology and Literature*, 3.

all non-Christians should be one of love. Many Southern Baptist leaders are missing this kind of narrative, yet it is this kind of narrative that can build upon shared values and beliefs, thus fostering just peace, love, understanding, and even substantive doctrinal discussions with Muslims. Below, I focus on the lived spirituality of the Prophet Muhammad, highlighting some of his teachings that significantly influence how Muslims live their lives. This reflection upon the Prophet Muhammad and his teachings can help shape a new perception of Islam that can spur kind, respectful, and meaningful conversations amongst Southern Baptists towards Islam as well as between Southern Baptists and Muslims. Many non-Muslims have pre-formed thoughts about Muslims; my hope is that this brief introduction into the lived spirituality of the Prophet will help forestall some of the negativity and the false narratives that we so often encounter.

The Concept of Lived Spirituality and Muhammad

The importance of understanding the lived spirituality of Muhammad can hardly be overestimated. As we saw in chapter 2, within the Southern Baptist denomination there is not only a lack of knowledge, but also considerable misperception of the Prophet Muhammad and his lived spirituality. Hence, in this section, I define what I mean by "lived spirituality" and in so doing offer what I take to be a more objective and scholarship-based view of the lived spirituality of the Prophet. In this context, I examine three different, though deeply interconnected, aspects of Muhammad's lived spirituality: the cultural and religious environment of Muhammad's early years, the life of the Prophet both pre- and post-revelation, and jihad. Collectively these three aspects of Muhammad's lived spirituality enable me to provide a framework for the pastor to have a deeper and perhaps more empathetic understanding and perception of the Prophet as well as Muslims. I have observed several recurring questions concerning the lived spirituality of the Prophet Muhammad that tend to surface among Southern Baptist pastors. They include: What is his ancestry? What made him think he heard from God? How did he understand and execute jihad, especially as it relates to the reasons and wisdoms of war and marriage? A lack of historical context surrounding these questions, along with a stereotyping of Muslims, has spurred much negative attention and hostile speech within Southern Baptist circles that has demonized the Prophet and his actions, and Muslims generally. This negativity and hostility greatly hinder interreligious dialogue and cooperation between Southern Baptists and Muslims.

Reflecting back on my college and seminary years, I did not receive a thorough and unbiased introduction to the study of the Prophet Muhammad and Islam. Instead, I received a very brief lecture on the historical Muhammad, followed by a lesson on why Islam is a false religion. No time was given to contextualizing the person of Muhammad or the reasons for his teachings. It was not until I pursued my doctoral studies at Catholic Theological Union in Chicago that I was offered semester-long classes on the study of the Prophet Muhammad and Islam—classes that significantly altered my pre-formed perceptions of the Prophet and Islam. As a pastor, I heard many of my colleagues both in social events and sermons from the pulpit say that the Prophet Muhammad was a man filled with a demonic spirit who should be classified as a pedophile, polygamist, warmonger, anti-Christ, and all around a bad man. Through the years, it has become apparent to me that very few Southern Baptist ministers have an objective historical understanding of Muhammad's early years and his lived spirituality. In many cases, what they heard and learned about the Prophet came from authors and speakers whose intention was to discredit the Prophet and in so doing discredit Islam. My intent is to present a more historical account of Muhammad and his lived spirituality as observed by his sixth- and seventh-century contemporaries and elaborated by modern scholars of Islam.

At this juncture, it is important to define what I mean by *lived spirituality*. Leading scholars in the field of spirituality, Elizabeth A. Dreyer and Mark S. Burrows, define lived spirituality as follows:

- The daily lived aspect of one's faith commitment in terms of values and behaviors.
- How one appropriates beliefs about God and the world.
- The process of conscious integration and transformation of one's life.
- The journey of self-transcendence.
- The depth dimension of all human existence.
- A dialectic that moves one from the inauthentic to the authentic and from the individual to the communal.
- The quest for ultimate value and meaning.[13]

13. Dryer and Burrows, *Minding the Spirit*, xv.

Taking into consideration Dreyer and Burrows's definition of lived spirituality and for the purpose of this endeavor, I understand lived spirituality as the interweaving of body, mind, and soul in the pursuit of life's meaning and purpose.

In my effort to understand and answer questions associated with Muhammad's pre-revelatory years, calling, and his pursuit of jihad—especially as it relates to his reasons and wisdoms of war and marriage—I found it important to observe that none of these issues, be they historical or contemporary, can be accurately addressed separately from the lived spirituality of Muhammad. Similarly, to have a contextual understanding of Judaism it is helpful to piece together the lived spirituality of Abraham, Moses, or David; of Christianity, Jesus, Paul, or John. (As a side note, we have at our disposal much more information on the day-to-day actions and words of Muhammad than we do on any of the Biblical characters.) The same symmetrical objectivity needs to be applied when trying to understand Islam and reconstruct (which really is a new construction) the life of the Prophet. Opinions and actions of Jews and Christians at times conflict with the teachings of Abraham and Jesus. The same is true of Muslims. Furthermore, while a religion's adherents have some things in common, it is a mistake to think they are all alike. As Aydin notes, "Muslims in different parts of the world are connected—through education, trade, pilgrimage, politics, and kinship, not just religion and not through collective competition with a non-Muslim other."[14] Thus, there is no "Muslim world," but instead a mosaic of Muslims from around the world, most of whom seek to understand their own lived spirituality by reflecting upon the Sunnah of the Prophet.

The Cultural and Religious Environment of Muhammad

Today, Islam is the second largest religion in the world and the predominant religion in the Middle East. As of 2010, Muslims were 23.2 percent of the world's population. It is estimated that by the year 2050, Muslims will be 29.7 percent of the world's population, with Christianity slightly ahead with 31.4 percent.[15] Given these trends, it behooves Southern Baptists, indeed it benefits them, to embark upon a more thorough understanding of Islam. Having defined the concept of lived spirituality and its

14. Aydin, *Idea of the Muslim World*, 16.
15. Pew Research Center, "Future of World Religions."

importance for the understanding of Islam, I now turn my attention to three different concepts associated with the Prophet's lived spirituality. If one is to understand Islam, the life of the Prophet must not be overlooked or underappreciated. Without the Prophet Muhammad there is no Islam.

Annemarie Schimmel writes, "All will agree that the personality of Muhammad is indeed, besides the Koran, the center of the Muslims' life; the Prophet is the one who forever remains the 'beautiful model' (Sura 33.21) for the life of all those who acknowledge in the profession of faith that he is truly 'the messenger of God.'"[16] Historians inform us that Muhammad was born into a world divided into tribal Arab cults with their fatalistic notions and pagan practices. The religious environment also included an assortment of primarily Christian sectarian beliefs, distinctive Jewish practices, and some Manichean ideas. The era prior to the introduction, cultivation, and spread of Islam in the seventh century is commonly known as the age of ignorance, against which Islam is contrasted as the age of enlightenment and knowledge.[17] Arabs were known for their strength, courage, indulgence, hospitality, drinking songs, and love poetry, as well as their polytheistic beliefs and practices. The center of worship at this time was the flourishing commercial city of Mecca. In the center of the city was a cubed structure made of granite called the Ka'bah, where over 360 idols were kept. According to the Qur'an, the Ka'bah was constructed by Abraham and Ishmael as the first house of worship dedicated to God.[18] Tribal cults, polytheistic systems, and versions of Judaism and Christianity churned in the political, religious and social milieu of Muhammad's time. Within a hundred years of his birth, this pluralistic milieu would come to an end.

Though some Arabs lived in major cities such as Mecca and Medina, most were Bedouin, or desert dwellers. During the time of Muhammad, the Bedouins were an ethno-cultural group with a culture based primarily in poetry and oral tradition. Poets were revered and thought to be divinely inspired; to have a poet in one's tribe was highly regarded in society. For entertainment, the nomads would give their time and attention to poets, as they would bring the world to life with their words and make meaning out of everyday situations. In the unlikely event that a nomad could write, he would write in the common tribal dialect; the poets, by contrast, would write in Classical Arabic, which would later

16. Schimmel, *And Muhammad Is His Messenger*, 8.
17. *The Princeton Encyclopedia of Islamic Political Thought*, s.v. "Muhammad."
18. The Cow 2:127 (The Qur'an).

influence the style of the Qur'an. The influence of the nomads extended throughout the vast deserts of northern Africa and the Middle East. They traveled in caravans and some of these caravans lacked scruples. For example, the caravan known as the vagrant-bandits roamed the desert pillaging whatever they needed or desired. Monferrer-Sala writes regarding these bandits, "One of the groups in pre-Islamic society that would disappear after the arrival of the new Islamic social model was that of the vagrant-bandits, who were traditionally depicted as vagrant bards or desperadoes without a fixed home, permanently moving throughout the Arabian milieu."[19]

The Arabs of Muhammad's time were very spiritual people, seeking meaning to life through various forms of pagan worship, idolatry, Judaism, Christianity, and other faiths and practices. During the expansion of the Byzantine Empire (fourth to sixth centuries), many Arabs converted to Judaism and Christianity and more would have converted to Judaism if the Jews had been less demanding of converts. As Kelen writes, "They [Arabs] might have turned in similar numbers to Judaism [than Islam], except that the Jews had a fancy that those who wished to join the People of the Book should be willing to submit to a certain amount of book learning in their Torah Schools. This was a hurdle. So was their requirement that all men be circumcised."[20] One surmises that had Judaism been willing to accept some of the Arab customs, Islam might not have found fertile ground to take root, grow, and become the second largest religion in the world. Judaism and Christianity played a major role in introducing the Arabs to prayerful meditation. It was not uncommon for Arabs to steal away to secluded areas in the desert and enter into a form of meditative prayer and solitude with the expectation of discovering new and deeper meaning to life.

The Arabian milieu, especially the Arabian Peninsula consisting of modern-day Saudi Arabia, Yemen, United Arab Emirates, and Oman, was an assortment of many faiths and cultures, characterized by tribal conflict and political and territorial disunity. Schimmel writes, "The pre-Islamic Bedouin religion most probably revered no images but rather stones, trees, and other objects, and the ancient Arabs seem to have been content, beyond that cult, with a general belief in an all-pervading fate."[21] Pre-Islamic Arabia was profoundly spiritual but lacked any one

19. In Fitzpatrick and Walker, *Muhammad in History*, 53.
20. Kelen, *Muhammad*, 39.
21. Schimmel, *And Muhammad Is His Messenger*, 12.

person or religion that could unite them in the way that Constantine the Great had united the Roman Empire. This lack of unification would soon come to an end. The cultural and religious environment that formed the context of Muhammad's life was complex. Its complexity allows one to understand and appreciate the life of the Prophet, both pre- and post-revelation, the topic of the following section.

The Life of Muhammad, Pre-revelation

In the year 570 CE, during a time of tribal distinctiveness and religious development, a baby was born to the Banu Hashim clan of the tribe Quraysh in the town of Mecca. The Quraysh tribe was a powerful merchant tribe that ruled over the city of Mecca and the Ka'aba. The baby born into this clan was a boy and he was given the name *Muhammad*, meaning "worthy of praise." Muhammad's father, 'Abdallah son of 'Abdul Muttalib, having died before his birth, his mother Amina and wet nurse raised him during his early years. At the age of six, his mother died and Muhammad was left an orphan. He grew up in poverty. Though Muhammad and his mother were under the protection of his grandfather, 'Abdul Muttalib, as fate would have it, he died when Muhammad was eight. He then passed into the custodianship of his uncle Abu Talib, whose son Ali was to become one of the first converts to Islam. Though Muhammad's ancestral lineage (as seen in the diagram below, figure 4.1) can be traced back to Ishmael, the son of Abraham, who worshiped the God of the Jews and the Christians, the Quraysh's main god was Hubal. In fact, the Quraysh tribe worshipped a multiplicity of idols and deities, including, among others Manaf and Na'ila.[22]

---

22. Johnson, *Oxford Handbook of Late Antiquity*, s.v. "Hubal."

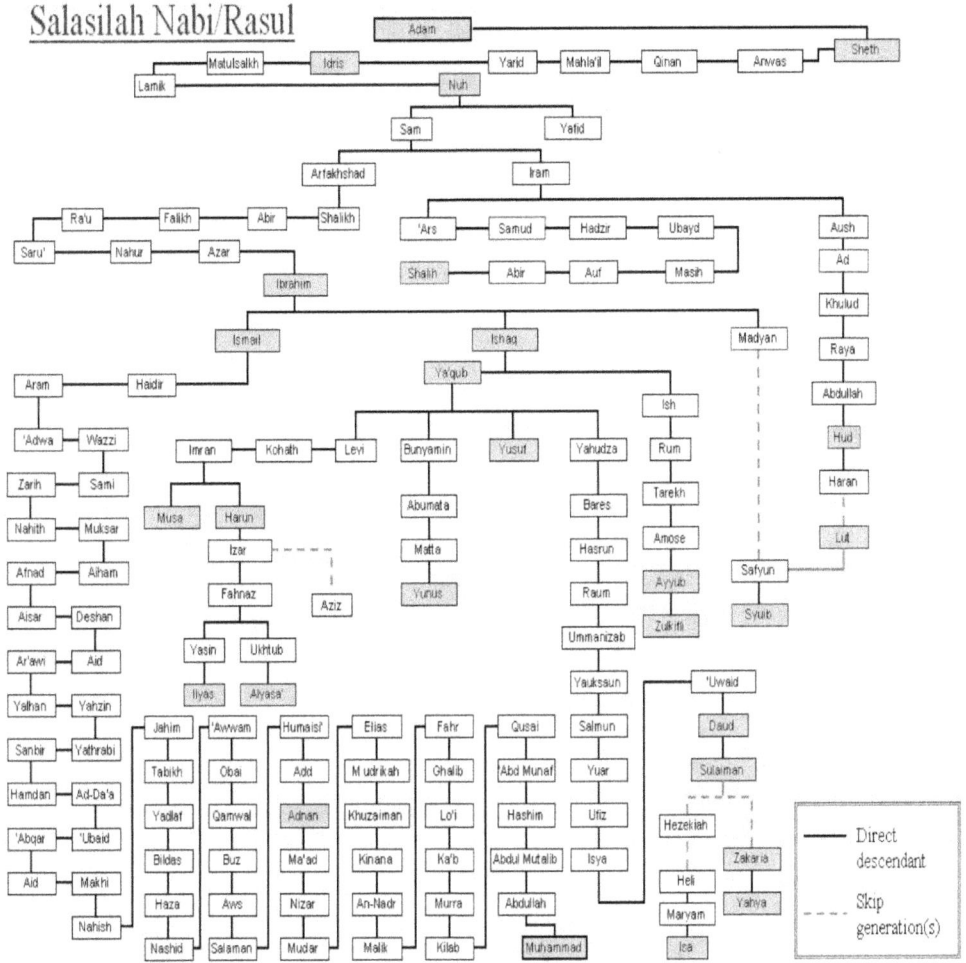

Figure 4.1. The family tree of the Prophet Muhammad.[23]

In contrast to Judaism and Christianity, Islam places primary emphasis upon Ishmael, the son of Abraham and Hagar. Hagar was the Egyptian slave that served Sarah, Abraham's wife. In the Biblical account, Sarah was barren, and it was determined by Abraham and Sarah that Abraham should take Hagar as a wife and have a child with her. Later Sarah became jealous of Hagar and so mistreated her that she fled from Sarah with the unborn child in her womb. During her wanderings in

23. Highlights indicate the important people of lineage of Jesus and Muhammad. Source: www.answering-christianity.com.

the desert an Angel of the Lord appeared and said to Hagar, "You have conceived and will have a son. You will name him Ishmael, for the Lord has heard your cry of affliction. This man will be like a wild ass. His hand will be against everyone, and everyone's hand will be against him; he will be at odds with all his brothers" (Genesis 16:11–12).[24] According to the Biblical account, Ishmael eventually lapsed into unbelief and became the progenitor of the Arabs. Before this, God spoke to Abraham regarding his son Ishmael, whom he loved very much, saying, "As for Ishmael, I have heard you. I will certainly bless him; I will make him fruitful and will multiply him greatly. He will father twelve tribal leaders, and I will make him into a great nation" (Genesis 17:20).[25] It is from the direct lineage of Ishmael that the Prophet Muhammad is born. Dr. C. I. Scofield, a leading Bible scholar of the twentieth century, noted in his commentary on this section of Scripture that Christianity and Islam have very much in common, and it is perhaps due to this reality that the two religions often spar with each other.[26] Incidentally, by the time of Muhammad, many within Muhammad's tribe were polytheistic and worshipped many of the idols found in the Ka'bah. Interestingly enough, the commonly held religious beliefs and traditions within his tribe as well as the greater beliefs of the Arabian Peninsula would not satisfy his quest for spiritual meaning and purpose.

As noted above, tragedy unfolded in the life of Muhammad; he had lost the dearest people in his life and had it not been for his uncle's custodianship, he would have been left to fend for himself. Though he grew up as an orphan and experienced poverty, he did not succumb to anger, resentment, fear, unbridled passion, hatred, or aggression. In the words of Schimmel, "His being an orphan, yatim, as pointed out in Sura 93—was to inspire many later poets to compare him to a yatima, a unique pearl."[27] Muhammad was indeed a unique person; rather than turning to the dark side of life, he would emerge as a seeker of truth and a successful merchant, a person trusted and respected by those who knew him. Perhaps this strength of character came from his time being raised in the desert. As a young baby, he was sent to live in the desert where he was cared for by a wet nurse. It is those years in the desert that helped shape Muhammad's character into the man he later became. Lings writes,

24. Genesis 16:11–12 (Holman Christian Standard Bible).
25. Genesis 17:10 (Holman Christian Standard Bible).
26. Commentary on Genesis 16:11–12 (Scofield Study Bible, King James Version).
27. Schimmel, *And Muhammad Is His Messenger*, 10.

Towns were places of corruption. Sloth and slovenliness lurked in the shadow of their walls, ready to take the edge off a man's alertness and vigilance. Everything decayed there, even language, one of man's most precious possessions. Few of the Arabs could read, but beauty of speck was a virtue which all Arab parents desired for their children. A man's worth was largely assessed by his eloquence, and the crown of eloquence was poetry. To have a great poet in the family was indeed something to be proud of; and the best poets were nearly always from one or another of the desert tribes, for it was in the desert that the spoken language was nearest to poetry. So the bond with the desert had to be renewed in every generation—fresh air for the breast, pure Arabic for the tongue, freedom for the soul; and many of the sons of Quraysh were kept as long as eight years in the desert, so that it might make a lasting impression upon them.[28]

Historically, much emphasis has been placed on the life and spirituality of Muhammad himself. However, I believe that his lived spirituality was deeply affected by the spirituality of his grandfather and father. Understanding his family background can also help us to understand the reasons for his choosing the path he chose later in life. Like most young men who were not privileged to know their father and grandfather, Muhammad was sure to ask questions about these absent figures—what were their likes and dislikes? what did they believe? what did they want to accomplish in life? etc. His grandfather 'Abd al-Muttalib, though the intertribal host of pilgrims to the Ka'bah, was a deeply religious and spiritual man who believed in and prayed to the God of Abraham and was responsible for discovering the Well of Zamzam. The well was anciently dug by Abraham to supply his son Ishmael with water. One night while 'Abd al-Muttalib was resting near the Ka'bah, he had a vision in which he was instructed,

> Dig her, thou shalt not regret,
> For she is thine inheritance From thy greatest ancestor.
> Dry she never will, nor fail
> To water all the pilgrim throng.[29]

Though 'Abd al-Muttalib encountered opposition in digging the well, he dug it as instructed, 20 meters east of the Ka'bah. At that very spot, water began to spring forth from the well and is still flowing to

---

28. Lings, *Muhammad*, 23.
29. Linds, *Muhammad*, 10.

this day. 'Abd al-Mattalib had ten sons, but prior to having these sons, he vowed to God that if He would bless him with ten sons and if they would all grow to manhood, then out of thanksgiving he would sacrifice one of his sons to Him at the Ka'bah. He remained true to his word and once all of his sons had grown to manhood, by the casting of lots, it was determined that his most beloved and youngest son, 'Abd Allah, be sacrificed at the Ka'bah. To honor God, 'Abd al-Muttalib and his son 'Abd Allah were willing to follow through with the sacrifice. Fortunately, once God saw that both were willing to obey, even unto death, God intervened and allowed for another sacrifice to take the place of 'Abd Allah.

During this time, many Jews and Christians believed that God was going to send another prophet to them. The Jews believed the prophet was to be of Jewish origins, but many of the Christian Arabs of the time saw no reason why the prophet could not be of Arab descent. Lings writes, "The Arabs stood in need of a prophet even more than the Jews, who at least still followed the religion of Abraham inasmuch as they worshipped the One God and did not have idols; and who but a prophet would be capable of ridding the Arabs of their worship of false gods?"[30] Waraqah, the son of 'Abd al-Muttalib's second cousin Nawfal, of the clan of Asad, was a Christian. He was also looking for the coming of another prophet with enough influence to rid the Arab world of many of its pagan practices. As a student of the Scripture, he was very familiar with one of Christ's promises recorded in chapter sixteen of John's gospel and believed it possibly paved the way for another prophet to come. Lings writes, "Generally interpreted by Christians as referring to the miracle of Pentecost, there were none the less certain elements which did not fit that miracle and must be taken to refer to something else—something which had not yet been fulfilled. But the language was cryptic: what was the meaning of the words: *he shall not speak of himself, but whatsoever he shall hear, that shall he speak.*"[31] Waraqah would later come to believe that this prophecy was fulfilled in the person of Muhammad.

'Abd Allah, the father of Muhammad, believed in God like his father before him. He was considered by many to be the Joseph of his time. He was smart, handsome, and well respected in Mecca. He held great respect for his father and sought to honor his father's wishes. This is evident in that he married Aminah, whom his father had chosen for him as

---

30. Lings, *Muhammad*, 17.
31. Lings, *Muhammad*, 17.

being a suitable wife. At the age of twenty-five, he and Aminah married; Islamic tradition says that on the night of their wedding, Muhammad was conceived. Unfortunately, less than one year later, 'Abd Allah would fall ill while traveling and die before his son was born. Muhammad and his mother came under the care of his grandfather on his father's side. Muhammad's father and grandfather belonged to the Hanifs faith, which was a native pre-Islamic belief that professed a rigid monotheism; followers dated their beliefs back to Abraham.[32] Upon the untimely death of his mother and grandfather, he came into the care of his uncle Abu Talib. Though his uncle would come to love Muhammad as his own, he did not share the beliefs of his brother and father.

At one time, Muhammad's clan was very well off financially, but that seems to have changed by the time Muhammad came under the care of his uncle Abu Talib. Abu Talib was not wealthy; Lings writes, "The fortunes of 'Abd al-Muttalib had waned during the last part of his life, and what he had left at his death amounted to no more than a small legacy for each of his sons. . . . But Abu Talib was poor, and his nephew felt obliged to do what he could to earn his own livelihood."[33] Notwithstanding the financial hardships the family was experiencing, Abu Talib shared what he had with Muhammad and Muhammad loved him very much. He taught Muhammad archery, shepherding, and business. Lings writes, "Muhammad had come to be known throughout Mecca as al-Amin, the Reliable, the Trustworthy, the Honest, and this was initially owing to the reports of those who had entrusted their merchandise to him on various occasions."[34]

Muhammad's lived spirituality was deeply influenced by the spirituality of his family members. While we have very little information about Muhammad's teenage years, we know that by the time he was twenty he was often invited to join with his kinsmen on their travels abroad. Along these journeys, he gained experience as a merchant and was said to have had a keen ability to trade. His wealth and stature grew steadily and his name became known and respected by many. On one such caravan, he caught the attention of a wealthy Meccan merchant named Khadijah. Khadijah had been married twice and both times widowed. Though fifteen years older than Muhammad, she fell in love with him and would later ask him to marry her. At the age of twenty-five, Muhammad obliged.

32. www.britannica.com, s.v. "Hanif."
33. Lings, *Muhammad*, 29.
34. Lings, *Muhammad*, 34.

With their wealth and influence combined, they were an affluent business couple throughout the Arab world. Shortly after marrying Khadijah, Muhammad's life would take on new meaning and purpose. Khadijah would prove to be a great supporter of his spiritual journey.

Theologically, Muhammad was inspired by certain aspects of the oneness of God, yet he was still uncertain of the definitive nature of God. Schimmel writes, "Muhammad was looking for something higher and purer than the traditional religious forms."[35] Kelen writes, "The mountains around Mecca held many caves, and thoughtful citizens formed the habit of retiring to these secluded places for solitary meditation and prayer. This custom, called tahannuth, was a religious exercise, and it had originated, like the word which is related to the Hebrew word for certain special prayers, with the Jews of the Old Testament."[36] It is common knowledge that Muhammad was a deeply spiritual man; one of the oldest surviving biographies of the Prophet Muhammad is that of Ibn Hisham (d. 833 CE), which is an edited version of Ibn Ishaq's (ca. 704–767 CE) biography of Muhammad. Ibn Hisham writes, "before the revelation of the Qur'an Muhammad used to retreat for a month every year in a mountain called Hira' in Mecca. When he would finish his seclusion, he would return to circumambulate the Ka'bah seven times before heading home."[37] Some years later, on one such meditative excursion, Muhammad ventured into the dessert to one of his beloved caves on a barren mountain called Hira. In times past, he had retreated to this place for days, weeks, and at times even a month, in order to fast, pray, and relish his solitude. At this cave, in 610 CE, at the age of forty, Muhammad had an irresistible encounter with a spiritual figure that would later be called Gabriel, in which he was impressed to go forth and speak the words given to him. This episode would put Muhammad on the path from trustworthy and deeply spiritual man to Prophet and leader of a new world religion.

At the approximate age of twenty-five, Muhammad began his spiritual journey of praying, fasting, and meditating in the desert. Muhammad longed to hear, see, and feel something more meaningful than what the current religions offered. Judaism, though appealing in many ways to Muhammad, was after all, a religion that favored the Jews and demanded not only spiritual but physical conversion to belong. Christianity, though accepted by some in the Arab world and deeply regarded

---

35. Schimmel, *And Muhammad Is His Messenger*, 11.
36. Kelen, *Muhammad*, 41.
37. Fatoohi, "One Night in a Cave."

by Muhammad, seemed to have strayed from the truth in Muhammad's view. Some 245 years prior to Muhammad's birth, in 325 A.D. the Council of Nicaea was called to order. One of the more prominent Christian doctrines to have been discussed and later confirmed by the council was the dogma of the trinity. Muhammad found this doctrine difficult to digest. It seemed to him that Christianity had become polytheistic and had compromised the divinity of God. This will be seen most vividly upon his receiving the Qur'an:

> People of the Book, do not go to excess in your religion, and do not say anything about God except the truth: the Messiah, Jesus, son of Mary, was nothing more than a messenger of God, His word directed to Mary, and a spirit from Him. So believe in God and His messengers and do not speak of a 'Trinity'—stop [this], that is better for you—God is only one God, He is far above having a son, everything in the heavens and earth belongs to Him and He is the best one to trust. The Messiah would never disdain to be a servant of God, nor would angels who are close to Him.[38]

Muhammad longed for clarity in a world of differing religions and doctrines. Some of his contemporaries and relatives had not embraced Judaism, Christianity (at least not the Trinitarian view), or the heathen practices of his time, instead following a rigid monotheism; these were called Hanifs. This group of Arabs along with their rigid beliefs is what helped pave the way for what would later become the religion of Islam. Muhammad's ritualistic practice of praying, fasting, and meditating was his way of finding solitude and discovering deeper meaning to life. In the next section I describe the spiritual encounter that changed his life and quickly unified the Arabian Peninsula under one religion.

The Life of Muhammad, Post-revelation

The spiritual, cultural, and religious environment, as well as Muhammad's pre-revelation experiences, deeply influenced his post-revelation life. Yet it is in the latter period that Muhammad's lived spirituality solidified. An in-depth historical narrative of Muhammad's post-revelation ministry constitutes the heart of this chapter. The majority of Southern Baptist critiques and misunderstandings of Islam deal directly with aspects of Muhammad's post-revelation life. In particular, many Southern

---

38. Women 4:171–72 (The Qur'an).

Baptists demonize the Prophet's professed encounters with Gabriel and accuse him of pedophilia. Consequently, this section aims to shed light on the first of these issues. The first encounter Muḥammad had with the extraterrestrial being was described later by the Prophet as being overwhelming and unpleasant; at times he felt as though he would surely die. Muhammad believed that he was hearing directly from God through Namus (Greek), meaning Gabriel. This encounter is recorded in the Qur'an: "Read! In the name of the Lord who created, who created man from a clot of blood: Read in the name of a merciful Lord, who taught by the pen, taught men what they knew not" (Surah 96:1–5). Prior to this encounter, Muhammad had been experiencing some unusual happenings. He had had visions in his sleep and at times while en route to the cave had heard his name called out. Lings writes, "During these few years it often happened that after he had left the town and was approaching his hermitage, he would hear clearly the words, 'Peace be on thee, O Messenger of God,' and he would turn and look for the speaker but no one was in sight, and it was as if the words had come from a tree or a stone."[39]

A series of similar events had transpired prior to the physical encounter and revelation; absent these events, Muhammad might not have been spiritually and mentally prepared for such a strange and overwhelming experience. Lest there be any doubt as to Muhammad's mental competence up to this time, it is important to note that the community viewed him as a rational person. His retreating into the desert during the month of Ramadan was commonplace in the Quraysh tribe dating back to the time of Ishmael; it was seen as a time of mental and spiritual purification.[40] When the moment of contact with the Angel came Muhammad described it as forceful, as Lings notes:

> "Recite!" and he said: "I am not a reciter," whereupon, as he himself told it, "the Angel took me and whelmed me in his embrace until he had reached the limit of mine endurance. Then he released me and said: "Recite!" I said: "I am not a reciter," and again he took me and whelmed me in his embrace, and again released me and said: "Recite!" and again I said "I am not a reciter." Then a third time he whelmed me as before, then released me and said: "Recite in the name of thy Lord who created."[41]

---

39. Lings, *Muhammad*, 43.
40. Lings, *Muhammad*, 43.
41. Lings, *Muhammad*, 44.

After the third command to recite, the Angel left him and Muhammad would later say, "It was as though the words were written on my heart."[42] After this frightening encounter, Muhammad ran out of the cave for fear that he had become a "jinn-inspired poet or a man possessed."[43] While fleeing the scene, the Angel called out to Muhammad, "O Muhammad, thou art the Messenger of God, and I am Gabriel."[44] Shaken by his encounter, Muhammad quickly returned to his house and sought solace from his wife, Khadijah.

Regaining his composure, Muhammad shared his experience with her. Seeking guidance on how to handle the news, Khadijah went to tell her cousin Waraqah. Waraqah was old and blind, but full of wisdom and knowledge. He had been trained as a Nestorian priest and had studied the Bible under Jews and Christians. He had even translated the Greek New Testament into Arabic. When he heard of the encounter he said, "Holy! Holy! By Him in whose hand is the soul of Waraqah, there hath come unto Muhammad the greatest Namus, even he that would come unto Moses. Verily Muhammad is the Prophet of the people. Bid he rest assured."[45] Though according to the Prophet Muhammad, the Angel identified himself as Gabriel, it is the affirmation of Waraqah that solidified what he had heard in his heart and mind. The Greek word Nomos, in the sense of Divine Law or Scripture, is here identified with the Angel of Revelation. Waraqah's position and interpretation of what had happened to Muhammad sealed the encounter and what would later become the Qur'an as the true doctrinal manifestation of God.

Here is a concise account of Muhammad's encounter with the Angel Gabriel, provided by 'Abd ar-Razzaq:

1. Muhammad's true dream visions appearing 'like the crack of dawn' as the first marks of his prophethood; his religious practices (tahannut) in solitude atop mount Hira (tahannut narration).

2. Unexpected appearance of the angel (Who calls Muhammad 'messenger of God') in a cave on mount Hira.

3. (Direct speech of Muhammad: The angel's request to recite and Muhammad's refusal: 'I am not one to recite.' The angel presses

---

42. Lings, *Muhammad*, 44.
43. Lings, *Muhammad*, 44.
44. Lings, *Muhammad*, 44.
45. Lings, *Muhammad*, 44.

Muhammad. The scene is repeated twice. After pressing Muhammad for a third time, revelation of surah 96:1–5).

4. Muhammad's dread and return to Hadigah. His exclamation: 'Wrap me up.' His dread subsides.
5. Muhammad's conversation with Hadigah ('I fear for my soul'). Hadigah comforts him. Her praise (expressed in parallel phrases of Muhammad) (Hadigah narration II).
6. Muhammad's and Hadigah's visit to Waraqah ibn Nawfal.
7. Discussion with Waraqah. Waraqah's identification of the angel as the Namus and his prophecy: the expulsion and eventual triumph of Muhammad.[46]

The unfolding of this scene helps to reveal why the occurrence was understood positively by Muhammad. What we know today as Islam was not viewed by Waraqah or Muhammad as a new religion, but a clarification and or renewal of the latest form of what it meant to submit to God and to follow God as they believe that Abraham did. Some Christian theologians (John of Damascus, Peter Pascual, Ramon Llull) from the Early Middle Ages to the High Middle Ages have argued that Muhammad did not receive a direct revelation from God via the Angel Gabriel, but instead heard from the devil himself. Interestingly, this belief is still prevalent in Southern Baptist circles today. However that may be, Muhammad believed that the God of Abraham had spoken to him via the Angel Gabriel. For the next twenty-three years, until his death at age sixty-two, Muhammad would continue to hear from God, recite what he heard, and have his companions record the sayings. After the death of the Prophet Muhammad in 632, one of his early successors, Uthman ibn Affan, commanded the redaction of the Qur'an, a redaction that is still used today.

Reflecting on his recent experiences and the counsel of his wife and Waraqah, Muhammad committed himself to the new revelation and set out to evangelize his fellow Arabs. Waraqah advised him to be prepared for persecution: "Thou wilt be called a liar, and ill-treated, and they will cast thee out and make war upon thee."[47] At first, Islam was established on the basis of ritual purification (ablution) and prayer, as the Angel had taught it to Muhammad. The prayer was, "Allahu Akbar, God is Most

---

46. Schoeler, *Biography of Muhammad*, 39.
47. Schoeler, *Biography of Muhammad*, 39.

Great, and the final greeting as-Salamu 'alaykum, Peace be on you."[48] The ideal that "God is Most Great" was not new to Arab Jews and Christians, but Muhammad's conviction that he had to establish this truth through evangelization and remove pagan worship from Arab culture was not well received by many within his tribe nor by the merchants of Mecca. At the center of Mecca was the Ka'bah, and for generations the tribe of Quraysh had ensured that pilgrims felt welcomed into the city and the inner sanctuary to worship as they saw fit and to place idols to overlooked deities in the Ka'bah if desired. Any interference with this hospitality was greeted by most in the region as harmful to their economy and political relations. The tribe and the region did not take well to this new threat.

Muhammad's first revelations were followed by a period of silence, causing Muhammad to fear that he had disappointed God in some way. At last the silence was broken, and God not only comforted him but gave him his first command:

> By the morning brightness, and by the night when still! Thy Lord has not forsaken thee; nor does He despise. And the Hereafter shall be better for thee than this life. And surely thy Lord shall give unto thee, and thou shalt be content. Did He not find thee an orphan and shelter, find thee astray and guide, find thee in need and enrich? So as for the orphan, scorn not. And as for one who requests, repel not. And as for the blessing of thy Lord, proclaim![49]

As time passed and the revelations became more concise and frequent, a spiritual fever came over Muhammad that compelled him to proclaim the message of God to all those he encountered. Some within his family as well as close friends converted to Islam, but many within his tribe and community vehemently resisted the revelation he was receiving and sharing. Some of his early converts and close companions, as they were called, wrote down the words Muhammad recited. They also kept records of his method of ritual cleansing, modes of prayer, and communications regarding matters of daily life. This information can be found in the Sunnah of the Prophet. Believing that Muhammad was the prophet of God they had been waiting for, some Arab Jews and Christians converted to Islam, as did some who had been contemplating converting to Judaism or Christianity. As Islam grew, non-Muslim leaders became more

---

48. Lings, *Muhammad*, 46.
49. The Morning Brightness 93:1–7 (The Study Qur'an).

intolerant of the Prophet and his followers. With the intensification of opposition, the Prophet was prompted by his followers to teach them how to respond; he taught them to respond via jihad.

Jihad

Jihad is perhaps the most important way the Prophet Muhammad realized his lived spirituality. Indeed, jihad was the means by which the Prophet Muhammad strived to please God by right thinking and action. To this day, Muslims are reminded to follow in his footsteps in order to be in good standing with God. Jihad is a somewhat abstract concept that is interpreted differently by non-Muslims and Muslims and at times creates a great deal of tension in intra-faith, inter-religious, and political discourse.[50]

It is not an overstatement to say that jihad constitutes one of the biggest obstacles in fostering inter-religious dialogue between Southern Baptists—indeed, Christians more generally—and Muslims. Most Southern Baptist leaders I interviewed deeply believe that Muhammad engaged in a violent offensive jihad with the militarized conquest of the non-Muslim world in view. To help remove this obstacle, in this section I outline the challenges in interpreting the concept of jihad. Next I elaborate on the genesis and the meaning of jihad, as these are widely understood in the scholarship on Islam. Third, I focus on jihad as the primary means of Muhammad's lived spirituality. Fourth, I offer some contemporary examples of the abuse of jihad and briefly present the accepted view of the majority of contemporary Muslims. Understanding jihad is particularly important in developing narrative empathy among Southern Baptists towards Muslims. Indeed, many Southern Baptists rely on faulty information, historical inaccuracies, and unreliable perceptions of jihad, which in turn significantly hinder the formation of a healthy narrative empathy. To better understand the concept of jihad, I refer to the teachings of Iman D. A. Rashied Omar, who writes: "In the contemporary period, Islam is frequently depicted as predisposed to conflict and violence. . . . In order to correctly understand the ethical norms of Islam represented in the Muslim sacred scripture, the Qur'an, and in the exemplary conduct of the Prophet Muhammad, it is necessary to analyze

---

50. Afsaruddin, "Views of Jihad," 165–69.

the historical milieu within which such norms were negotiated."[51] Below, I examine the historical context of jihad and how I believe the term is generally understood and employed by the majority of Muslims.

Interpreting Jihad

Interpretation of concepts is a challenging enterprise and scholars understand the very process of concept interpretation in different ways.[52] Nevertheless, understanding what concepts mean to individuals, as well as societies, nations, and other collectivities, is an endeavor worth pursuing. After all, it is often the divergence in how societies understand and interpret concepts that leads to conflict. In the context of legal texts, concepts, rules, and norms, Andrei Marmor defines interpretation as "the imposition of meaning on a[n] object," and the goal of interpretation is to identify the appropriate notions of meaning.[53] Marmor specifies three available notions of meaning: (1) the *meaning* of the object; (2) what the author means by the object (*meaning faith*); and (3) what the object specifically means to the interpreter (*meaning for*).[54] Marmor dismisses the third understanding of meaning, *meaning for*, as an inherently emotional response to an object/concept that is simply irrelevant to the process of interpretation. According to Marmor, the most important element of interpretation is the *meaning faith* since "interpretation is the attribution of communication intention to an author."[55] While Marmor's work addresses in the most direct sense notions embedded in Western legal philosophy and jurisprudence, his conceptualizations provide much insights into concepts deeply embedded in Islam.

I argue that in the context of understanding the concept of jihad, the *meaning for* notion of interpretation, although not as important at the author's meaning, is still of great importance. In order to more fully capture the meaning of jihad, as a political as well as an inherently religious concept, one needs to pay close attention to the specific connotations jihad has for individuals and groups that engage in interpretation of the concept. The basis of my argument is that Marmor's *meaning faith*, which

51. Oman, *Islam beyond Violent Extremism*, 9.
52. Dworkin, *Law's Empire*; Marmor, *Interpretation and Legal Theory*; Raz, "Relevance of Coherence," 273–74; Endicott, "Putting Interpretation in Its Place."
53. Marmor, *Interpretation and Legal Theory*, 13.
54. Marmor, *Interpretation and Legal Theory*, 30.
55. Marmor, *Interpretation and Legal Theory*, 30.

inherently focuses on author's intentions, falls short in that it fails to take into account the emotional response of the interpreter. It is the *meaning for* notion of interpretation that can fundamentally elucidate how jihad can indeed get lost in interpretation.

The act of jihad is an inherently abstract and often intangible process; it is therefore subject to a wide variety of interpretations. Thus, using a theoretical approach to the interpretation of sociological process or concepts, that is interpretation of intangible processes, can be much more effective than the "scientific interpretation."[56] In the latter process, a scientist simply explains or observes what information can be extracted from data, and how it can inform human understandings of certain processes. In other words, a scientist is engaging in a process of explanation. In the case of jihad—which as a concept cannot be subject to a *sensu stricto* scientific interpretation—the very process of interpretation involves more than just explanation, elucidation, or clarification of data. In the context of interpretation of a broad concept or an intangible process, interpretation does not only extract meaning, but can also impose meaning.[57] This can be clearly seen with regard to jihad, as different schools of thought may understand the concept of jihad in quite different ways; hence the theoretical approach seems to be the most useful process in interpreting jihad. In addition to jihad being a profoundly general concept, as well as a legal term, it also has deep religious connotations. Its origins are directly linked to Muhammad's lived spirituality.

Genesis and Meaning of Jihad

The scholarship suggests that interpretation is much more difficult when dealing with abstract ideas such as jihad, Islam, love, or justice. It is obvious that concrete concepts such as "bread," "stone," or "dog" will naturally yield a smaller number of possible interpretations than more abstract concepts pertaining to ideas, terms, or processes. Speaking of abstract concepts, Islam teaches there is a continual struggle of good vs. evil in this world. Decisions must be made at every turn in life; the decisions we make, make us who we are. In Islam, the Holy Qur'an teaches that Muslims must struggle daily to live righteously and that every person is responsible for his or her own actions. Moreover, every person will give

---

56. Dworkin, *Law's Empire*, 51.
57. Endicott, *Putting Interpretation in Its Place*, 457.

an account to God on the final day of judgment and depending upon his or her actions, be granted access into heaven or everlasting punishment in hell. The word jihad means struggling or striving. According to Shaykh Muhammad hisham Kabbani (Chairman, Islamic Supreme Council) and Shaykh Seraj Hendricks (Head Mufti, Cape Town, South Africa), "In a religious sense, as described by the Qur'an and teachings of the Prophet Muhammad (s), 'jihad' has many meanings. It can refer to internal as well as external efforts to be a good Muslim or believer, as well as working to inform people about the faith of Islam."[58] As a general concept, the term jihad is open to various interpretations and a few Muslims use it to justify certain actions they deem necessary to take against the non-Muslim or Muslim who is not following their particular interpretation of the Holy Qur'an. It is therefore crucial to discover how the vast majority of Islamic scholars and Muslims interpret jihad. I propose that the most fruitful way to approach jihad is to study it in the context of the lived spirituality of the Prophet Muhammad.

Jihad is mentioned over 160 times in the Qur'an and each reference must be understood in its historical context. For example, any use of jihad to mean "fight" must be juxtaposed with this verse of the Qur'an: "Fight in the way of God against those who wage war against you, but do not commit aggression—for verily, God does not love aggressors!"[59] To fight in the way of God is to fight with the utmost integrity and only when there appears no other way. This act of self-defense is the least of what jihad means: self-defense is the lesser of two highways for the Muslim to tread. Most importantly, jihad is historically understood to be a personal struggle within the life of the Muslim as he or she seeks to submit to the will of God and live in peace with one's neighbors, be they Muslim or non-Muslim. An example of such peace existed during the time of the Prophet Muhammad. In Medina—the city of the Prophet—Jews, Muslims, and polytheists were coexisting in peace. This largely took place because the Prophet Muhammad had introduced what some historians have called the first constitution of the world—the Medina Accord in 622 CE. This accord granted freedom of religion to Muslims and non-Muslims. Moreover, it ensured certain rights such as equality, protection from foreign invaders, and justice. In the diagram below, Sayyid Muhammad Rizvi illustrates the significance of the major and minor struggles

---

58. Kabbani and Hendricks, "Jihad: A Misunderstood Concept."
59. The Cow 2:190 (The Qur'an).

in Islam—of particular importance is that the name "Islam" comes from "silm" which means two things: submission and peace.

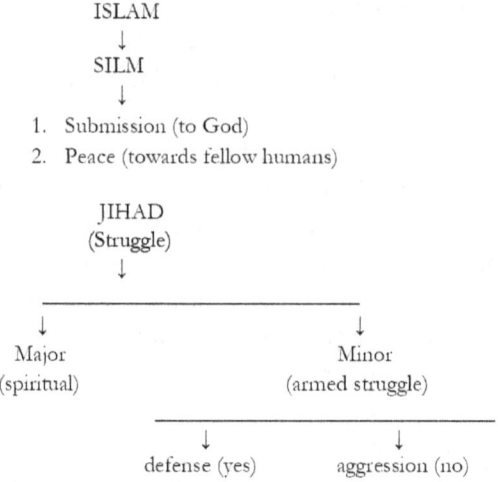

Rizvi writes,

> The word jihad literally means striving and working hard for something. In Islamic terminology, it retains the literal meaning in two different dimensions, which are expressed by 'major jihad' and 'minor jihad.' The major jihad is known as the spiritual struggle, a struggle between two powers within ourselves: the soul and the body. . . . Islam expects its followers to give preference to the soul and the conscience over the body and its desires. The minor jihad is the armed struggle. However, that does not automatically mean unjustified use of violence. The minor jihad may be divided into two: aggression and defense. Aggression against any people is not permitted in Islam: however, defense is an absolute right of every individual and nation. Islam has allowed the minor jihad only to defend the Muslim people and their land, and to maintain peace in Muslim societies.[60]

Some scholars argue that Rizvi's categorization has at least one problem that needs to be addressed—offensive armed struggle. For example, professor of Islamic Studies at Catholic Theological Union Scott Alexander writes, "The one problem with Rizvi's typology is that it has no place for unprovoked 'offensive' armed struggle—a valid interpretation of jihad in a wide variety of medieval legal sources. According to classical Islamic

60. Rizvi, *Peace and Jihad in Islam*.

legal interpretation, this would not constitute 'aggression' any more than the Bush Administration considered its pre-emptive invasion of Iraq to be an act of 'aggression.' Nonetheless, many objective observers would consider expansionist uses of jihad to be 'aggressive' much as most of the world and many in the U.S. looked upon the 2003 U.S. invasion of Iraq."[61] Noting this concern, I cannot locate any passage in the Qur'an that allows for the "initiation" of a fight by a Muslim or Muslim community. It is my understanding that any act of aggression towards an enemy is unjustified unless there is a real and present danger to the community, moreover the enemy must start the fight. Asma Afsaruddin writes, "A number of commentators after Mujahid (d.722) continued to uphold this categorical Quranic prohibition against initiating fighting. [The] late twelfth-century exegete Fakhr al-Din al-Razi makes it very plain in his Quran commentary that the divine command 'Do not commit aggression!' in Quran 2:190 is directed at actual, not potential, combatants, meaning that the verse allows fighting only against those who have actually started to fight and not against those who are able and prepared to fight but have not yet resorted to violence."[62] In the subsection below, I offer some historical and contemporary examples of jihad that often create an atmosphere of distrust, anger, and even hatred of Islam by many Southern Baptists, then I give an example of what the majority of Muslim scholars believe regarding the concept of jihad.

Muhammad's Personal Jihad

The Arabs of the early seventh century were submerged in oppressive social relations and caught up in a vicious cycle of violence. When the Prophet Muhammad began to spread the message of the Qur'an, he and his followers were met with hostility. Dr. Omar writes, "Muhammad's egalitarian message quickly began to threaten the Makkan elite. They opposed his teachings with great vehemence, to the point of brutally torturing the whole family of 'Ammar ibn Yasir, one of Muhammad's followers, to death."[63] For fifteen years, Muhammad and his followers were persecuted. They would flee from one city only to be persecuted in the next. The early Muslims responded to this abuse with passive resistance.

---

61. Alexander, "Muhammad and the Qur'an."
62. Afsaruddin, *Jihad*, 20.
63. Omar, *Islam beyond Violent Extremism*, 9.

They pleaded with Muhammad to allow them to protect themselves and their families from assault. The Prophet petitioned God for an answer and God responded in their favor but with strict guidelines:

> Permission [to fight] is given to those against whom war is being wrongfully waged. God has indeed the power to succor them. (They are) those who have been evicted from their homelands for no other reason than their saying, "Our Lord and Sustainer is God! For, if God had not enabled people to defend themselves against one another, monasteries and churches and synagogues and mosques—all in which God's name is abundantly extolled—would surely have been destroyed. God will surely support those who support Him. Indeed, God is All-Powerful and Exalted in Might." (22:39–40)

This passage alone reveals the mind of the Prophet as it pertains to minor jihad. In the event that one must physically engage in battle, it is to protect himself and his family from harm and protect religious freedom. Notice that this verse calls upon Muslims to be proactive in safeguarding monasteries, churches, and synagogues from evil doers. In the early years of Islam, the Abrahamic religions were viewed by most as monotheistic faiths that ultimately believed in the same God, only with differing doctrines. In large part, this alliance of the three faiths is what provided the pathway for monotheistic growth in the Arab world. Islam, in particular, took into account the Arab milieu and offered what was perceived to be a newfound hope and clarification to the familiar faiths of Judaism and Christianity. As mentioned above, Judaism—by and large—was not sensitive to the Arab culture, and certain schools of thought within Christianity had appeared, at least in the mind of Muhammad, to embrace a polytheistic view of God—the Trinity. Muhammad and the revelations he recited were of a timely nature and both Judaism and Christianity, as well as many monotheistic believers in the Arab world, such as the Hanif, were in need of a Prophet.

As more Arabs converted to Islam, it became common practice for the believers to listen to the most recent revelations given to the Prophet Muhammad from God and receive them as their own.[64] The revelations began to flow more copiously, and they were immediately transmitted by the Prophet to those who were around him. As the new religion began to take form, the early Muslims, following in the path of Muhammad,

---

64. Lings, *Muhammad*, 49.

would prepare their bodies and garments for daily ritual prayers and via the greater jihad strive to live a life that was not defiled by the sins of the world around them. They would also intently listen to the words of the Prophet, memorize those words, and recite them among themselves to ensure they not be forgotten. The Prophet Muhammad and his early followers, via greater jihad—the disciplined life—sought to rid themselves of impure thoughts and actions and to peaceably spread the message of the oneness of God throughout the Arab world to rid it of idolatry. The Angel Gabriel instructed the Prophet on matters of religion. For instance, there is to be no coercion in religion, but people who convert should do so freely.[65] Moreover, if God had willed it, all on earth would have been of one religion.[66] Though Islam became the predominant religion in the Arab world, it was first met with disdain, but through greater and lesser jihad, the message of God would spread, take root, and grow into the world religion it is today.

It is important to understand the concept of jihad in the broader context of a disciplined life as embodied in Islam's Five Pillars. According to the Muslim faith, the Five Pillars of Islam are crucial for leading the disciplined life and thus fulfilling the greater jihad. These Five Pillars of Islam are mentioned individually in the Qur'an as well as in Hadith when the Prophet was asked to describe what Islam is. Though the Five Pillars are of utmost importance in Islamic life, preachers of Islam are careful to point out that just as the pillars alone do not make up a whole building, so the pillars of Islam do not describe all of the acts and practices of Islamic faith. Below is a list and description of the Five Pillars:

1. Shahāda—the testifying or witnessing that there is only God and that Muhammad is God's messenger.
2. Iqāmat al-salāt—establishing the ritual prayer.
3. Itā' al-zakāt—the giving of alms.
4. Sawm Ramadān—fasting in the month of Ramadan.
5. Hajj al-bayt—making the pilgrimage to the Ka' bah in Mecca.

In addition to the fifth pillar, the Sunnis add a sixth pillar—jihad—the struggle in the cause of Islam. The Five Pillars represent the fundamental beliefs of Muslims. At least once in a Muslim's lifetime, he or she is

---

65. The Cow 2:256 (The Study Qur'an).
66. Jonah 10:99–100 (The Study Qur'an).

required to utter the shahada, the first pillar. For converts, "this testimony marks an entrance into and membership in the Muslim community and polity, resulting in the immediate obligation to practice the remaining four pillars."[67] The second pillar, salat, refers to five daily prayers offered by Muslims while facing the city of Mecca where the Ka' bah is located. Zakat, the third pillar, requires that each Muslim (those that have an income) give 2.5 percent of their accrued wealth, goods, and stock to those in need. This practice was instituted by the Prophet Muhammad and this practice has "continued into modern times; in some Muslim countries, ministries or departments are in charge of collection and distribution; in others, nongovernment organizations do so. Recipients include not only the needy but also sometimes poorer countries."[68] The fourth pillar, sawm, or fasting, takes place during the entire month of Ramadan; Ramadan is the ninth month in the Islamic lunar calendar. During this fast, which last from daybreak until sunset, Muslims will not eat any food and will instead reflect upon the first revelations revealed to the Prophet Muhammad. To draw a comparison, I liken their act of fasting to the discipline of fasting that is sometimes practiced in Christian circles in hopes of being drawn closer to God.

Finally, the fifth pillar, the hajj, is a pilgrimage that all able-bodied Muslims are to take at least once in their lifetime. "It takes place between the 8th and 12th days of the 12th Islamic month, Dhu alHijjah, or 'pilgrimage month,' which together with the months preceding and following were regarded as a time of 'sacred truth,' during which none were permitted to bear arms in the sacred precincts."[69] With regard to Islamic soteriology, participating in these five pillars bears witness to the fact that one is truly Muslim. The Prophet Muhammad participated in these rituals and instructed his followers do likewise to continually strive to be in a right standing with God. Jihad—living the disciplined life—was the foundation of his lived spirituality. In the section below, I highlight what I see as the most contested aspects of Muhammad's life: warfare and his marriages. Muhammad saw both of these issues as fundamentally linked to his pursuit of jihad, and thus to his acceptance by God. Southern Baptists' misunderstanding and in many cases lack of historical knowledge about these two aspects are the main obstacles to constructive inter-religious dialogue with Muslims.

67. *Princeton Encyclopedia of Islamic Thought*, s.v. "Pillars of Islam."
68. *Princeton Encyclopedia of Islamic Thought*, s.v. "Pillars of Islam."
69. *Princeton Encyclopedia of Islamic Thought*, s.v. "Pillars of Islam."

Warfare and Marriage: Fulfillment of Jihad

From about 610 to 622 Muhammad's emphasis was on composing the Qur'an, evangelizing his community, and leading new converts to Islam. For twelve years, the Prophet Muhammad was primarily understood to be a spiritual leader, engaging in minor jihad only when forced to defend Islam and its followers. In 620, at the age of sixty-five, Khadijah—Muhammad's first wife—passed away, followed shortly by his uncle Abu Talib. This marked the tenth year into his prophetic ministry, and looking back the Prophet called it his year of sorrow. Muhammad said, "She believed in me while the people disbelieved in me. And she trusted in me while the people belied me. And she helped and comforted me in person and in wealth when the people would not. God provided me with children by her, and He did not with others."[70] In all the Prophet Muhammad had six children with Khadijah, two sons and four daughters; later a son was born to him through Maria al-Qibtiyya. With the exception of Fatimah, all of his children died before his death in 632. In the years following the death of Khadijah, Muhammad would take on a more influential role as a political leader. From 622, when he and the early Muslims migrated to Medina, until his death in 632, Muhammad strived to find the balance between his role as the spiritual prophet of Islam and his position as an emerging political leader of the Arab world. Western historians describe his journey in terms of his implementation of the major and minor jihad.

Many of his contemporaries, as well as later scholars, have observed that the Prophet Muhammad possessed great political acumen. As a political leader, he was astute at negotiation: "The negotiations he held with the emissaries of the Medinans and the pledges he made with them shortly before the hijra paved the way for his subsequent political leadership in Medina."[71] He was competent in drawing up legal documents that were just and fair for Muslims and non-Muslims, specifically Jews and Christians. He was also a competent military leader, showing composure before, during, and after battle, including at the Battle of Badr, the War of the Trench, the truce of Hudaybiyya. The quality of Muhammad's political leadership is perhaps best captured by the following: "Muhammad was led by a sense of flexible and adaptable pragmatism rather than by preset principles of political theory and may thus be considered a genius

---

70. *Musnad Imam Ahmad* 6:118.
71. *Princeton Encyclopedia of Islamic Thought*, s.v. "Muhammad."

in the field of applied political practice."⁷² However, it is no secret that Muhammad engaged in many military operations that resulted in lives lost, including civilian.

Every pastor that I interviewed for this book and every pastor that I have had personal conversations with regarding the Prophet Muhammad has stated in unequivocal terms that Muhammad was a man of violence and was responsible for the slaughter of those who did not convert to Islam. Having spent considerable time, in and outside the classroom, reflecting upon the lived spirituality of the Prophet as well as studying in some depth his military career, it has become apparent to me that Muhammad's actions were more or less justified. In the event that he and his followers were forced into battle, it was either to defend themselves or to prevent a greater war from taking place. When the principles of Islam are taken into consideration, it becomes clear that "the relationships among individuals and states are based on the principle of peace. War is an unwanted obligation that is temporary; it can take place as a struggle of existence."⁷³ As the messenger of God and the spiritual leader of Islam, the Prophet Muhammad was fully aware that all of his actions, both active and passive, were being observed and followed. Dr. Veysel Nargul, professor of Theology at Igdir University, offers twelve reasons and wisdoms as to why the Prophet Muhammad engaged in warfare and why they were deemed just in accordance with the Qur'an and the Sunnah:

1. In order to make the enemy feel they have enough power to fight.
2. Preventing the financial sources of attacks.
3. Defending against attacks.
4. Gathering information about the enemy.
5. The breach of treaties and punishing betrayal.
6. Punishing the raid and plunder.
7. Preventing the enemy to gain supporters.
8. The military interventions performed upon receiving the news of attack.
9. Helping Muslims that are persecuted.

---

72. *Princeton Encyclopedia of Islamic Thought*, s.v. "Muhammad."
73. Nargul, "Purposes of Wars."

10. Eliminating the barriers that prevent tabligh (conveying the message of Islam).
11. Punishing those who mistreated and killed envoys.
12. Answering the declaration of war by the enemy.[74]

I find it noteworthy that, as mentioned above, these reasons and wisdoms of war practically mirror the reasons and wisdoms of war used today by the United States Congress. It also resembles the Christian theory of just war propounded by Augustine of Hippo and Thomas Aquinas. It seems that Muslims were taking necessary precautions to protect themselves from the hostiles of their time. Islam had become a major disruption to commerce in the cities of Mecca and Medina, as well as the other major trade routes in Arabia. The Prophet Muhammad consistently preached against the many gods worshiped by Arabs of his time. Not to mention the fact that Jews, Christians, and polytheists were converting to Islam, many of whom were poor and in need of hope, security, and wealth. This angered the non-Muslim Arab leaders of the time, and in their attempts to put a stop to Muhammad, personal attacks on Muslims were becoming commonplace. For example, one of the early martyrs of Islam was Sumayyah bint Khayyat, a slave of a prominent Meccan leader. She was killed by her master with a spear because she refused to renounce her faith.[75] Another story is told of Bilal, a Muslim slave, who was tortured by Umayyah ibn Khalaf. Umayyah ibn Khalaf placed a heavy rock on Bilal's chest trying to force his conversion—he did not convert, and his chest caved in due to the pressure of the rock.[76] Furthermore, certain wealthy political actors at the time would hire outside forces such as the Syrian army or the Ahzab troops to attack the Muslims. Most of the battles resulted in success for Muhammad and were viewed by Muslims as God blessing them in their submission to Him. Two years prior to his death, he managed to organize an army of 10,000 troops and in response to ongoing persecution, he led them to Mecca and seized the city with little bloodshed. Many Muslims had been forced to flee the city because of their religion; now they were able to come home.

Muhammad's multiple marriages are vehemently criticized by most within the Southern Baptist denomination—and not only Southern

---

74. Nargul, "Purposes of Wars."
75. *Encyclopedia of the Qur'an*, vol. 4, s.v. "Slaves and Slavery."
76. *Encyclopedia of Islam*, 3rd ed., s.v. "bilal b. Rabah."

Baptists but the larger Christian community. All the Southern Baptist pastors I interviewed stated that the Prophet Muhammad was both a polygamist and a pedophile. It is true that after Khadijah passed, he went on to remarry and had multiple wives. It is also true that he was betrothed to a young girl named Aisha. Tradition holds that she was either six or seven years old—more discussion on her age below. In medieval and early modern times, the Western sensibility has frowned upon the Prophet for having multiple wives and being betrothed to such a young girl. Schimmel writes, "In Europe, where Muhammad has at times been understood as an idol worshiper or transformed into Mahound, the Spirit of Darkness, his historical biography was studied from the eighteenth century onward, and although he was generally depicted as a kind of Antichrist or a Christian heretic and arch-schismatic, he also appeared to some philosophers of the Enlightenment period as representative of a rational religion, one devoid of speculations about Trinity and Redemption and, even more importantly, a religion without a powerful clergy."[77] More often than not the Western view of him was marred by prejudice and failed to do justice to the role of the Prophet Muhammad as seen by devout Muslims. Schimmel notes that the majority of Muslims were not aware of what the Western thought and teachings were about the Prophet Muhammad until the British colonized India and began to evangelize them through educational institutions and missionary schools. The images depicted and stories told by the British to the Muslim Indians horrified them. It is perhaps at this point in history that Muslim scholars began to conduct more thorough research and writing on the Prophet by examining hadith that documented the life of Muhammad and provided a more legitimate defense of his moral character and integrity to the West. Owing in large part to scholarly work carried out in the last century by Muslims and non-Muslims alike, a more thorough contextual understanding can be reached concerning the marriages of the Prophet.

Historians cannot say for certain how many wives the Prophet Muhammad had; most biographical resources I consulted described him as having at least eleven and no more than fifteen wives. However, as noted above, when Muhammad was approximately twenty-five years of age, "the woman for whom he had been carrying out business and who was impressed by his honesty and sincerity married him. Her name was Khadija, and though she was considerably senior to him, their marriage

---

77. Schimmel, *And Muhammad Is His Messenger*, 5.

proved very happy."[78] Khadija was Muhammad's first love, best friend, first convert to Islam, and only wife until her death in 619. Together "they had four daughters who grew to adulthood and at least three sons, all of whom died in infancy."[79] All early historical sources revealed that Muhammad and Khadija were faithful to each other for twenty-five years, good parents, and worthy spiritual leaders. When Khadija died, Muhammad was sickened with grief and to make the situation worse, his beloved uncle Abu Talib also passed. It would not be until about the year 623 that he would marry his second wife Sawdah bint Zam'ah and shortly thereafter 'A'isha.

Among Christians and the larger secular society, there has been much controversy surrounding Muhammad's marital life, especially his marriage to 'A'isha. I found that many Southern Baptist leaders will use this marriage to discredit the Prophet Muhammad as a godly leader by labeling him a pedophile. As before mentioned, according to traditional historical resources, 'A'isha was only nine or ten when she entered into marriage with the Prophet.[80] Although in modern times this sort of marriage arrangement to such a young girl is viewed by most to be at best taboo and at worst pedophilic, it was not uncommon for such arrangements to be made in the seventh century, especially in the Arab culture. However, in light of the great controversy this has caused in modern times, historians have renewed their efforts to uncover documents that might produce a more objective and comprehensive understanding of this marriage. Sayyid Muhammed Jasmin, a scholar in the field of Sharia, writes regarding the Prophet's marriage to 'A'isha, "naturally most people today consider a nine year old as a child, and straight away start criticizing the Prophet (PBUH). However, this kind of response is due to Presentism, an anachronistic misinterpretation of history based on present day circumstances not existing in the past. We misjudge when we assume that the ways in which our ancestors viewed childhood and marriage are the same as the contemporary Western ideas imposed upon them. In fact, they are completely diverse and quite different from each other."[81] Additionally, many will criticize the Prophet for polygamy. A leading scholar in Islamic studies, Sayyid Muhammad Rizvi, addresses the concept of polygamy and the Prophet's marriages. He writes, "Let it

78. Schimmel, *And Muhammad Is His Messenger*, 11.
79. *Oxford Dictionary of Islam*.
80. *Princeton Encyclopedia of Islamic Thought*, s.v. "Aisha"; Lings, *Muhammad*, 132.
81. Jasmin, "Marriage of Prophet Muhammed."

be known that Islam did not initiate the system of polygamy; it existed from the early dawn of human history. When Islam came on [the] world scene in the seventh century of the Common Era, it inherited the existing marriage system. Condoning of polygamy should not be seen as a piece of pure male chauvinism. In [the] words of Karen Armstrong, 'polygamy was not designed to improve the sex life of the boys—it was a piece of social legislation.'"[82]

Scholars point out that polygamy or to use a more concise term polygyny had been practiced throughout history and by some very noteworthy people tied to the Jewish and Christian faiths. Some examples are Lamech, the grandson of Adam, who took two wives; Abraham was married to Sarah and Hagar; Jacob had four wives and concubines; King David had at least eight wives, many of whose identities were never recorded; Solomon had 700 wives and over 300 concubines. Moreover, some historians place Mary, the mother of Jesus, between the ages of 12 and 14 when she was betrothed to Joseph. Furthermore, the Prophet Muhammad put limitations on how many women a man should be married to at any one time: the Qur'an states, "If you fear that you will not deal fairly with orphan girls, you may marry whichever [other] women seem good to you, two, three, or four. If you fear that you cannot be equitable [to them], then marry only one" (4:3).[83] The ideal marriage arrangement in Islam has always been that one man should live in a monogamous relationship with his wife throughout the entirety of his life. There were very stringent conditions that allowed for a man to have multiple wives as is seen in table 4.1 below. The Prophet Muhammad's marriages fell into the appropriate and culturally accepted categories. Rizvi offers four categories that were appropriate for a man, in this case the Prophet, to be married to multiple wives at the same time: to provide protection and dignity to widows so that others may follow that example, to set the slaves free, to forge friendly relations for the sake of Islam, and the desire to be related to the Prophet.[84]

---

82. Rizvi, "Concept of Polygamy."
83. Women 4:3 (The Qur'an).
84. Rizvi, "Concept of Polygamy."

Table 4.1. Marriages can be divided into four categories

Providing protection and dignity to widows so that others may follow that example	*Lady Sawdah bint Zam'ah*: a Muslim lady whose husband had died in Abyssinia. When she returned to Mecca, she was a *widow*; and her father and brother were not only infidels but also enemies of Islam. She could not seek shelter with them; they were so much opposed to Islam that they could even torture her to death. The Prophet, now a widower himself, married Sawdah in order to provide protection to her as well as to forge important link of kinship with his opponents. *Lady Zaynab bint Khuzaymah*: a *widow* for the second time when her second husband 'Abdullah bin Jahsh was martyred in the Battle of Uhud. She was known for her generosity, and was famous as "Ummul masākīn, mother of the poor." Now she herself faced hard times. The Prophet wanted to maintain her prestige, and so he married her in the 3rd year AH. She died less than a year after this marriage. *Lady Zaynab bint Jahsh*. She was a cousin of the Prophet; and she was a *widow* and a *divorcee*. The circumstance of her marriage to the Prophet was very unusual. Islam had come to end all the material and social criterion of distinction. Every Muslim was equal to the other. While preaching this equality, the Prophet, as an example, gave his three female relatives in marriage to persons of so-called low birth or status. Among those three relatives was Zaynab bint Jahsh. She was given in marriage to Zayd son of Hāritha, an Arab slave whom the Prophet had freed and then adopted as a son. After that adoption, Zayd was being called, Zayd bin Muhammad—Zayd the son of Muhammad. The marriage of Zaynab to Zayd soon turned sour. Zaynab could not overcome the fact she was of nobler descent than her husband. No matter how much the Prophet counseled them, Zaynab's attitude did not change. So finally Zayd divorced her. At the same time, verses 4 and 5 of Chapter 33 (Surah al-Ahzaab) were revealed which declared that adoption was not recognized in Islam. After these verses, the people started calling Zayd by his real father's name: Zayd bin Hāritha. But in order to fully abolish the system of adoption, Almighty God ordered the Prophet to marry Zaynab, the divorcee of Zayd. In the pre-Islamic society of Arabia, an adopted son was considered to be like a real son: with the same rights and duties: for example, an adopted son's wife was considered like a real daughter-in-law with whom marriage was forbidden forever. And so to break that taboo, the Prophet married Zaynab, the divorcee of his former adopted son. Both the marriages of Zaynab bint Jahsh served to enforce two important social principles of Islam: First, equality among Muslims irrespective of their ethnic or social distinctions; and second, it demonstrated the fact that a fostering or adoptive relationship was not a tie of blood and should not be a barrier in marriage. *Lady Umm Salamah*. She was first married to 'Abdullah Abu Salamah. She migrated to Abyssinia with her husband. She was known for her piety and wisdom. When she became a *widow* and had orphan children, the Prophet married her in the 4th year A.H. She was also the sister of the chief of a powerful Meccan tribe of Makhzum. This marriage had the element of forging the link of kinship with his opponents in Mecca.

To set the slaves free	*Lady Juwayriyyah bint al-Hārith*. After the Battle of Banu Mustaliq in the 5th year AH, the Muslims took two hundred families of that tribe in slavery. Juwayriyyah, the daughter of the chief of that tribe, had become a *widow*. The Prophet set her free and married her. Why? The Muslims, who had made the two hundred families of Banu Mustaliq their slaves, realized that by Juwayriyyah's marriage to the Prophet, all these two hundred families were now related to the Prophet by marriage. Out of courtesy to the Prophet, the Muslims set them free. Impressed by this nobility, the whole tribe of Banu Mustaliq became Muslim. By this marriage, the Prophet was able to transform a hostile tribe into an ally.
To forge friendly relations for the sake of Islam	*Lady 'Āisha bint Abi Bakr*. Although the betrothal was done in Mecca, she came into the household of the Prophet after his migration to Medina. She was the *youngest* wife of the Prophet. This marriage sealed the alliance with Abu Bakr so that he would be on the side of Muslims during the confrontation against the idol-worshippers of Mecca. *Lady Hafsah bint 'Umar ibn al-Khattāb*. She became a *widow* after her husband was killed in the Battle of Badr. The Prophet married her in the 4th year AH. This marriage was also done to seal the Prophet's alliance with 'Umar. *Lady Umm Habibah*, daughter of Abu Sufyan. She was married to 'Ubaydullah ibn Jahsh and had migrated to Abyssinia. He became a Christian; while she continued the Islamic faith and *separated* from him. Her father, Abu Sufyan, was a bitter enemy of Islam and planned battles after battles against Muslims. When she returned to Medina, the Prophet married her in order to provide protection for her and also to soften the heart of Abu Sufyan. However, that marriage did not have the desired effect on Abu Sufyan. *Lady Safiyyah bint Huyaiy ibn Akhtab*. She was the daughter of the chief of Banu Nadhir, a Jewish tribe of Khaybar. She became a *widow* when her husband was killed in the Battle of Khaybar. She was taken as a captive by the Muslim forces. The Prophet married her in the 7th year AH to maintain her noble status and also to establish marriage ties with her Jewish tribe.
The desire to be related to the Prophet	*Lady Maymunah bint al-Hārith al-Hilaliyyah*. Her second husband died in 7 AH. She came to the Prophet and "gifted" herself to him if he would accept her. She only desired the honour of being called "the wife of the Prophet." The Prophet (based on verse 33:50 of the Qur'ān) accepted her as his wife.

As noted above, while pre-Islamic Arab culture allowed for a man to have multiple wives, Muhammad was faithfully married to Khadija for twenty-five years; it was only after her death that he remarried. It is evident from the Sunnah of the Prophet that the Prophet Muhammad strived to please God in every aspect of his life. In the case of his marriages, it was no different. As Rizvi shows in table 4.1, Muhammad married for honorable reasons. Furthermore, he was fair and just to the women he married; however, he had a special bond with 'A'isha—a bond similar to the one he had previously enjoyed with Kadijah. Schimmel writes, "Among his wives only 'A'isha, the daughter of his friend Abu Bakr, a mere child still playing with her dolls, was a virgin when she was married to him; he was apparently particularly fond of the young woman."[85] The other women that Muhammad married were widows. There has been much controversy, primarily among non-Muslim Western scholars, as to the exact age of 'A'isha when she was married to Muhammad. Was she a young girl still playing with dolls, probably around the age of seven as many have suggested, or was she older? The renowned Muslim scholar Ibn Kathir (d. 1373) proposes that she was not of such a young age when given to Muhammad, but was instead upwards of fifteen, sixteen, or maybe even eighteen years old. These findings are derived from researching the age of her older sister Asma bint Abu Bakr, who was ten years older than 'A'isha. Ibn Kathir, in his *al-Bidayah wa' n-Nihayah*, states that Asma died in the year 73 AH at the age of 100; based on this calculation, 'A'isha would have been eighteen or nineteen at the time of her marriage.[86] Scholars, both Muslim and non-Muslim, continue to debate her approximate age. No one can with certainty identify the exact age of 'A'isha upon her marriage to the Prophet. However, with regard to the ethics of this marriage union and in consultation with Islamic scholars, I have been able to ascertain the following:

1. Her father Abu Bakr was a close companion of Muhammad and the future caliph, or successor, to the Prophet. Abu Bakr held deep respect for the Prophet and was glad to have his daughter marry Muhammad.

2. Every indication is that 'A'isha was betrothed to Muhammad when she was a young girl, specific age unknown. After studying the moral character of the Prophet Muhammad, especially regarding children and women, it would have been contrary to his moral teachings to have engaged in intercourse with a young girl prior to her menstrual cycle, therefore she would have lived at home until coming of age. Incidentally, she had already been pledged to another man at the time that the Prophet Muhammad requested her hand in marriage, once again suggesting she had come of age.

3. The Prophet Muhammad loved 'A'isha and confided in her until his death in 632. Denise Spellberg claims that "when the Prophet was

---

85. Schimmel, *And Muhammad Is His Messenger*, 15.
86. Ibn Kathir, *Bidaya wa-al-Nihaya*, vol. 8, 31.

ill toward the end of his life in 632, 'A'isha, only 18 and with no children, was acknowledged to be his favorite wife, and thus she nursed him in her quarters, where he died and was buried beneath the house."[87] Historical writings confirm that the two were extremely close companions and their relationship was one of mutual love and respect.

4. I have not been able to locate any scholarly Islamic documents suggesting that his marriage to 'A'isha was pedophilic or even taboo in nature.

Therefore, my conclusion as to the morality of his marriage to 'A'isha is that, though taboo in most cultures today, it was a perfectly acceptable engagement at that time. Furthermore, the argument that she was not of age to marry conflicts with marriage principles found in the Sunnah of the Prophet. For example, in regard to accountability, the Prophet said, "The Pen has been lifted from three: from the child until he reaches puberty, from the sleeper until he wakes up, and from the one who has lost his mind until he recovers."[88] Moreover, the Prophet said, "Virgin girls are like fruits on trees. If not plucked in time, the sun will rot them and the wind will disperse them. When girls reach maturity and their sexual instincts arise, like that of women, their only remedy is marriage. If they aren't married, they are prone to moral corruption. It is because they are human beings and human beings are prone to making mistakes."[89] Both remarks speak to the age of accountability, both sexually and spiritually— 'A'isha seemed to possess both of these qualities prior to her marriage to the Prophet.

Information in the Qur'an and Sunnah enables me to discern that the Prophet Muhammad strived daily in all matters of his life to please God. In matters of war and marriage, I have articulated his reasons and wisdoms for engaging in warfare and marrying multiple wives. In the context of his cultural environment, both socially and religiously, and in the context of his lived spirituality, Muhammad strived to live a life above reproach. Jihad—as a spiritual discipline—was the means by which he accomplished many of his God-given and personal goals. Below I offer some contemporary examples of major and minor jihad and address some controversies surrounding the concept.

87. *Princeton Encyclopedia of Islamic Thought*, s.v. "Aisha."
88. Sunan an-Nasa'i, vol. 4, book 27, Hadith 3462.
89. Sadooq, *Uyun Akhbar Al Reza*, 28:36.

Contemporary Issues and Clarity Relating to Jihad

The major jihad, understood to be the inner spiritual struggle to find acceptance with God and peace with neighbors, is the primary concern of the Muslim majority throughout the world. This struggle is perhaps the greatest contributing factor that promotes the growth of Islam. That said, in our current moment, jihad is being misinterpreted and abused by certain extremists within Islam, such as al Qaeda and the so-called Islamic State of Iraq and the Levant (ISIL). The difficulty in understanding jihad appears to lie not in the literal meaning of the term but in its interpretation. In most circles of faith, it is the perceived leader of a group who determines how a word of theological significance is to be interpreted. That leader has the power to influence his followers in ways that often incite negative emotions such as fear, anger, resentment, hopelessness, etc., which can and often do lead to conflict.

Jihad can provide a tool for a leader to fulfil his personal goals that are often detached from orthodox faith. With the minor struggle (fighting), the oppressed must be mindful when enacting the minor jihad not to become the aggressor. Osama bin Laden and Dr. Abu Bakr al-Baghdadi (who earned a doctorate in Islamic studies in history and was an Islamic preacher) are both examples of leaders who, though apparently sincere in their belief that they were following the right path, did indeed leave the realm of the afflicted and became the afflicters. The world is teeming with such leaders who become so ensnared by hatred and anger that they devolve into political and religious leaders that they once campaigned against. Hence, precisely, the need for major and minor jihad, as prescribed by God and the Prophet Muhammad: a striving to be in right standing with God and one's neighbor; a struggle that requires a scholarly consensual understanding and interpretation of the Qur'an and Sunna. The words and deeds of the now deceased Osama bin Laden, directed against Muslims and non-Muslims alike, offer contemporary examples of jihad being personalized, politically influenced, and abused by a leader.

In the case of Osama bin Laden, he lashed out at some of his fellow Muslims (those who he believed were aligning themselves with the U.S.), as well as the Crusaders and Zionists, because "he believed that these people were actively engaged in an assault upon Islam and attempting to dominate the Muslim world by non-Muslim powers, consequently inflicting their values and ideas upon Muslims."[90] Osama bin

---

90. Alexander, "Muhammad and the Qur'an."

Laden—who was educated in economics, business, and engineering (not theology)—believed that his act of war upon the United States was justifiable. In a videotape addressed to the American people on the September 11, 2001, attacks he said, "People of America this talk of mine is for you and concerns the ideal way to prevent another Manhattan and deals with the war and its causes and results. Before I begin, I say to you that security is an indispensable pillar of human life and that free men do not forfeit their security, contrary to Bush's claim that we hate freedom. If so, then let him explain to us why we don't strike, for example, Sweden?"[91] Osama bin Laden and Abu Bakr al-Baghadadi subscribed to what is called jihadism. With regard to jihadism, Mary Beck writes, "Jihadism is an extreme version of Islamism. Less than one percent of Islamists are jihadists. The jihadist ideology holds that they are the only true believers. The rest of the world is made up of hostile unbelievers whose sole purpose is the destruction of Islam. These people are thus worthy of attack."[92] It is important to note that the actions taken by Osama bin Laden are not accepted by ninety-nine percent of Muslims worldwide and are considered abhorrent. The prominent Muslim view of jihad seeks to discover and promote true religion of heart, soul, mind, and actions that please God and pursue peace with all. Yet it is the horrific acts of Islamic militant extremist groups that are frequently used by members of the Southern Baptist denomination to justify their lack of tolerance towards Muslims and the belief that the religion of Islam is violent.

The minor jihad is only to be engaged in when the one or the many are being spiritually and/or physically oppressed or attacked by a force that is unwilling to allow the Muslim the freedom to worship God. Leaving aside discussions about requirements of justice, there is no evidence in the Qur'an to support the intentional killing of innocents, even if, in times of war, innocent lives are often caught in the crossfire. God stated in the Qur'an, "And do not kill the soul which God has forbidden except for the requirements of justice; this He has enjoined you with that you may understand" (6:151).[93] Alexander says, "this is true not only of the Qur'an, but of the jurisprudence as a whole."[94] Furthermore God states,

---

91. Osama bin Laden in his October 2003 videotaped address to the American people on the September 11, 2001 attacks, www.aljazeera.com, "Full Transcript of bin Ladin's Speech."

92. Habeck, "Knowing the Enemy."

93. Livestock 6:151 (The Qur'an).

94. Alexander, "Muhammad and the Qur'an."

"whoever slays a soul, unless it be for manslaughter or for mischief in the land, it is as though he slew all men; and whoever keeps it alive, it is as though he kept alive all men; and certainly Our messengers came to them with clear arguments, but even after that many of them certainly act extravagantly in the land" (5:32).[95] At its very core, Islam was founded as a religion of peace and justice—indeed, of the Just Peace. Acts of terrorism that are being carried out around the world in the name of Islam are a great crime against humanity, as well as the spirit and law of Islam as exemplified by the Prophet Muhammad and in the Sunnah of the Prophet.

Southern Baptists frequently associate jihad with the term "holy war." The United States and Western Europe have coined the phrase "holy war" to describe the minor (or physical) struggle of jihad; however, my findings suggest that this minor jihad described in the West as "holy war" has no basis in the Qur'an. Amir Ali speaks to this misconception in Western thought: "In the West, 'jihad' is generally translated as 'holy war,' a usage the media has popularized. According to Islamic teachings, it is UNHOLY to instigate or start war, however, some wars are inevitable and justifiable. If we translate the words 'holy war' back into Arabic, we find 'Harbun Muqaddasatu,' or for 'the holy war,' 'Al Harbu Al Muqaddasatu.' WE CHALLENGE any researcher or scholar to find the meaning of 'jihad' as holy war in the Quran or authentic Hadith collections or in early Islamic literature.... The Arabic words for 'war' are 'Harb' or 'Qital,' which are found in the Qur'an and Hadith."[96] Owing to the term "holy war" being coined and misused by popular media outlets to describe jihad, it has inadvertently caused many Southern Baptists to conclude that jihad is an act of aggression instead of defense and offense against those who seek to inflict some form of oppression or harm upon a Muslim or Muslim community. Regarding the minor jihad, which may require armed conflict, Amir Ali, among other notable scholars, concludes that jihad as defense is proper in the following realms: defending Islam and the community, helping allied people who may not be Muslim, banishing those who act treacherously, defending through preemptive strikes and gaining freedom to inform, educate, and convey messages of Islam in an open and free environment. God declares in the Qur'an, "To those against whom war is made, permission is given (to defend themselves), because they are wronged—and verily, God is Most Powerful to give

---

95. The Feast 5:32 (The Qur'an).
96. Ali, "What Is Jihad?"

them victory—(they are) those who have been expelled from their homes in defiance of right—(for no cause) except that they say, 'Our Lord is God (22:39–40) . . . 'fight in the cause of God against those who fight against you, but do not transgress the limits. Lo! God loves not aggressors. . . . And fight them until persecution is not more, and religion is for God. But if they desist, then let there be no hostility except against transgressors'" (2:190, 193).[97] At no point does God mandate or allow for an unjust war and in the event that war is inevitable, there are limits to the extent of violence that should be enacted upon the aggressor(s).[98] Hence, the misnomer among many Southern Baptists that jihad is justified by the Qur'an or the Sunnah of the Prophet to unleash an unjust act of aggression towards non-Muslims is not supported by the Qur'an, or the lived spirituality of the Prophet Muhammad as seen in the Sunnah of the Prophet.

In stark contradiction to the claims of those who attack Islam as a violent religion and who characterize all Muslims as actual or potential terrorists, on September 25, 2014, more than 120 Muslim scholars condemned the acts of violence being carried out by ISIS in an open letter to the Islamic State.[99] Ayman S. Ibrahim writes, "The letter is meticulously composed, and contains twenty-four sections in twenty-eight pages in Arabic and English. These sections attempt to refute the awful deeds and claims of ISIS—deeds including killing unarmed innocents, slaying prisoners of war, mutilating dead bodies, taking women as concubines, forcing non-Muslims to convert to Islam; and claims including the 'Prophet Muhammad was sent with the sword as a mercy to all world' and Yazidis 'are Devil's worshippers.'"[100] There has been a global outcry from Muslims and non-Muslims against the extreme ideologies of ISIS. Though ISIS uses the Qur'an and Sunnah to claim legitimacy in carrying out their war against the United States and her allies, the larger Islamic sociopolitical world denounces them as terrorists.

Though jihad is an abstract, vague legal concept dealing with an intangible process, it is also a deeply religious term securely anchored in Islamic religious sources. Accordingly, I argue that when the term jihad is being used to further a cause, one must look not only to the historical contextual meaning of the term and what the author(s) (God and the

97. The Pilgrimage 22:39–40; The Cow 2:190, 193 (The Qur'an).
98. Symes, "Osama bin Laden's Fatwa."
99. See Appendix 3.
100. Ibrahim, "Muslim Scholars vs. Isis."

Prophet) meant but also take into consideration what the object specifically means to the interpreter of the concept. The greater concern does not seem to be with the intangible process of understanding jihad, but with the psychological well-being of the one interpreting it. Therefore, no religion should be prematurely judged and the adherents stereotyped based upon a few people of ill-will, who act outside the norm. The official statement of the group Islam Awareness regarding jihad is "that Islam does not call for violence; rather it abhors all forms of violence and terrorism, whether against Muslims or non-Muslims. Islam, moreover, calls for peace, cooperation, and maintaining justice, and provides for the happiness and welfare of humanity as a whole."[101] Support for this statement can be found in the Qur'an and the lived spirituality of the Prophet Muhammad. The Qur'an reads, "Truly God commands justice, virtue, and giving to kinsfolk, and He forbids indecency, wrong, and rebelliousness. And he admonishes you, that haply you may remember" (16:90).[102] I believe that the negative perceptions embodied by many leaders, and consequently laity, within the Southern Baptist denomination towards Islam can be significantly improved when weighed against the lived spirituality of the Prophet Muhammad. It is clear to me when reading the Qur'an, Sunnah, and contemporary scholarly sources, that Islam is a religion of peace and justice. Interestingly, every chapter in the Qur'an with the exception of one begins with the phrase—In the Name of God, the Compassionate, the Merciful.

Conclusion

As the spiritual and political leader of Islam, the Prophet Muhammad had a great deal of responsibility placed upon him by God, the Muslim community, and his own volition, and it was via jihad that he struggled or strived to do right and to please God. The Oxford Dictionary of Islam sums his life up in the following way: "Muhammad served as administrator, legislator, judge, and commander-in-chief as well as teacher, preacher, and prayer leader of the Muslim community. For the scholars of Islamic law he is the legislator-jurist who defined ritual observance; for the mystic he is the ideal seeker of spiritual perfection; for the philosopher and statesman he is the role model of both a conqueror and a just ruler; for

---

101. Islam Awareness Homepage (2014), "Types of Jihad."
102. The Bee 16:90 (The Study Qur'an).

ordinary Muslims, he is a model of God's grace and salvation."[103] Within the Islamic religion, Muhammad is the beloved Prophet through whom God spoke and brought about positive change in the Arab world of the seventh century. These changes include restoring to the weak and oppressed their rights, freeing slaves, elevating the social status of women and the poor, and doing away with oppressive practices against women and children. He exposed the darkness of superstition, fortune telling, and divination. He dispelled the people's wantonness and sexual exploitation. He did away with tribal boasting and rivalries. He opposed all forms of polytheism and only preached the oneness of God, the Creator of heaven and earth—all things seen and not seen. The lived spirituality of the Prophet Muhammad reveals the life of a mere man who was humble, kind, wise, teachable, honest, earnest, and desiring to hear from God seemingly to find unadulterated meaning and purpose to life.

Many Christian scholars and Southern Baptist leaders reject the divine origin of Muhammad's revelations, emphasizing the differences in historical accounts and doctrines found in the Bible and Qur'an, not to mention his denouncing of the Holy Trinity for reasons mentioned above. Be that as it may, I believe that it is possible for the Southern Baptist leader, a leader much like myself, to develop a narrative empathy of the Prophet that can appreciate what he genuinely believed to be a calling from God to usher in positive changes in the Arab world of his time. An article published in the Arab News sums up how the spirit of the Prophet is understood, appreciated, and embraced by most within the Arab world today:

> During the many eras of Islamic rule in history, the rights of the various religious communities and denominations were upheld and protected within the context of a strong social fabric. They were not forced to change their religion or their denominational affiliation. The Muslims continued to engage them in polite debate and discussion.

This social fabric can be torn apart by conflicts spurred on by political interests who instigate the ignorant people and play on their prejudices. When this happens, when neighbor turns against neighbor, people abandon our Prophet's teachings, which stress neighborly rights even with those you disagree with.

> At times of conflict, people behave irrationally and suspiciously. Sensible people know that this state of affairs is temporary and

---

103. *Oxford Dictionary of Islam.*

can—must—be surmounted. People can settle back into living together in peace and cooperation for their mutual wellbeing.[104]

A thorough, impartial study of the lived spirituality of the Prophet Muhammad is beneficial to all, especially those who are students and practitioners of history, theology, religion, and preaching. Yet many of the pastors I interviewed possessed minimal knowledge and understanding of the founder of Islam, and furthermore did not appreciate the need to more adequately study the life and times of the Prophet. In some instances, laity within the denomination expressed great discomfort with the mere notion of reading the Qur'an, much less studying the life of the Prophet. To be blunt, they perceived the action to be a sin of unfaithfulness to Christ. On a side note, when I teach Muslim-Christian Dialogue, I encourage my predominantly Christian students to read parts, if not all, of the Qur'an. At the end of the semester, I inquire whether they have read the Qur'an and to my great disappointment, ninety-nine percent of them say no. When I ask why, they tell me they feel at best uncomfortable and at worst sinful for reading it. While writing this book, I had dinner with a very devout Christian lady from my home state of Mississippi regarding my pursuit of objectively studying the lived spirituality of the Prophet and consequently engaging in a critical historical understanding of Islam. My actions concerned her and with a very troubled countenance, she looked me in the eyes and with distress in her voice, asked whether I had converted to Islam. Though I tried to assure her that I had no intentions of converting to Islam, I could sense she was still uncomfortable with my area of research. Time and again, I have been met with suspicion by fundamental evangelical Christians.

Interestingly enough, many of my casual conversations held with Southern Baptist pastors and laity have revealed that they are not interested in learning about Islam—they are however interested in Muslims learning about Christianity. One of the pastors I interviewed said, "If more people within my congregation were interested in learning about Muhammad, then I might consider studying more about the prophet and teaching about him."[105] My personal conversations, interviews, and interactions with leaders and laity within many of the Southern Baptist churches suggest that there simply is not a perceived pressing need or even desire at this time to objectively explore the religion of Islam. Of

---

104. "How the Prophet Brought about Positive Change," *Arab News*, October 4, 2013.
105. Interview by author, northwest Florida, 5 April 2018.

course, I argue that now is the time to engage in dialogue with Muslims. Though Islam is growing in the United States, it is exponentially growing in Africa and in many Asian countries. I am encouraged that some of the top leaders within the Convention are showing more interest in studying Islam and understanding the complexities of Muslim communities throughout the world—especially as it relates to the 10/40 Window.[106] Hopefully, this movement will continue and thus trickle down to regional leaders, pastors, and laity. For example, former SBC President J. D. Greer encouraged religious dialogue between Muslims and Southern Baptists. Furthermore, my pastoral experience within the Southern Baptist denomination informs me that pastors will study Islam and seek to educate their congregations on the basic tenets of the religion if pressed. However, my familiarities also tell me that many pastors, though they will present select facts about Islam and Muhammad, will often fall short of having a personal narrative and/or historical context in which to be objective. This lack of narrative empathy and context among many pastors has inadvertently promoted defamation, partiality, inaccurate reporting, and a lack of trust towards the religion of Islam and Muslims.

In the process of researching and writing this book, I developed Muslim friendships with imams, lawyers, government leaders, professors, members of the working class, and college students from Afghanistan, Bahrain, Great Britain, Indonesia, Iraq, Jordan, Oman, Pakistan, Egypt, Israel, United Arab Emirates, and the United States. Without exception, these people welcomed me into their lives and shared personal narratives that positively impacted my perception of Muslims and bequeathed to me a far greater understanding of how diverse Muslims are, how distinct the religion of Islam is (at times) from Christianity, and also how similar our values are. My Muslim friends, acquaintances, and colleagues represent a diverse group of Muslims who wake up every day and give praise to God and often request the same types of blessings to be upon them as Christians do, such as health, protection from evil, wealth, joy, peace, and hope for a peaceful and just world. They are people of deep faith, who attend the local mosque, voice daily prayers, read, study, and memorize large sections of their Holy Qur'an, seek to have good familial relations, hold down a good job, and provide a future for their family that is right, just, and prosperous. I perceive that these people are good and genuine and like many Christians they are also concerned with

---

106. Mohler, "Don't Just Support Missions."

the religious violence in the world—especially certain countries in the Middle East and North Africa—the lack of religious tolerance, and the political propaganda that goes on by those elected and appointed leaders, both political and religious, who so often do not reflect the law and spirit of their faith as prescribed by the Prophet Muhammad and contained in the Qur'an.

I believe Southern Baptists have been given an incredible opportunity to welcome Muslims into their homes and communities. By knowing Muslims and developing a more thorough understanding of Islam, Southern Baptists can more effectively communicate the love and salvific message of Christ and share their own personal narratives and religious beliefs. For various reasons, one being geographic, most Southern Baptists will not have the opportunity to travel to Muslim-majority countries. Thus few have the prospect of developing non-American Muslim friendships; and I do mean friendships, not simply acquaintances. However, due to Muslims immigrating into the United States and with the growth of families already here, I believe now is the right opportunity for Southern Baptist leaders to encourage and even lead their churches to discover Islam, get to know the people of Islam in their community, and cultivate a more thorough understanding of the founder of Islam by consulting both religious and contemporary scholarly literature; literature that I referred to in this chapter and further elaborate upon in the next.

5

What Do We Do about It

The Much Needed Reflective Conversation

Introduction

IN THIS CHAPTER, I deploy Osmer's pragmatic task[1] to develop concrete strategies to promote a scholarly, more objective understanding of Islam, the Prophet Muhammad, and jihad. My goal is to present concrete ideas that will help Southern Baptists to design, coordinate, and implement opportunities to peaceably and respectfully encounter Muslims. Most importantly these strategies will help engender an environment that provides the space for good and worthwhile dialogue, thus creating narrative empathy (capacity to understand and feel what the other person is experiencing via reading, hearing, observing, etc.). I demonstrate how leaders within the church can respond in love and in truth to the pressing concerns, questions, and perceptions to which the growth of Islam in the United States and around the world gives rise.

In chapter 2, I employed Osmer's descriptive-empirical task to gather information that helped us to discern patterns and dynamics in particular episodes, situations, and contexts within the Southern Baptist

---

1. Osmer, *Practical Theology*, 176.

denomination regarding its view of Islam—particularly Islam in the United States. I then used the interpretive task to draw on theoretical approaches to better understand and explain why certain patterns and dynamics are occurring. Next, using the normative task, I consulted the historical and contemporary scholarly literature to interpret specific episodes, situations, and contexts in light of modern Islamic doctrine. The hope is to construct an ethical norm, grounded in historical facts, that will help guide Southern Baptists' responses to Islam, Prophet Muhammad, and jihad. Finally, employing the pragmatic task, I intend in this chapter to foster a narrative empathy that will significantly reduce many of the misperceptions about Islam held by Southern Baptists. Moreover, my aim is to cultivate a spirit of learning that is more objective of Islam and simultaneously respectful of Muslims. In the words of Osmer, "these four tasks constitute the basic structure of practical theological interpretation."[2] My research has important implications, as it reveals that most Southern Baptists and Muslims share a common interest in building and sustaining communities of peace and justice where human beings can flourish and religion can serve as a catalyst of mutual interest.

Methodology

In an important way this chapter fulfills the goals of practical theology, which provides concrete models of constructive behavior, practice, and rules. In the words of Osmer, "Models of practice offer leaders a general picture of the field in which they are acting and ways they might shape this field toward desired goals. Rules of art are more specific guidelines about how to carry out particular actions or practices."[3] I first engage in a more theoretical aspect of this issue by asking several questions: What shared concepts can Southern Baptists focus on to bring about more peaceful relations with Muslims? What are some of the common values and beliefs between the two faiths? Finally, are the two faiths profoundly disparate from each other? In providing answers to these questions, I focus on confronting the fear of Islam and emphasizing common values and beliefs. After elaborating on the theoretical aspect, I propose some concrete strategies of action that implement this learned theoretical knowledge: consulting historical literature, small conferences

2. Osmer, *Practical Theology*, 4.
3. Osmer, *Practical Theology*, 176.

and workshops, and personal encounters with Muslims. As a whole, this chapter fulfills the goals of Osmer's practical task, "the task of forming and enacting strategies of action that influence events in ways that are desirable."[4]

Theoretical Level: A Pivotal Adjustment in Missional Thinking

In chapter 3, I examined plausible explanations as to why there is so much negative rhetoric being employed by leaders within the Southern Baptist denomination towards Islam. I examined the larger political and sociological context and then offered theories that helped to explain the negative rhetoric. We saw that the negative rhetoric often derived from anger, fear, and insecurity within the denomination. I made reference to the fact that politically and sociologically, the Southern Baptist denomination is by and large held together by the Baptist Faith and Message, a document that explicitly outlines the fundamental doctrines of their faith community.[5] These doctrines represent certain beliefs that in their view should not be compromised: salvation through Christ alone, *Sola scriptura*, total depravity of man, and so forth. Furthermore, the denomination elects' leaders who endorse the Baptist Faith and Message and are prone to be evangelical. Within the denomination there are three attitudinal clusters that play important roles in the day-to-day dynamics: authoritarian submission, authoritarian aggression, and conventionalism. In the event that these three attitudinal clusters are commonplace within an organization, psychologists give the group a name: Right Wing Authoritarians. As stated earlier, this description may or may not have any ties to a group's political affiliation. It is, however, a way to better understand the social dynamics within the organization. For example, among Southern Baptists, there is a high degree of compliance to the authorities that are perceived to be established and legitimate within the denomination. Furthermore, there is a general aggressiveness directed against deviants, outgroups, and other people that are perceived to be targets according to established authorities, e.g., left-wing liberal democrats (who are often viewed as socialists and secularists) and Muslims (especially Muslims of Arab descent). Finally, there is a high degree of

---

4. Osmer, *Practical Theology*, 176.
5. Hobbs, *Baptist Faith and Message*.

adherence to the traditions and social norms that are perceived to be endorsed by the majority of followers and their established authorities.[6] These attitudinal clusters must be taken into consideration when seeking to design, coordinate, and implement ways of creating a narrative empathy among Southern Baptists that promotes a more positive image of Islam, the Prophet Muhammad, and jihad.

If more of the authorities, i.e., leaders within the denomination, are receptive to the idea of expanding their evangelical spirit of love to encompass followers of Islam—which my experience says they are, then my research and writing holds very practical implications. Southern Baptist leaders and laity tend to think of themselves as friendly and eager to spread the gospel of Christ throughout the world, so this is not some novel idea that I am presenting. But it does require intentional action. If denominational leaders familiarize themselves with a historically objective rendering of the Prophet Muhammad and Islam and engage in friendly encounters with Muslims, these practices are likely to influence the greater denomination. If one of the goals of the denomination is to make their interpretation of Jesus known, loved, and served among Muslims, then the leaders must set a new norm of positive understanding and implementation. This norm must replace the existing paradigm—the norm of suspicion, hostility, surveillance, and resentment. For the new norm to take hold, fear, anger, and insecurity must be replaced with trust, compassion, and confidence. The leaders have the power to educate and form a denomination that has the competence to see and the courage to act in ways that promote human solidarity, without which tribal instincts flourish.

Historically, when Southern Baptists come together, they have been able to feed the hungry, empower global missions, curtail HIV/Aids in Africa, influence foreign affairs, mobilize disaster relief groups, serve at-risk children and their families, and educate thousands of ministry-minded adults via their six seminaries and numerous colleges.[7] Moreover, Southern Baptists influence local, state, and federal elections and policies. Through the International Mission Board and North American Mission Board, Southern Baptists engage in an array of mission activity whose primary goal is to lead people to a saving knowledge of Christ. Though Baptists have been effective in engaging with people groups

6. Altemeyer, *The Authoritarians*, 27.
7. "Fast Facts about the SBC," June 16, 2018.

throughout the world, Islam (the second-largest religion in the world) is the one religion that seems impenetrable to many Baptists. Some Southern Baptist scholars have argued, rightly, that the challenge to reaching Muslims is "multidimensional, with three primary categories of theological, ethical, and historical concerns."[8] My argument in this book has been that the overarching reason behind this failure is a lack of encounter between the two faiths and, consequently, a lack of understanding, trust, and collaboration. This lack of encounter has opened the door to negative emotions and attitudes among Southern Baptists towards Islam and Muslims. Without the literary and personal encounter, there is no narrative empathy. And without narrative empathy it is difficult to cultivate warmth towards Muslims, and consequently, a foundation of trust and friendship that can foster an effective sharing of the Gospel of Jesus. Religious leaders, be they Christian or Muslim, from the 10/40 Window can attest to this. The 10/40 Window classifies a section of the world map encircling North Africa, the Middle East, and Asia. It extends from latitude 10 degrees N to 40 degrees N of the equator. In terms of Christian missions, this area represents the most unreached people groups. Missionaries often relocate to areas within the 10/40 Window and live among the people learning their language, culture and religion, all the while, developing authentic friendships.

The idea of Muslims converting to Christianity in droves is unrealistic. A more practical approach is to promote concrete strategies of action to Southern Baptist leaders to encourage interreligious dialogue, mining for religious commonalities that foster human solidarity and collaboration. This dialogue can lay the foundation for the much-needed reflective conversation between the two faiths on issues large and small. I believe the social and religious dynamics in the United States place the responsibility of contact with Muslims upon the Southern Baptists. Southern Baptists constitute a much larger group than Muslims. Indeed, Muslims represent the minority and have been the target of much verbal abuse over the course of the last few decades. As previously discussed, in the United States, Muslims feel victimized by the greater population. In the spirit of reconciliation, it is necessary for the perceived perpetrator or offender to listen to stories of the victims. Moreover, the perceived perpetrator should engage in constructive dialogue that seeks to heal broken relationships and forge new, more positive ones. Ideally, in this

---

8. Chancellor and Wasserman, "Religions of the Middle East," 391.

process of reconciliation, both parties will be able to share their stories and begin the process of building mutual trust. In turn, a stronger mutual trust generates respect for future conversations, which can and often do lead to shared understanding, trust, and collaboration between Southern Baptists and Muslims.

This notion of creating a new perception of Islam, the Prophet Muhammad, and jihad within the framework of the Southern Baptist denomination requires a change of attitude, in some cases a deep-rooted change. Without this change, the Southern Baptist denomination will be found wanting when it comes to fostering accord with Muslims and engaging in opportunities for discussing doctrinal views. As Osmer points out, "[leaders] must confront their own hypocrisy in failing to embody the values they espouse and must alter their behavior to model with integrity the sorts of changes they would like to see in their organization."[9] Furthermore, he writes, "deep change is messy. . . . As the organization moves through a period in which old patterns no longer work and new ones have not yet emerged, it often feels chaotic. . . . During such periods, transformational leaders must remain committed to their internal vision, even as they empower others to reshape their vision."[10] At times, pivotal changes must take place in order to continue to meet the goals of the organization's mission. Without necessary reform, the Southern Baptist denomination will likely falter in its missional endeavors towards Muslims.

To put this in perspective, "between 1990 and 2000 the total membership of the Presbyterian Church (USA) shrank by 411,769 people, a decline of 11.6 percent."[11] Osmer writes, "During the same decade, the membership of the Episcopal Church declined by 5.3 percent, the United Methodist Church by 6.7 percent, the Evangelical Lutheran Church in America by 2.2 percent, and the United Church of Christ by 14.8 percent."[12] There are a few reasons for this decline in these mainline Protestant churches, such as low birthrates, death of older members, and lax congregational vitality, but the crux of the problem is the reality that change was not timely and substantial enough to prevent the decline. According to Bill Day, associate director of New Orleans Baptist Theological Seminary's Leavell Center for Evangelism and Church Health, 70

---

9. Osmer, *Practical Theology*, 178.
10. Osmer, *Practical Theology*, 178.
11. Marcum, "Trends and Changes."
12. Osmer, *Practical Theology*, 175.

percent of Southern Baptist churches have plateaued or are declining.[13] In the same vein, former president of the New Orleans Baptist Theological Seminary Chuck Kelly said, "And what we are seeing right now out on the field . . . is that the passion of Southern Baptists for reaching lost people for Christ is fading, that focus on the necessity of people to be born again through faith in Jesus Christ is fading in Southern Baptist life."[14] Moreover Kelly stated, "Every denomination in America has experienced what Southern Baptists are currently going through. Every denomination has grown, plateaued, and drifted into decline, but Southern Baptists can avoid the tragic decline that other denominations have faced. I believe that God is capable of doing a great and mighty work such as this nation has ever seen, God is able, and God is willing. The question is: 'Are we available?'"[15] Bobby Welch, former president of the Southern Baptist Convention and former pastor of First Baptist Church in Daytona Beach, Florida, likewise issued a call to action in his 50-state bus tour in 2004: "We cannot wait any longer, we have got to get serious about it [evangelism] and put our shoulder and heart to this wheel."[16] When asked about how to grow churches in the twenty-first century, Kelly said, "The Bible tells us how, the Lord has shown us the possibilities. The cold reality is that the only hindrance to greatness is the hindrance of my heart and yours."[17]

Chuck Kelly and Bobby Welch have influenced and shaped the Southern Baptist Convention in palpable ways. Both of these men conclude that the growth of the Southern Baptist church is dependent upon its leaders and members engaging with the world around them. Though I don't foresee a lot of American-Muslims converting to Christianity, it should not deter Southern Baptist from engaging with the Muslim population in the United States. Southern Baptist believe in the power of the Holy Spirit to awaken non-Christians to the gospel message of Christ. Therefore, by engaging with Muslim-Americans more opportunities of spreading the gospel presents the prospect of some Muslims converting to Christianity. The traditional methods of communication embraced by the denomination, at least within the United States as opposed to the foreign mission field, need to be modified. Such reforms will undoubtedly

13. McCormack, "Study Updates Stats."
14. McCormack, "Study Updates Stats."
15. McCormack, "Study Updates Stats."
16. Welch, report to the SBC Executive Committee, September 20, 2004.
17. McCormack, "Study Updates Stats."

constitute an incredible challenge that will take years. As Phil Pharshall writes, "criticism, both from friend and foe, we must be willing to re-evaluate what has come to be regarded as sacrosanct methodology. 'Change' must not be a dreaded word. Can the missionary to Islam be more effective? What is the Muslim's perception of the missionary? How can it be changed for the better?"[18] If Southern Baptist leaders and congregations fail to act in building bridges of understanding, trust, and collaboration with Muslim-Americans, then I believe they will miss out on the biggest missional opportunity of the twenty-first century. In this context, it is important to recognize the many practical hurdles Southern Baptists are likely to encounter while ministering to Muslims. Consider two examples. First, most Southern Baptists have been taught that the God of Islam is different from the God of Christianity, yet according to the Prophet Muhammad, the Qur'an, and the Muslim community, Muslims worship the same God as Abraham, Moses, Mary the mother of Jesus, and Jesus. My Arabic speaking Christian friends call God by the name of Allah. Second, Muslims venerate Mary the mother of Jesus and believe that she was a virgin when she gave birth to Jesus. In fact, a whole chapter in the Qur'an is devoted to Mary, it is called Maryam. Moreover, they believe that Jesus performed many miracles and was a great prophet of God. They do not believe that Jesus was/is equal with God and savior of the world, but Islamic tradition does hold that Jesus is with God now and is coming back at the end of time on earth to fight and defeat the False Messiah and establish peace and justice on earth. What these points suggest is that many of the traditional methods of missiology will have to be nuanced when one is conversing with Muslims. The whole encounter will be much more constructive if Southern Baptists seek first to know, respect, and love Muslims as people who are made in the image of God and trace their lineage back to Abraham.

Theoretical Level: Recognizing Common Values and Beliefs

Recognizing Common Values

One way to produce institutional change in the Southern Baptist denomination is to disseminate the knowledge of shared values between Muslims and Christians. In chapter 4, I reflected upon the lived spirituality of the

---

18. Parshall, *New Paths in Muslim Evangelism*, 98.

Prophet Muhammad with the intent to reveal the life of a very spiritual man who wanted peace with God and peace with his neighbors. Both values—achieving peace with God and peace with one's neighbors—are an important part of the Southern Baptist narrative. Based on the sayings and actions of Muhammad it appears that he was genuinely convinced that he had encountered God in the cave of Hira. His family and friends were also convinced by his experiences. Indeed, Muhammad's encounter forever changed his life as well as the religious landscape of the world. Based on the Qur'an and Sunna, the Prophet Muhammad valued his relationship with God, his family, his friends, and neighbors. As pointed out in chapter 4, his mission was to establish a more just and peaceful Arab community that worshiped the God of Abraham, the sole Creator and presider over heaven and earth. Muhammad's goal was to peacefully yet persistently communicate what he believed to be a direct message from God to him to make known the ways of God, train disciples, increase followers, and put an end to idolatry, polytheism, and injustices against humanity, especially the vulnerable and weak. Whether you believe he encountered the angel Gabriel or not, perhaps you can empathize with his longings to make straight the path that he believed had been made crooked intentionally and unintentionally by many, especially since the time of Jesus. He accomplished his mission through jihad, that is, he strived to please God in his everyday thoughts, words, and actions. For obvious reasons, Southern Baptists do not use the term "jihad" to describe their daily striving to live an exemplary life that honors God. However, the dynamics of jihad, as a concept, are very similar to spiritual disciplines practiced by Southern Baptists. The Prophet Muhammad engaged primarily in the major jihad, in which he communed with God via the disciplines of prayer, fasting, worship, evangelism, serving, stewardship, silence, solitude, and learning. He did this to live a more righteous life and to pursue godliness. I know from my own experience with colleagues within the Southern Baptists denomination that most leaders engage in such disciplines and teach their congregations to do the same. Indeed, Southern Baptist leaders encourage their congregants to seek to honor God by doing His will as found in Scripture and to try to refrain from any acts of violence, calling to mind the words of Jesus in the Gospel of Matthew: "You have heard that it was said, 'An eye for an eye and a tooth for a tooth.' But I tell you, do not resist an evildoer. On the contrary, if anyone slaps you on your right cheek, turn the other to him also" (5:38).[19] Both religions support and promote peaceful dispute resolution when possible. Yet both Christianity and Islam allow for circumstances when one can defend him- or herself from acts of violence or threatening behavior.

Many of the rudimentary values for Christian living are found in the message preached by Jesus in the Sermon on the Mount.[20] Here Jesus taught the early followers how to pray, how to fast, whom to serve, the cure for anxiety, the importance of not judging, how to enter the Kingdom of Heaven, neighborliness, evangelism, love for enemies, love for family, among other things. Interestingly enough, similar themes can be found in the final message that the Prophet Muhammad shared with his followers before his death. Regarding this last sermon by the Prophet Muhammad, Imam Abdullah Antepli writes, "The Prophet of Islam addresses some of the core universal values in a society where those values are long forgotten and violated in a systemic basis. . . . In this sermon, Muslims find their deep commitment to the universal human values such as sacredness of life and property, equality, justice, peace and more."[21] Below are some excerpts from the Prophet's last sermon.

> O People, just as you regard this month, this day, this city as Sacred, so regard the life and property of every Muslim as a sacred trust. Return the goods entrusted to you to their rightful owners. Treat others justly so that no one would be unjust to you. Remember that you will indeed meet your LORD, and that HE will indeed reckon your deeds. God has forbidden you to take usury (*riba*), therefore all riba obligation shall henceforth be waived. Your capital, however, is yours to keep. You will neither inflict nor suffer inequity. God has judged that there shall be no riba and that all the riba due to `Abbas ibn `Abd al Muttalib shall henceforth be waived.
>
> Every right arising out of homicide and blood-killing in pre-Islamic days is henceforth waived and the first such right that I waive is that arising from the murder of Rabi`ah ibn al Harith ibn `Abd al Muttalib.
>
> Beware of the devil, for the safety of your religion. He has lost all hope that he will ever be able to lead you astray in big things, so beware of following him in small things.

19. Matthew 5:38 (Holman Christian Standard Bible).
20. Matthew 5–7 (HCSB).
21. Antepli, "Last Sermon."

> O People, it is true that you have certain rights over your women, but they also have rights over you. Remember that you have taken them as your wives only under God's trust and with His permission. If they abide by your right then to them belongs the right to be fed and clothed in kindness. Treat your women well and be kind to them, for they are your partners and committed helpers. It is your right and they do not make friends with anyone of whom you do not approve, as well as never to be unchaste.
>
> O People, listen to me in earnest, worship God (The One Creator of the Universe), perform your five daily prayers (*Salah*), fast during the month of Ramadan, and give your financial obligation (*zakah*) of your wealth. Perform Hajj if you can afford to.
>
> All mankind is from Adam and Eve. An Arab has no superiority over a non-Arab nor a non-Arab has any superiority over an Arab; also a white has no superiority over a black nor a black has any superiority over white except by piety and good action. Learn that every Muslim is a brother to every Muslim and that the Muslims constitute one brotherhood. Nothing shall be legitimate to a Muslim which belongs to a fellow Muslim unless it was given freely and willingly. Do not, therefore, do injustice to yourselves.
>
> Remember, one day you will appear before God (The Creator) and you will answer for your deeds. So beware, do not stray from the path of righteousness after I am gone.
>
> O People, no prophet or messenger will come after me and no new faith will be born. Reason well, therefore, O People, and understand words, which I convey to you. I am leaving you with the Book of God (the Quran) and my Sunnah (the life style and the behavioral mode of the Prophet). If you follow them you will never go astray.
>
> All those who listen to me shall pass on my words to others and those to others again; and may the last ones understand my words better than those who listen to me directly. Be my witness O God, that I have conveyed your message to your people.[22]

This last sermon clearly shows the value the Prophet Muhammad placed on religion, life, family, mind, wealth, and justice. Furthermore, Imam Kamil Mufti writes,

> Classical scholars of Islam have condensed the teachings of Prophet Muhammad into a few statements. These comprehensive

---

22. Schih Muslim, book 15, Hadith 159; Sunan al-Tirmidhi, vol. 1, book 7, Hadith 1163; Sunan ibn Maja, vol. 3, book 9, Hadith 1851.

statements touch every aspect of our lives. Some of them are: Actions are judged by the intention behind them; God is pure and does not accept anything unless it is pure and God has commanded the faithful with what He commanded the prophets; Part of a persons good observance of Islam is to leave aside what does not concern him; A person cannot be a complete believer unless he loves for his brother what he loves for himself; One should not harm himself or others; Don't let your focus in this life to be to amass worldly gain and God will love you—don't be concerned with what people have, and they will love you.[23]

The last sermon and the statements made by classical scholars of Islam reveal that the ideal Muslim is one who seeks and strives to serve, worship, and lovingly submit to God by way of living a virtuous life. In contrast, as I discuss in chapter 2, Muslims who oppress fellow Muslims and non-Muslims, who rape, plunder, steal, and kill without just cause, simply do not mirror the lived spirituality of Muhammad and the Holy Qur'an. Many Islamic militant extremists may officially subscribe to Islam and even proclaim that they represent the true Muslim community; however, it is clear from my research conducted on the lived spirituality of the Prophet Muhammad and reading of the Qur'an that their words and conduct are not congruent with historical and modern interpretations of Islam. Again, in this context it is important to recall the message conveyed in 2007 by spiritual leaders of Islam, "A Common Word between Us and You."[24] Historically, Christians and Muslims have championed many of the same values. In modern times, many Muslims have concluded that the Christian West has broken its moral compass. When conversing with Muslims, Southern Baptists may need to underscore that their Christian values are at times at odds with perceived Western values—especially some values that are reflected in politics, pop-culture, and music, such as Madonna dancing provocatively on stage with a cross dangling from her neck and making statements that Jesus is sexy. James Chancellor and Jeffery Wasserman write, "This call [within many Muslim communities] to a renewed moral and ethical life based on Islam is considered a response to the economic exploitation of the poor, breakdown of the family, drug and alcohol abuse, materialism, and rampant sexual

---

23. Mufti, "Core Values of Islam."

24. "A Common Word between Us and You" is an open letter, dated October 13, 2007, from leaders of the Islamic religion to leaders of the Christian religion.

immorality associated with the modern Christian West."[25] In the process of interreligious dialogue, both Southern Baptists and Muslims will have to seriously examine their own spiritual shortcomings and recognize that both have room for improvement.

Recognizing Common Beliefs

Not only do Christians and Muslims share many common values, they also share some common beliefs about God, angels, creation, blessings, prophets, and eschatology. Of the nearly two billion Muslims worldwide, most can be said to share a few fundamental beliefs. These beliefs are known as the Articles of Faith. This compilation of Islam's tenets forms the foundation of the Islamic belief system. Below is a list of these articles with a brief explanation offered by Imam Kamil Mufti:

1. Belief in One God: The most important teaching of Islam is that only God is to be served and worshipped. Also, the biggest sin in Islam is to worship other beings with God. In fact, Muslims believe that it is the only sin that God does not forgive if a person dies before repenting from it.

2. Belief in Angels: God created unseen beings called angels who work tirelessly to administer His kingdom in full obedience. The angels surround us at all times, each has a duty; some record our words and deeds.

3. Belief in Prophets of God: Muslims believe that God communicates His guidance through human prophets sent to every nation. These prophets start with Adam and include Noah, Abraham, Moses, Jesus and Muhammad, peace be upon them. The main message of all the prophets has always been that there is only One true God and He alone is worthy of being supplicated to and worshipped.

4. Belief in Revealed Books of God: Muslims believe that God revealed His wisdom and instructions through 'books' to some of the prophets like the Psalms, Torah, and the Gospel. Over time, however, the original teachings of these books got distorted or lost. Muslims believe the Quran is God's final revelation revealed to Prophet Muhammad and has been fully preserved.

---

25. Chancellor and Wasserman, "Religions of the Middle East," 391.

5. Belief in Day of Judgment: The life of this world and all that is in it will come to an end on an appointed day. At that time, every person will be raised from the dead. God will judge each person individually, according to his faith and his good and bad actions. God will show mercy and fairness in judgment. According to Islamic teachings, those who believe in God and perform good deeds will be eternally rewarded in Heaven. Those who reject faith in God will be eternally punished in the fire of Hell.

6. Belief in Destiny and Divine Decree: Muslims believe that since God is the Sustainer of all life, nothing happens except by His Will and with His full knowledge. This belief does not contradict the idea of free will. God does not force us, our choices are known to God beforehand because His knowledge is complete. This recognition helps the believer through difficulties and hardships.[26]

Reflection on these six articles of faith reveals important commonalities between Southern Baptists and Muslims. Both religions believe in the oneness of God (though Southern Baptists can find it challenging when defining the Holy Trinity) as well as angelic beings. Both appreciate the contributions of Adam, Abraham, Moses, David, Mary the mother of Jesus, and Jesus. Southern Baptists and Muslims believe in and teach from some of the revealed books of God such as the Torah and Psalms. Muslims believe that some of the words of Jesus are contained in the New Testament, though they believe the gospel of Jesus has been lost. They also share a common understanding that there will be a final day of judgment before God, followed by all the righteous spending eternity with God. Furthermore, Muslims believe that God alone is the Creator and Sustainer of the universe and that the Virgin Mary gave birth to Jesus. Moreover, Muslims view Jesus as a great prophet, miracle worker, and messenger of God and believe he is coming back at the end of time on earth to fight and destroy the false messiah, liar, deceiver, known in Arabic as Al-Masih ad-Dajjal. Finally, he will establish peace on Earth. Jesus is venerated and mentioned at least 187 times in the Qur'an.[27] Though there are distinct doctrinal differences, most Christians and Muslims fail to appreciate that Christianity and Islam have much in common. Recognizing these commonalities can act as a starting point for

---

26. "A Common Word."
27. Barker and Gregg, *Jesus beyond Christianity*, 84.

the much-needed reflective conversation—a conversation that allows both sides to see, hear, and feel what the other is saying without fear of trepidation.

Competition for resources and a lack of cross-cultural knowledge and understanding, coupled with greed, hunger for power, and lack of narrative empathy, all contributed to the historical conflict between Christians and Muslims, especially in Europe and Upper Mesopotamia. Throughout history, followers of Christianity and Islam have strayed from the orthodox teachings of Jesus and Muhammad, a departure that resulted in much bloodshed and hatred of the religious other. Some of these propensities have been aggravated in recent years; hence, I believe that now is an opportune time to engage in a much-needed reflective conversation, one that nurtures the healing of memories and sets out to form a more peaceful path forward between Christians—especially Southern Baptists—and Muslims. Below, I set forth some concrete strategies of action that can foster a narrative empathy among Southern Baptists towards Muslims (particularly Muslims-Americans and Arab Muslims). These strategies can also foster a narrative empathy among Muslims towards Southern Baptists and Christians in general.

When I embarked upon my research for this book, I did not personally know any Muslims. In fact, I lacked narrative empathy towards Muslims. My deep awareness of this reality caused me to set out on this reflective journey to encounter Muslims both in the United States and abroad. My goal has been to personally put my research to the test and discover whether my experiences would indeed change me. They did! For the last several years, I have consulted with interfaith dialogue scholars and practitioners and developed relationships with many Muslim-Americans and Arab Muslims. During this time, I have also had many casual conversations as well as formal interviews with Southern Baptist pastors. As a result, I have personally discovered concrete practices that can enable Southern Baptists to have meaningful and constructive encounters with Muslims. Before considering these strategies of action, it is useful to consider Muhammad's respect for Jesus. Indeed, a reflection upon his attitude towards Jesus can cultivate a sincere desire within Southern Baptists to continue, renew, or begin the process of healing, understanding, appreciation, respect, and dialogue that has periodically existed between Muslims and Christians. Ibrahim Hooper writes, "The Prophet Muhammad himself sought to erase any distinctions between the message he taught and that taught by Jesus, who he called God's 'Spirit and word.'

Prophet Muhammad said: 'Both in this world and in the Hereafter, I am the nearest of all people to Jesus, the son of Mary. The prophets are paternal brothers: their mothers are different, but their religion is one."[28] Every Muslim I have spoken with has honored Jesus by calling him prophet Jesus and saying "peace be upon him" (a traditional sign of veneration among Muslims) after using his name.

Concrete Strategies of Action

There are several concrete strategies of action that Southern Baptists can employ when seeking to create and foster long-lasting relationships with Muslims both in the United States and abroad. These include cultural immersion trips, workshops and seminars for the purpose of gaining knowledge and understanding of Islamic history, personal and strategic or thoughtful encounters with Muslims, collaborative interaction, and a more objective and responsible approach to preaching and teaching about Islam within the confines of the local church. All of these strategies will help to create narrative empathy for Muslims. My conversations with practitioners of interreligious dialogue reveal that dialogue only for the purpose of converting Muslims will be rejected by the majority of Muslims. If, however, dialogue is rooted in dignity and respect for the Muslims and takes into account the *spirit* of the Great Commission, then it lays the foundation for understanding, trust, and collaboration. Such respect can develop into in-depth discussions between Southern Baptists and Muslims about the person of Jesus and why Southern Baptists believe that Jesus is the way, the truth, and the life for all humankind and necessary for everlasting salvation. How Southern Baptists share the Gospel with Muslims must be carefully thought out and implemented; attempts to proselytize Muslims will only further inflame the current relationship of distrust between the two religions. I have also discovered that a well-educated Christian theologian debating a well-educated Muslim theologian is likely to come to an impasse, although it can help the two participants, as well as any onlookers, understand the similarities and the peculiarities of each religion.

Let me add, as a side note, that the idea of evangelism is not new to Muslims; like Christians, they believe that it is important to proclaim one's faith in the hope of converting the recipient. In other words,

---

28. Hooper, "Muslims and Christians."

evangelism—sharing one's good news with the anticipation of transforming the other—is viewed positively in both Christianity and Islam. To my knowledge, most religious groups appreciate the freedom to share their own version of what it means to have faith in God or gods, or no gods at all, and what that particular group believes is the true meaning of life. In the United States, Christian evangelism has historically been very effective among those of white European descent, owing to a common culture and worldview. However, as the American populace changes and increasingly welcomes individuals of different ethnic and cultural backgrounds, traditional methods of evangelism employed by the Southern Baptist denomination, and other mainline religious denominations of European descent, must change. Otherwise, religious intolerance will continue to drive deep wedges within the religious milieu of the United States.

Specific methods for sharing the orthodox salvific message of Christ with the world, especially the Muslim population, must evolve. Southern Baptists will need to take precautions against a type of "crusade evangelism" whereby direct proselytizing seeks to convert Muslims by coercion or demonization of Islam. Thus, I propose that via intentional interreligious dialogue, Southern Baptists have the potential to create a narrative empathy that will help shape an improved, if not entirely new, perception of Islam, the Prophet Muhammad and jihad. It is this altered perception that will in truth foster respect and love for Muslims. I have personally experienced that this respect and love can be and often is reciprocated. One morning, I received a text message from a Shia Muslim in Bahrain wishing me a beautiful day and closeness to God. That same afternoon, I received a phone call from a Sunni Muslim from Afghanistan who just wanted to check in with me and make sure that I am doing okay.

Here, then, are some concrete strategies of action that I have discovered while visiting Arab countries, befriending Muslims, participating in interreligious dialogue, speaking to professors in the academy, listening to directors and practitioners of interreligious centers, and engaging in conversations with Southern Baptist pastors. As a former pastor myself, I believe these particular actions can prove chiefly effective for Southern Baptists leaders. I recommend three ways for Southern Baptist leaders to grow in their understanding of Islam and personal narratives of Muslims: (1) become familiar with the religious and scholarly literature on Islam, (2) attend small conferences and workshops on Muslim-Christian relations, and (3) commit to friendly personal encounters with Muslims. I believe the trickle-down effect, from leader to lay person, will begin to significantly alter the biased perception of Islam and its adherents among Southern Baptists, and vice versa. Ultimately, it will enable a more objective discussion and understanding of the question of how to work together to bring about a more peaceful and just world via our shared values, beliefs, and eschatology.

Develop a More Objective Rendering of Early Islamic History

There are many literary sources on Islam for the pastor to consult. Below are a few sources recommended to me by academic friends who study and teach on Islam at the Catholic Theological Union, the University of Notre Dame, the University of Chicago, and Oxford University, among other institutions. These works represent a broad scholarly consensus among Muslims and non-Muslims, and have provided me with a solid foundation for extended studies in the pastorate and academy. I recommend that every Southern Baptist pastor familiarize himself with some of the scholarly literature on Islam. Two of the most important resources are the Qur'an (i.e. *The Study Quran: A New Translation and Commentary* by Seyyed Hossein Nasr—an excellent English translation) and the Sunnah of the Prophet (particularly the eighth and ninth centuries works of Muhammad ibn Ishaq and Muhammad ibn Sa'd). In addition, I have found these four sources extremely helpful in my study of Islam: *The Princeton Encyclopedia of Islamic Political Thought*, *And Muhammad Is His Messenger* by Annemarie Schimmel, *Muhammad: His Life Based on Earliest Sources* by Martin Lings, and *Islam beyond Violent Extremism* by Imam Dr. A. Rashied Omar. To be sure, there are many scholarly works to consult, but based on my own personal experience, I have confidence that these six sources will prove invaluable resources for any Southern Baptist pastor as he seeks to better understand Islam. Likewise, these sources will help any pastor engage with the Muslim population and educate his congregation on Islam and Muslims. The importance of reading the primary sources of Islam—the Qur'an and Sunnah—can hardly be overestimated. Indeed, any pastor should possess basic firsthand knowledge of what the Prophet said and how the Prophet lived. Otherwise, one cannot objectively speak about Islam. These readings can prove to be an anchor of truth and knowledge about the Muslim faith, which in the words of Osmer, can guide the pastor in a more objective interpretation and response to particular episodes, situations, and contexts. As such, these readings are indispensable for an attempt to construct ethical norms to guide the Southern Baptist leader's responses and learning from good practice.[29] A copy of *The Princeton Encyclopedia of Islamic Political Thought* is an irreplaceable resource that references numerous central terms, concepts, personalities, movements, places, and schools of thought across Islamic history. The information included in this encyclopedia should be juxtaposed against the frequently misleading rhetoric in US politics and media; this work will help distinguish fact from fiction. To garner a thorough appreciation for the life and times of the Prophet Muhammad, the works by Schimmel and Lings are paramount. These are contemporary yet timeless portals by which the pastor can gain understanding of the pre-Islamic milieu and of the much-needed societal changes brought about by the Prophet Muhammad. Schimmel's book especially lays bare the love for the Prophet Muhammad that Muslims enjoy. Finally, I highly recommend Imam Omar's *Islam beyond Violent Extremism*. Omar's work, a compilation of modern essays and sermons, shows that Muslim scholars and practitioners are committed to ending political violence. By consulting with such scholarly works, the pastor will be better equipped in promoting truth over lies. The goal of this endeavor is for education to trump indoctrination and thus provide a better, more historical, worldview of Islam that takes into account the Arabic milieu of the Prophet Muhammad's time.

Participate in Small Group Learning Activities

Though personal reading and research cannot be underestimated, it is also vital to engage in dialogue with those who are well versed in Islamic thought and practice, both in the United States and abroad. Indeed, individual-level encounters with Islamic scholars and practitioners foster a more substantive understanding and appreciation for the Islamic milieu than reading along can offer. Most pastors and leaders within the Southern Baptist denomination are practical theologians, theologians who seek to provide biblical answers to problems and questions facing their congregations and communities. What better way for the pastor to be informed and consequently provide answers to questions his congregation has about Islam than to attend and or provide "safe" spaces for scholars and practitioners of Islam to expound upon the beliefs and

---

29. Osmer, *Practical Theology*, 4.

practices of Muslims? Such interaction can foster a narrative empathy among Southern Baptists—a narrative empathy that can fuel human solidarity and collaboration. Simultaneously these so-called safe spaces can provide for a more objective interpretation of Islamic thought and practice as Islamic history is explored. These meetings can take place in local churches, Islamic centers, or religiously neutral places, where other pastors are invited to attend and to participate in asking relevant, thought-provoking, and respectful questions. Regardless of its location, it is conducive for such a meeting to be held in an intimate setting that allows pastors to deepen conversations with Muslims and Islamic scholars.

I cannot overemphasize how important intimate group sessions are. Research has found that the most conducive size of a group is between four to five people, especially as it relates to meaningful discussions that require performance and thought-provoking questions.[30] In larger group settings there is often a personal disconnect between the speaker and the listener. Most importantly, however, in the large group setting, peer pressure can contaminate the value-free dialogue. In the small setting, people are—simply put—more likely to be truthful and honest. My experience is that pastors have access to many Islamic scholars and practitioners throughout the United States. Potential speakers include Muslim and non-Muslim professors and graduate students in our colleges and universities who are specialists in Islamic theology and history, imams from local mosques, and imams who have traveled from afar and are studying or preaching/teaching in the United States. In the spirit of learning, educational presentations, weekend retreats, and conversations over dinner, as well as small group studies—such as Scriptural Reasoning—a method of interfaith dialogue founded by Peter Ochs[31], can greatly aid Southern Baptist leaders in becoming more knowledgeable of Islam and more loving towards Muslims. Of course, each party will continue to hold its distinctive beliefs, but a greater appreciation of our commonalities can spur good and worthwhile collaboration.

When designing, organizing, and implementing small conferences and workshops, it is helpful to provide not only a respectful environment but also specific topics of study that will allow for a deeper discussion and understanding of Islam. Examples of such topics might include Islam and the Bible, Islam and Jesus, Muslims and jihad, pre-Islamic

---

30. Hackman and Vidmar, "Effects of Size and Task Type."
31. Ochs, *Religion without Violence*.

beliefs in Mecca, and the history of the Ka'bah. The majority of Muslims I scheduled appointments with, asked me beforehand what I wanted to get out of the meeting. They found it very helpful and less threatening to be prepared for the conversation. The lack of a well-defined topic can leave room for many random and unexpected questions from the audience with not enough time to answer them in a constructive manner. A precise topic allows the speaker to be more concise and provide a better framework for participants to ask questions and receive thoughtful answers. It is crucial that these meetings be conducted in a respectful manner. A debate style, where one tries to prove the other one wrong, can result in arguments that prevent understanding, trust, and collaboration to flourish. The purpose of these meetings is to genuinely gain more insight into the Islamic milieu so as to engage in constructive dialogue and develop a narrative empathy towards Muslims—an empathy that is rewarding for both dialogue partners. It is helpful when the audience and the speaker listen to each other to converge on commonalities and respect their differences. Such meaningful dialogue can prove to be the foundation for civic-solidarity between Southern Baptists and Muslims. Such dialogue can simultaneously provide a vehicle for sharing Christian beliefs with Muslims. As this inter-faith relationship is cultivated, Southern Baptist pastors are likely to find still more opportunities to engage with the Muslim community, thus creating a united community of respect, appreciation, and learning. Knowledge changes a person. I strongly believe that small conferences and workshops provide a non-threatening way for Muslims and Southern Baptists to share their faith beliefs and humanitarian concerns and to offer strategic methods to address these concerns. In 2021, I met with several members of the Muslim community in Mobile, Alabama. My goal was to hear their stories about living in America. I discovered that most of them had immigrated into the United States as either high-achieving college students or white-collar professionals. My takeaway from those conversations was that there is barely a hair difference between their wants and needs and mine. In most cases they came to America and have remained in America to pursue a good education, find meaningful employment, raise a family, and worship without fear of persecution; they want freedom of religion. In every story shared, they voiced how proud they were to be Muslim-Americans and to live in a democracy.

Engage in Personal Encounters

In the late spring of 2018, I met and subsequently developed a friendship with a Muslim man from Afghanistan, whom I will identify as Mohammad (I will conceal his name for his protection). He was attending the University of Notre Dame Law School to gain a better understanding of international and humanitarian law. Upon completion of his law degree, he returned to Afghanistan and prior to the Taliban takeover, was working for the United States government in educating Muslim leaders in his region on matters of international law. As our friendship developed, it became apparent to me that my friend is one of the leading imams in Afghanistan teaching Islamic law. In an effort to better understand Islam, I engaged in several conversations with Mohammad. We frequently spoke of matters relating to everyday life and religion. One day, Mohammad asked if I could drive him into town to pick up a new computer since his had malfunctioned the night before. It was on this trip that our comfort level naturally grew enough to speak about our daily interactions with God. I will never forget when Mohammad teared up and smiled and said, "I never knew how wonderful Christians were until I met you, I will never be the same again and I will tell others of your Christian love." My friend had been "around" Christians for quite some time while at the University of Notre Dame. Yet, he had never truly encountered a Christian on a personal level. It was this personal encounter between Mohammad and me that created a narrative empathy toward Christianity and Christians in Mohammad. To this day we correspond via email and will hopefully remain friends for life. Did he share his faith with me? Yes. Did I share my faith with him? Yes. Most importantly, this sharing of time and thoughts has brought us closer together. I understand and appreciate the Muslim faith better and Mohammad understands and appreciates the Christian faith better. Small conferences and workshops held within one's own community can foster friendships such as the one between me and Mohammad. After all, communities and societies comprise individuals. Interreligious dialogue starts from an interpersonal encounter.

In the summer of 2018, I traveled to Oman for two purposes: cultural immersion and to meet with Aaro Rytkonen, at that time the Executive Director of the Al Amana Centre in Muscat, Oman. He now serves as their Director of Strategic Planning, Development, and Partnerships—henceforth is my experience. Christian leaders who have visited the Holy Land often say to me that it vastly improved their understanding of and appreciation for many of the people, places, and stories found within the Bible. Likewise, Christian leaders who have immersed themselves in a Muslim culture, particularly in the Middle East, have found it helpful in both understanding and empathizing with Muslims in general. The Al Amana Centre is located in the heart of Old Muscat near the Muttrah Souq, a place where family, friends, and visitors come together and experience cultural immersion. Step outside the gate of the Centre and step onto the hustling and bustling walkways and streets as Muslims engage in daily activities—peaceably, happily, and respectfully. Observe children playing on the sidewalks, the elderly sitting and having conversations, the local business community greeting customers and selling goods, or hear the sound of clanging pots and dishes of local restaurants serving the locals Omani cuisine. In the midst of this lively community sits the Al Amana Centre, a place of interreligious dialogue for over 125 years.[32] This is one of the safest places for Christian leaders, more specifically, Southern Baptist leaders, to come, learn, and encounter a Muslim community. It is a safe place to ask questions, contemplate answers, and speak with local Christians and Muslims alike. Most importantly, Oman—the home of Ibadi Islam—provides a welcoming environment, where one can discover that life is good in many Muslim communities throughout the Arab region. I found these Muslim communities to be very similar to communities in the United States. Sure, the language is different, the facial features are distinctive, the dress is unique to the culture, but the human interaction is similar.

The Al Amana Centre provides space designed for daily encounters that promote interreligious dialogue and cultural immersion.[33] The leaders of the Centre offer invaluable experiences for representatives of all world religions. I believe that the Centre constitutes an invaluable resource for Southern Baptist leaders. In the words of Director Rytkonen,

> The world is in need of dialogue. In order to provide peaceful coexistence, prevent conflicts as well as resolve them, we need to understand each other. This means we are open for dialogue. Dialogue is a process that can lead us to something new. Dialogue can be a process where people understand more about each other. Dialogue is entering to joint path with others. It

---

32. More information about the Al Amana Centre can be found at alamanacentre.org.

33. For more information on intercultural immersion visit alamanacentre.org, "Our Programs."

means sharing thoughts about values and beliefs. But it also gives us a possibility to understand oneself better. Because many times through discussions with others you begin to understand yourself better.[34]

This sort of immersion experience can deepen and clarify the Southern Baptist leader's understanding and appreciation of the Islamic milieu. Arguably, the experience lends more credibility to any pastor as he preaches his sermons and engages in conversations with his congregation, colleagues, and community about Islam. Such an immersion experience communicates to any church and community that the pastor values Muslims, moreover appreciates them as being created in the image of God and is himself aware of the particularities of Islam. Most importantly, as a leader in the local church, the pastor can more effectively dialogue with Muslims in his community.

In chapter 2, I discussed the reality that there is a great deal of negative rhetoric in the United States directed towards Islam. Rytkonen substantiates this in an email to me by writing, "From the movies we watch to social media, many of these are promoting a stereotype about cultures, religions, and regions of the world that are largely unfounded and often harmful to peaceful cohabitation of the planet we call home."[35] I believe that one of the best ways for Southern Baptist leaders to offer influential and effective leadership within their respective communities on Islam, is for them to personally engage with an institution like the al Amana Centre that offers such programs and intentionally develop a meaningful relationship with its staff—a staff that has been immersed in Muslim-Christian dialogue.

Though I highly recommend a personal immersion experience in Oman (I personally know the Centre is non-threatening to evangelical Christian leaders seeking more knowledge and understanding of Islam), there are certainly other locations both in the United States and the Arab region that can help immerse the Christian leader in Muslim culture and faith. Some examples include Multifaith Neighbors Network[36] in Keller, Texas; Georgetown University's Center for the Study of Islam and Muslim-Christian Understanding;[37] and the Royal Institute for Interfaith

34. Al Amana Centre website, alamanacentre.org (accessed March 2, 2022).

35. Aaro Rytkonen, personal email, November 17, 2022.

36. More information about Multifaith Neighbor's Network can be found at mfnn.org/.

37. More information about the Prince Alwaleed Bin Talal Center for Muslim-Christian

Studies in Amman, Jordan.[38] This type of encounter can help Southern Baptist leaders correct misperceptions and misunderstandings about Islam, learn about Islamic beliefs and practices, and identify false cultural stereotypes. From my visits to the Al Amana Centre in Oman in 2018, 2019 and 2022, I can attest that the Centre is strategically located and thoroughly equipped to effectively educate Southern Baptist leaders on the Islamic milieu. The Centre was founded by the Reformed Church in America and works closely with Christian denominations in the United States.[39] Subsequently, the Centre has an informed understanding of the many missional needs in the Protestant circles. Though the educational immersion trip can be tailored around the needs of a specific group, most leaders and church groups spend a week to ten days in Oman. During this time, participants not only engage in interreligious dialogue and cultural immersion, but they also enjoy the cultural aspects of the Omani context. As participants travel into the heart of this Islamic culture and encounter the many varied people of Islam, their perception of the Muslim people changes. Furthermore, such an immersion experience cultivates a true narrative empathy, which can foster a more positive and unbiased view of Muslims. Additionally, these experiences can significantly support Southern Baptist leaders in developing a greater appreciation for the shared values and beliefs between the two faiths as well as more clearly comprehend the humanness in the "religious other."

While writing this chapter, I reached out to Rytkonen, then director of the Al Amana Centre, for a few words about why he believes the Al Amana Centre is an effective place for Southern Baptist leaders to gain practical knowledge and understanding of Islam. "I think there are three main reasons," he said. "First, Al Amana Centre is a great place for church leaders to build their own narrative about Islam in a safe environment through encounters with local Muslims. Second, those encounters give also a possibility to be an example of a Christian to Muslims here in the Middle East. Finally, meetings with Christians living in Oman is a great possibility to understand some of the challenges minority religions have. All of these experiences will definitely change your approach to your own

---

Understanding can be found at www.globalministries.org.

38. More information about the Royal Institute for Interfaith Studies can be found at riifs.org.

39. More information about the history of the Centre can be found at alamanacentre.org.

faith as well as to other believers after returning home!"[40] My visit to the Al Amana Centre, conversations with religious and government officials (Muslim and non-Muslim), and practitioners of interreligious dialogue both in the United States and abroad, all lead me to conclude that the Centre captures the spirit of the Sermon on the Mount, the Great Commission, and the words of the Apostle Peter: "Always be ready to give a defense to anyone who asks you for a reason for the hope that is in you. However, do this with gentleness and respect."[41] In the summer of 2019, I traveled back to Oman and participated in the Global Symposium on Interreligious Dialogue, hosted by the Al Amana Centre. I presented some of my research from this book and it received a warm reception. Moreover, both Christian and Muslim leaders from the United States and Europe, commended the research and echoed the call for the fostering of narrative empathy between Christians and Muslims. Furthermore, I discovered at this conference that many of the Islamic leaders are actively engaged in helping Muslims better understand Christians and the West in much the same way. Make no mistake, many Muslims are engaged in Christian-Muslim dialogue.

Conclusion

I believe that one of the greatest missional opportunities for Southern Baptists in the twenty-first century is getting to know the people of Islam. Taking a "getting to know" approach will plant and cultivate a much-needed reflective conversation with Muslims in the spirit of interreligious dialogue. As a result, friendships and partnerships can bridge the gap between the world's two most populace religions. The specific methods of immersion I offer in this chapter—informational literature, small conferences and workshops, and personal encounters—will provide a great deal of substance to the intentional and reflective conversation. This type of meaningful conversation reaches deep into the participants' seat of emotions. It involves significant thinking, communicating, and reflecting. In a short article titled "Phases of Reflective Conversation" Mara Brenner highlights the importance of thinking, communicating, and reflecting. Brenner writes:

---

40. Aaro Rytkonen, personal correspondence, October 16, 2018.
41. 1 Peter 3:15-16 (HCSB).

Thinking

- Sees and can explain the "big picture" when analyzing situations. Sees and can explain the interactions of various factors

Communicating

- Uses appropriate non-verbal behavior correctly; interprets others' non-verbal behavior
- Actively listens to others; asks questions for clarification

Reflection

- Remains open and curious
- Regularly examines own thoughts, feelings, strengths and growth areas[42]

This type of deep, true, interpersonal conversation, along with the concrete strategies of action I propose, helps rekindle a fellowship that was once enjoyed between Christians and Muslims during Muhammad's leadership. The renewing of such a fellowship holds the potential of bringing Southern Baptists and Muslims together to increase mindfulness of each other, as well as promote shared values and beliefs. As a result, Muslims and Southern Baptists working together can effectively reduce religious intolerance and militant religious extremism in the United States and abroad. Together, Muslims and Southern Baptists can tackle many of the crises of our time—genocide, human trafficking, climate change, poverty, disease, urban crime, etc. I truly believe that this dialogue can be accomplished without Southern Baptist leaders compromising any of their religious beliefs. Remember the goal of interreligious dialogue is civic plurality not theological plurality. Though my focus in this book is not on evangelization, I do believe that it is in engaging in such actions that Baptist leaders can communicate their understanding of the Gospel of Christ with Muslims in a benevolent way. Additionally, lead Southern Baptist congregations to a deeper understanding of what it means to love God and one's neighbor as oneself.

---

42. Brenner, "Phases of Reflective Conversation."

6

Conclusion

I was raised in a fundamental evangelical Southern Baptist family. I attended church regularly and developed a great appreciation for the authority of the Bible and recognized early on the importance of studying it. As a young man I attended a Bible college and seminary with hopes of becoming an effective preacher, teacher, theologian, and Christian example of God's Word. I was taught to love God with all my heart, soul, mind, and strength and to love my neighbor as myself. The first instruction came easy; however, the second instruction was more of a challenge. Furthermore, I did not fully come to appreciate the depth of this instruction until much later in life. Through the years, I have contemplated on the commandment to "love one's neighbor." Moreover, I questioned "Who is my neighbor?" I came to understand that the neighbor Christ was referring to was not so much the person in close proximity to me or my immediate community, but the greater world—a complexly populated world which, according to Orthodox Christianity, He came to save from sin and death. A world inhabited with people who Christians believe are in need of hearing the Good News of Christ so as to begin the most rewarding spiritual journey any man or woman can embark upon. Because of this conviction shared by many, I believe it is important for me and other Christian leaders to partner with practitioners of interreligious dialogue and for Southern Baptist leaders, particularly, to promote these concrete strategies of action in the denomination. My experiences as a former Southern Baptist pastor and now as a scholar-practitioner of interreligious dialogue and multi-faith engagement has provided me with a unique perspective that can inform a constructive dialogue between Southern Baptists and Muslims. When the Southern Baptist leaders employ these practical strategies of action, their missional endeavors to Muslims will arguably reflect the mandate of Christ to love your neighbor as yourself. Baptist pastor and chancellor of Bethlehem College and Seminary John Piper summed up the love of neighbor well when he said,

> Now those are the two stupendous things we need to ponder [that is on the two greatest commandments depend the whole law and the prophets] before we dive into the overwhelming commandment to love our neighbor as we love ourselves. I say it is overwhelming because it seems to demand that I tear the skin off my body and wrap it around another person so that I feel that I am that other person; and all the longings that I have for my own safety and health and success and happiness I now feel for that other person as though he were me. It is an absolutely staggering commandment. If this is what it means, then something unbelievably powerful and earthshaking and reconstructing and overturning and upending will have to happen in our souls. Something supernatural. Something well beyond what self-preserving, self-enhancing, self-exalting, self-esteeming, self-advancing human beings like John Piper can do on their own.[1]

"That I tear the skin off my body and wrap it around another person so that I feel that I am the other person"—these words capture the essence of narrative empathy. This process of being Christ-like takes courage and love, a courage and love that are largely untapped in Southern Baptist circles towards Muslims.

Education, travel, teaching, research, friendships, and personal conversations with Muslims and Islamic scholars continue to inform my worldview. These activities provide me with a narrative that transcends my own Christian and American milieu. Walking the streets of Warsaw, Berlin, Copenhagen, Manama, Muscat, or Doha, engaging in conversation with people from different cultures, observing families playing together in parks, reading local newspapers in foreign countries, and simply immersing myself in the culture of another has significantly increased my

---

1. Piper, "Love Your Neighbor."

ability to form a more global narrative empathy. I view myself differently. I grew up hearing about the "others" in the world, only to discover that I am somebody else's "other." I am the religious other. I am the stranger. I am the perceived enemy. I am the one with the foreign language. I am the neighbor that Jesus and the Prophet Muhammad instructed their followers to love. I am the one in the crowd. I am the statistic. I am the problem. I am the solution. I am the one that people in other countries are trying to develop a narrative empathy towards. This startling reality is what fosters my view that I need to further develop my ability to listen critically, observe more objectively, walk humbly, and speak kindly, so that I can better empathize with all people, especially as a scholar-practitioner of interfaith dialogue. Narrative can be used as a tool or a weapon. Narrative can bring unity, but it can also bring division. Responsible implementation of narrative empathy in the lives of Southern Baptist leaders can significantly actualize and humanize their perception of Muslims and the story of Islam, and thereby improve the quality of speech and interaction with Muslims. The implications of forming and developing one's ability to empathize can lead to greater human solidarity.

I opened this book by stating that there is a lack of narrative empathy in the Southern Baptist denomination towards Islam, especially towards Middle Eastern, Northern African, and Indonesian Muslims, a lack of empathy that I had personally observed while pastoring churches in the denomination. Let me be clear: some Southern Baptists and members of the greater Evangelical community are educated in the history of Islam, know and enjoy friendships with Muslims, and have traveled to Muslim-majority countries. I presented some of the primary reasons why narrative empathy towards Muslims is lacking in the denomination and considered whether any actions can be taken to remedy this lack of empathy. To develop a more concise understanding of the perceived lack of empathy, which fosters negative rhetoric within the denomination, I referred to Osmer's four tasks of practical theological interpretation—descriptive-empirical, interpretive, normative, and pragmatic. These four tasks allowed me to make sense of my experiences and then develop concrete actions to bring about the desired outcome: fostering narrative empathy in the Southern Baptist denomination towards Muslims, all the while providing Southern Baptists with a more historical and thus a more objective view of Islam and the Prophet Muhammad.

Narrative empathy for Muslims can emerge and flourish in the Southern Baptist denomination. I expect the actions I recommend will be challenging to most pastors, especially those who lean towards fundamentalism. Indeed, for many Southern Baptist leaders, these actions are likely to require a shift in their missional focus and a financial sacrifice. Most importantly, the implementation of these strategies will entail for many pastors a willingness to step outside their personal comfort zone. An in-depth study of Islam calls for an open mind and an open heart as leaders within the denomination seek to establish deep-rooted and friendly relationships with Muslims. Furthermore, in this process, pastors will be challenged to confront the biased narrative and rhetoric that seems to be prevalent throughout much of the denomination. This process is related to what Osmer calls the pragmatic task. It is the ability for the leader to recognize the issue and then determine strategies of action that will influence the situation in a desirable way. In his book "Deep Change" Robert Quinn puts forth a four-stage model of organizational change, which he calls the transformational cycle:[2]

1. Initiation—a leader, group, or leadership team develops a strong sense of the need for change and begins to form a vision of the desired future; it starts acting on this vision and taking risks.

2. Uncertainty—those leading change begin to engage in more serious forms of experimentation and innovation; likely, at least some of these new initiatives fail, leading to doubt and uncertainty on the change agents' parts and strengthening resistance; leaders feel lost, but if they (and the organization) can tolerate this period of uncertainty, it depends their vision and opens up new lines of action.

3. Transformation—innovation gradually spreads to the organization as a whole, leading to deep change in its identity, mission, culture, and operating procedures; new energy is released and relationships formed.

4. Routinization—the organization moves into a new state of equilibrium; new roles and structures have been developed and mastered; specific problems can be handled by the new organizational system.

At the end of the day, historians remind us that change is inevitable. The Southern Baptist denomination has historically been a vibrant and healthy organization, in large part because its leaders have not wavered from its core values and beliefs. I believe that the success of the

---

2. Quinn, *Deep Change*, 167–69.

denomination throughout the years has been and continues to be its love for people. Not always in practice, but in theory, every Southern Baptist leader and lay person I have met believes that Jesus lived, died, and was resurrected so that all people might have the opportunity to receive God's love and salvation. In this vein, I hope that this book will renew that love for all people, especially Muslims, and in so doing establish a new and respectful initiative that entails "getting to know" Muslims. Education, encounter, and intentional dialogue help to begin the transformation towards addressing the larger systemic problem of Islamophobia that I addressed in chapter 2.

Orthodox Christianity and Islam teach that in the beginning God created the heavens and the earth and everything in them, and sustains them. They teach that we are all descendants of Adam and Eve. At a certain point in time, sin entered the world, sowing division between God and humankind and between human beings themselves. At various moments in history God raised up prophets to guide people in the right way. However, the world has been riddled with wars and rumors of war since earliest recorded history. Christians and Muslims believe that God has instructed them to spread seeds of peace, justice, mercy, and compassion. However, war, injustice, cruelty, and indifference have for far too long come between the two descending families of Abraham and the world has suffered deeply for it. My hope is that my research and findings illuminate this large-scale problem and in so doing foster narrative empathy towards Muslims among Southern Baptists and Christians more generally. Though the relationship between Southern Baptists and Muslims is outright hostile at worst and tense at best, I have proposed concrete strategies of action that can significantly improve these relations. Of course, many of the concerns I raised and strategies I promoted can be applied to many of the Christian denominations in the United States and Europe.

In my introduction, I stated that the Southern Baptist denomination has a great missional opportunity—to learn about Islam, develop a more thorough appreciation for Islamic history and culture, and foster meaningful relationships with Muslims in a way that promotes trust and collaboration. Scarboro Missions, A Canadian Roman Catholic Mission Society, identifies five types of dialogue that can improve human relations: informational, confessional, experiential, relational, and practical. Informational—learn about your dialogue partner. Confessional—listen to their story and try to empathize. Experiential—discover their faith tradition and the meaning it brings to your dialogue partners life.

Relational—develop and foster friendship. And practical—collaborate with your dialogue partner in ways that promote the integral human development of people all over the world.[3] Taken together these five types of dialogue have strong potential to help Southern Baptist engage constructively with their Muslim counterparts. My research leads me to conclude that the biggest obstacle to this missional opportunity is a lack of personal encounter, followed closely by a lack of knowledge about Islam. Most leaders within the Southern Baptist denomination simply do not know any Muslims. This lack of narrative allows for a biased perception and understanding of Islam to flourish. My research on narrative empathy shows that it can alter one's perception and indeed improve one's ability to not only sympathize but empathize with others, especially those that have a distinct culture and religion from ours and live in a region of the world that is distant from our own.[4] Hence, I argue that a better understanding of Islamic history, combined with personal encounters with Muslims, can significantly improve relations between Southern Baptists and Muslims. The interviews I conducted with Southern Baptist leaders revealed that leaders who have relations with Muslims, even if minimal, significantly improved their perception of Islam, and are less likely to engage in negative rhetoric towards Islam and Muslims.

In chapter 2, I demonstrated that Muslim Americans are a diverse group of people. There is no single person or group that speaks for all Muslims in the United States. It is estimated that there are 3.5 million Muslims living in the United States. These Muslims vary in ethnicity, culture, and political views, and they adhere to different schools of thought in Islam. Four in ten Muslim Americans are white.[5] Twenty-six percent of Muslim Americans are currently enrolled in college compared to only thirteen percent of non-Muslims and most Muslims live in metropolitan cities. Moreover, Muslim Americans tend to vote Democrat, in large part due to the immigration policies and negative rhetoric used towards them by the Republican Party. Within the Southern Baptist denomination, I reveal that there is a systemic bias against Islam, especially among those leaders who do not know any Muslims. Leaders who have personal encounters with Muslims speak more favorably of Islam, though they disagree with many of their doctrinal beliefs. The majority of the denominational leaders I interviewed said they are concerned about the increase

3. Scarboro Missions, "Principles and Guidelines."
4. Keen, *Empathy and the Novel*, 88–89.
5. Pew Research Center, "Demographic Portrait of Muslim Americans."

in the Muslim population in the United States. They believe many of the cultural norms will be challenged. Furthermore, they fear Islam will be attractive to many young Americans who are not grounded in a Biblical worldview—more specifically, *their* Biblical worldview.

In chapter 3, I built upon my in-depth qualitative interviews with pastors and revealed that many Southern Baptists are experiencing emotions of anger, fear, and insecurity. I observed that these three emotions were at the root of much of the negative rhetoric being used in the denomination towards Islam—negative rhetoric that significantly increased after 9/11. Furthermore, these negative emotions, combined with a lack of encounter, allowed space for misperceptions and misunderstandings to grow in the denomination. For example, many Southern Baptists have an unsubstantiated fear of Sharia usurping US constitutional law. Moreover, there is a profound and yet completely ungrounded fear of Muslims engaging in a bloody religious battle against Jews, Christians, and the non-religious in the United States. Yet, most violent crimes in the United States are carried out by non-Muslim white and black males. In fact, Muslims are often the target of religious hate crimes in America. I observed that the emotions of anger, fear, and insecurity in the Southern Baptist denomination are fueled by biased news coverage, an absence of personal encounter with Muslims, a shortage of in-depth knowledge about Islam, and the intention of some leaders to create an "us against them" mentality in order to contain and perhaps increase church attendance within their congregation. Furthermore, I show that Muslims in the Middle East as well as those Muslims who immigrated to the United States overwhelmingly reject many of the teachings and actions of Islamic militant groups. Moreover, opinion polls have shown that Muslims rank as the most likely to say that violence targeting civilians is never justified—ranking higher, incidentally, than Protestants and Catholics. My findings suggest that most Muslims, like most Christians, seek peace with neighbors and justice for all. The belief that a one-world Muslim organization is actively seeking to rid the United States of democracy and its religious traditions is not grounded in any scholarly work. While Muslims believe that Islam is the one true faith, the Qur'an embraces religious diversity as evidenced in chapter 49 and verse 13: "O humanity! Indeed, We created you from a male and female, and made you into peoples and tribes so that you may get to know one another. Surely the most noble of you in the sight of Allah is the most righteous among you. Allah is truly All-knowing, All-Aware. Furthermore, 94 percent of terrorist attacks carried out in the United States between 1980 and 2005 were by non-Muslims.[6] As more Southern Baptist develop personal narratives with Muslims, new, more positive perceptions will be fostered, friendships will be cultivated, interreligious dialogue will be more effective, and overall relationships between the two religious groups will significantly improve.

In chapter 4, I returned to the sources of Islam (the Qur'an and the Sunnah of the Prophet) in order to develop a better understanding of the Prophet Muhammad and his lived spirituality. The end result revealed that Muhammad was a deeply spiritual individual who sought to live a virtuous life. Early on he devoted himself to praying and fasting in hopes of discovering deeper meaning to life and a better understanding of his belief in one God—creator, sustainer, and judge of all human beings. At the age of 40, Muhammad believed he received a direct revelation from God through the angel Gabriel. The words he received from the angel, he recited and his closest companions recorded them in the Qur'an. The revelations he would receive sealed his belief in monotheism, leading him to teach the oneness of God. Moreover, via jihad he exposed and curtailed injustices to humanity, promoted peaceful interactions between neighboring communities, encouraged interreligious dialogue and cooperation between Jews, Christians, and Muslims, and constructed a political system that would eventually unite the Arab tribes into a Muslim community. The early Muslim community has a respect for Jews and Christians and sought positive relations. With time however, these relationships suffered due to tribal animosities and broken trust, for example, the Battle of the Ditch.[7] Today the majority of Muslims seek peace, justice, and human solidarity, just like their Jewish and Christian counterparts. Muslims are not a people for Southern Baptists to fear and speak negatively about; instead they are a people to know, love, respect, and work together with to promote shared values and beliefs. Many of these shared values and beliefs can be traced back to Abraham and his relationship with his first two sons, Ishmael and Isaac.

Finally, in chapter 5, I set forth reasons why Southern Baptists should make Muslims the focus of their mission. The Muslim population is growing, both within the United States and in the broader world. More than 24 percent of the world's population is Muslim. In some Muslim-majority countries, it is extremely difficult for Southern

---

6. Information can be found at www.fbi.gov.
7. Brown, *Muhammad*, 43.

Baptist missionaries to engage in interreligious dialogue. While in most Muslim-majority countries it is forbidden to openly evangelize, informational, confessional, experiential, relational, and practical methods of dialogue are often welcomed. Certain challenges related to travel can hinder this much needed dialogue from taking place. But in the United States, Southern Baptists have many opportunities and resources to promote interreligious dialogue with Muslims and make significant progress in making their understanding of Jesus and the Bible known to Muslims. Because of this great opportunity, I spoke to some of the shared values and beliefs enjoyed between Southern Baptists and Muslims. These commonalities can spur meaningful dialogue and mutual partnerships that both religions believe are important for the well-being of humanity. Additionally, I offered concrete ways for Southern Baptists to foster long-lasting relationships with Muslims. The strategies of dialogue included cultural immersion trips, workshops and seminars for the purpose of gaining knowledge and understanding of the history of Islam, collaborative interaction, and personal encounters. These dialogue strategies will create and sustain a narrative empathy for Muslims. A side-effect is that the Muslims encountered will also form a narrative empathy towards Southern Baptists. Indeed, this pivot in missional thinking requires a reflective conversation to take place—a conversation that will allow Southern Baptists to eagerly welcome and foster generational friendships with Muslim Americans. Taken in their entirety, my findings in this book offer an understanding of why there is such negative rhetoric being used in the Southern Baptist denomination. They shed light on why many Baptist leaders feel the need to defame the Prophet Muhammad. I employed the four tasks of practical theological interpretation by Osmer in order to explain these patterns and dynamics and, moreover, to better understand the missional dilemma within the denomination as it relates to its biased perception and understanding of Islam. As Southern Baptist leaders contemplate and hopefully embark upon this missional journey, I think some of the most encouraging words for such an endeavor come from Christ—words that the writer of Matthew's gospel say that Jesus spoke to His disciples prior to His earthly departure: "And remember, I am with you always, to the end of the age."[8] I conclude my book with the wise words of Fred McFeely Rogers who said, "As different as we are from one another, as unique as each

---

8. Matthew 28:20b (HCSB).

one of is, we are much more the same than we are different. That may be the most essential message of all, as we help our children grow toward being caring, compassionate, and charitable adults."[9]

---

[9]. Quote can be found at www.misterrogers.org.

Appendix 1

"I think Islam hates us": A Timeline of Trump's comments about Islam and Muslims[1]

March 30, 2011

For years, Trump publicly questioned then-President Barack Obama's religious beliefs and place of birth. As he debated running for president in the 2012 election, Trump said in a radio interview: *"He doesn't have a birth certificate, or if he does, there's something on that certificate that is very bad for him. Now, somebody told me—and I have no idea if this is bad for him or not, but perhaps it would be—that where it says 'religion,' it might have 'Muslim.' And if you're a Muslim, you don't change your religion, by the way."* (Obama is a Christian, and state records show he was born in Hawaii.)

Sept. 17, 2015

At a campaign town hall in New Hampshire, a man in the audience shouted out: "We have a problem in this country; it's called Muslims. We know our current president is one." The man mentioned Muslim "training camps" and asked: "When can we get rid of them?" Trump responded: "We're going to be looking at a lot of different things. *You know, a lot of people are saying that, and a lot of people are saying that bad things are happening out there.* We're going to be looking at that and plenty of other things."

---

1. Johnson and Hauslohner, "'I Think Islam Hates Us.'"

Sept. 30, 2015

At a New Hampshire rally, Trump pledged to kick all Syrian refugees—most of whom are Muslim—out of the country, as they might be a secret army. "They could be ISIS, I don't know. This could be one of the great tactical ploys of all time. A 200,000-man army, maybe," he said. In an interview that aired later, Trump said: "This could make the Trojan horse look like peanuts."

Oct. 21, 2015

On Fox Business, Trump says he would *"certainly look at" the idea of closing mosques in the United States.*

Nov. 20, 2015

In comments to Yahoo and NBC News, *Trump seemed open to the idea of creating a database of all Muslims* in the United States. Later, he and his aides would not rule out the idea.

Nov. 21, 2015

At a rally in Alabama, Trump said that on Sept. 11 he "watched when the World Trade Center came tumbling down. *And I watched in Jersey City, N.J., where thousands and thousands of people were cheering as that building was coming down."*

Nov. 30, 2015

On MSNBC, a reporter asked Trump if he thinks Islam is an inherently peaceful religion that's been perverted by a small percentage of followers or if it is an inherently violent religion. Trump responded: "Well, all I can say . . . there's something going on. You know, there's something definitely going on. I don't know that that question can be answered." He also said: "We are not loved by many Muslims."

Dec. 3, 2015

The morning after Syed Rizwan Farook and Tashfeen Malik killed 14 people in San Bernardino, Calif., Trump called into Fox News and said: *"The other thing with the terrorists is you have to take out their families, when you get these terrorists, you have to take out their families."* (Killing the relatives of suspected terrorists is forbidden by international law.) Later, in a speech to the Republican Jewish Coalition, Trump criticized Obama for not using the phrase "radical Islamic terrorism" and commented: "There's something going on with him that we don't know about."

Dec. 6, 2015

On CBS News, Trump said: *"If you have people coming out of mosques with hatred and death in their eyes and on their minds, we're going to have to do something."* Trump also said he didn't believe the sister of one of the San Bernardino shooters who said she was crestfallen for the victims, saying: "I would go after a lot of people, and I would find out whether or not they knew. I would be able to find out, because I don't believe the sister."

Dec. 7, 2015

Trump's campaign issued a statement saying: *"Donald J. Trump is calling for a total and complete shutdown of Muslims entering the United States until our country's representatives can figure out what is going on."* Trump read this statement aloud at a rally in South Carolina.

Dec. 8, 2015

On CNN, *Trump quoted a widely debunked poll by an anti-Islam activist organization that claimed that a quarter of the Muslims living in the United States agreed that violence against Americans is justified as part of the global jihad.* "We have people out there that want to do great destruction to our country, whether it's 25 percent or 10 percent or 5 percent, it's too much," Trump said.

Dec. 13, 2015

On Fox News, Trump was asked if his ban would apply to a Canadian businessman who is a Muslim. Trump responded: *"There's a sickness. They're sick people. There's a sickness going on. There's a group of people that is very sick."*

Jan. 12, 2016

At a rally in Iowa, Trump shared his suspicions about Syrian refugees and then read the lyrics to Al Wilson's 1968 song *"The Snake,"* the story of a *"tender woman"* who nursed a sickly snake back to health but then was attacked by the snake. Trump often read these lyrics at rallies.

Feb. 3, 2016

Trump criticized Obama for visiting a mosque in Baltimore and said on Fox News: *"Maybe he feels comfortable there. . . . There are a lot of places he can go, and he chose a mosque."* (It was Obama's first visit to a mosque during his presidency, and it was made in an effort to encourage religious tolerance in light of growing anti-Muslim sentiment.)

Feb. 20, 2016

After Obama skipped the funeral of Supreme Court Justice Antonin Scalia, Trump tweeted: "I wonder if President Obama would have attended the funeral of Justice Scalia if it were held in a Mosque? Very sad that he did not go!" (Obama did pay his respects when Scalia's body lay in repose in the Supreme Court.) That night at a rally in South Carolina, Trump told an apocryphal tale that he would return to repeatedly about U.S. Gen. John J. Pershing fighting Muslim insurgents in the Philippines in the early 1900s and killing a large group of insurgents with bullets dipped in pigs' blood.

March 9, 2016

On CNN, Trump said: *"I think Islam hates us. There's something there that—there's a tremendous hatred there. There's a tremendous hatred. We have to get to the bottom of it. There's an unbelievable hatred of us."*

March 22, 2016

Soon after three suicide bombings in Brussels tied to a group of French and Belgian Muslims, Trump told Fox Business: *"We're having problems with the Muslims, and we're having problems with Muslims coming into the country."* Trump called for surveillance of mosques in the United States, saying: "You have to deal with the mosques, whether we like it or not, I mean, you know, these attacks aren't coming out of—they're not done by Swedish people."

On NBC News, Trump added: *"This all happened because, frankly, there's no assimilation. They are not assimilating. . . . They want to go by sharia law. They want sharia law. They don't want the laws that we have. They want sharia law."*

March 23, 2016

In an interview with Bloomberg TV, Trump said that Muslims "have to respect us. *They do not respect us at all.* And frankly, they don't respect a lot of the things that are happening throughout not only our country, but they don't respect other things."

March 29, 2016

During a town hall in Wisconsin, CNN's Anderson Cooper asked Trump: "Do you trust Muslims in America?" Trump responded: "Do I what?" Cooper again asked: "Trust Muslims in America?" Trump responded: "Many of them I do. Many of them I do, and some, I guess, we don't. Some, I guess, we don't. We have a problem, and we can try and be very politically correct and pretend we don't have a problem, but, Anderson, *we have a major, major problem. This is, in a sense, this is a war."*

May 20, 2016

On Fox News, Trump said this of Muslims: *"They're going to have to turn in the people that are bombing the planes. And they know who the people are. And we're not going to find the people by just continuing to be so nice and so soft."*

June 13, 2016

The day after the mass shooting at a gay nightclub in Orlando, Trump declared in a speech in New Hampshire that *"radical Islam is anti-woman, anti-gay and anti-American."* He criticized his Democratic rival, Hillary Clinton, for refusing to use the term "radical Islam" and for speaking positively of Islam. *"Hillary Clinton's catastrophic immigration plan will bring vastly more radical Islamic immigration into this country, threatening not only our society but our entire way of life. When it comes to radical Islamic terrorism, ignorance is not bliss. It's deadly—totally deadly,"* Trump said. Later he added: "I want every American to succeed, including Muslims—but the Muslims have to work with us. They have to work with us. They know what's going on."

June 15, 2016

On Fox News, Trump said this of Muslims who immigrate to the United States: "Assimilation has been very hard. It's almost—I won't say nonexistent, but it gets to be pretty close. And I'm talking about second and third generation. *They come—they don't—for some reason, there's no real assimilation."*

July 21, 2016

In accepting the Republican Party's presidential nomination, Trump focused heavily on "brutal Islamic terrorism" and promised: *"I will do everything in my power to protect our LGBTQ citizens from the violence and oppression of a hateful foreign ideology."*

July 24, 2016

On NBC News, Trump defended his proposal for a Muslim ban, despite some of his aides insisting he had rolled it back. "People were so upset when I used the word Muslim. 'Oh, you can't use the word Muslim,'" Trump said. ". . . But just remember this: *Our Constitution is great, but it doesn't necessarily give us the right to commit suicide, okay? Now, we have a religious—you know, everybody wants to be protected. And that's great. And that's the wonderful part of our Constitution. I view it differently. Why are we committing suicide? Why are we doing that?*"

Aug. 11, 2016

At a meeting of evangelical leaders in Orlando, Trump said: "If you were a Christian in Syria, it was virtually impossible to come into the United States. If you were a Muslim from Syria, it was one of the easier countries to be able to find your way into the United States. Think of that. Just think of what that means."

Aug. 18, 2016

During a rally in North Carolina, Trump said that *"all applicants for immigration will be vetted for ties to radical ideology, and we will screen out anyone who doesn't share our values and love our people."*

Sept. 19, 2016

At a rally in Florida, Trump reacted to explosions over the weekend in New York and New Jersey and said: "There have been Islamic terrorist attacks in Minnesota and New York City and in New Jersey. These attacks and many others were made possible because of our extremely open immigration system, which fails to properly vet and screen the individuals and families coming into our country. Got to be careful."

Jan. 27, 2017

Within a week of becoming president, Trump signed an executive order blocking Syrian refugees and banning citizens of seven predominantly Muslim countries from entering the United States for 90 days. This order goes into effect immediately, prompting mass chaos at airports, protests and legal challenges. Rudolph W. Giuliani, a close adviser to the president, later said on Fox News: "So when [Trump] first announced it, he said, 'Muslim ban.' He called me up. He said, 'Put a commission together. Show me the right way to do it legally.'"

Feb. 28, 2017

Despite urging from some of his Cabinet members, *Trump continues to use the term "radical Islamic terrorism,"* including in a speech to a joint session of Congress.

March 6, 2017

Trump issues a new travel ban for citizens from six majority-Muslim countries, which is also challenged in the courts.

April 29, 2017

At a rally celebrating his 100th day in office, Trump once again dramatically read "The Snake."

May 17, 2017

At a commencement ceremony, Trump previewed his upcoming overseas trip and said: "I'll speak with Muslim leaders and challenge them to fight hatred and extremism and embrace a peaceful future for their faith. And they're looking very much forward to hearing what we, as your representative, we have to say. We have to stop radical Islamic terrorism."

Appendix 2

The Baptist Faith and Message 2000

Article I.

The Scriptures

The Holy Bible was written by men divinely inspired and is God's revelation of Himself to man. It is a perfect treasure of divine instruction. It has God for its author, salvation for its end, and truth, without any mixture of error, for its matter. Therefore, all Scripture is totally true and trustworthy. It reveals the principles by which God judges us, and therefore is, and will remain to the end of the world, the true center of Christian union, and the supreme standard by which all human conduct, creeds, and religious opinions should be tried. All Scripture is a testimony to Christ, who is Himself the focus of divine revelation.

Article II.

God

There is one and only one living and true God. He is an intelligent, spiritual, and personal Being, the Creator, Redeemer, Preserver, and Ruler of the universe. God is infinite in holiness and all other perfections. God is all powerful and all knowing; and His perfect knowledge extends to all things, past, present, and future, including the future decisions of His free creatures. To Him we owe the highest love, reverence, and obedience. The eternal triune God reveals Himself to us as Father, Son, and Holy Spirit, with distinct personal attributes, but without division of nature, essence, or being.

A. God the Father

God as Father reigns with providential care over His universe, His creatures, and the flow of the stream of human history according to the purposes of His grace. He is all-powerful, all knowing, all loving, and all wise. God is Father in truth to those who become children of God through faith in Jesus Christ. He is fatherly in His attitude toward all men.

B. God the Son

Christ is the eternal Son of God. In His incarnation as Jesus Christ He was conceived of the Holy Spirit and born of the virgin Mary. Jesus perfectly revealed and did the will of God, taking upon Himself human nature with its demands and necessities and identifying Himself completely with mankind yet without sin. He honored the divine law by His personal obedience, and in His substitutionary death on the cross He made provision for the redemption of men from sin. He was raised from the dead with a glorified body and appeared to His disciples as the person who was with them before His crucifixion. He ascended into heaven and is now exalted at the right hand of God where He is the One Mediator, fully God, fully man, in whose Person is effected the reconciliation between God and man. He will return in power and glory to judge the world and to consummate His redemptive mission. He now dwells in all believers as the living and ever present Lord.

C. God the Holy Spirit

The Holy Spirit is the Spirit of God, fully divine. He inspired holy men of old to write the Scriptures. Through illumination He enables men to understand truth. He exalts Christ. He convicts men of sin, of righteousness, and of judgment. He calls men to the Saviour, and effects regeneration. At the moment of regeneration He baptizes every believer into the Body of Christ. He cultivates Christian character, comforts believers, and bestows the spiritual gifts by which they serve God through His church.

He seals the believer unto the day of final redemption. His presence in the Christian is the guarantee that God will bring the believer into the fullness of the stature of Christ. He enlightens and empowers the believer and the church in worship, evangelism, and service.

Article III.

Man

Man is the special creation of God, made in His own image. He created them male and female as the crowning work of His creation. The gift of gender is thus part of the goodness of God's creation. In the beginning man was innocent of sin and was endowed by his Creator with freedom of choice. By his free choice man sinned against God and brought sin into the human race. Through the temptation of Satan man transgressed the command of God, and fell from his original innocence whereby his posterity inherit a nature and an environment inclined toward sin. Therefore, as soon as they are capable of moral action, they become transgressors and are under condemnation. Only the grace of God can bring man into His holy fellowship and enable man to fulfill the creative purpose of God. The sacredness of human personality is evident in that God created man in His own image, and in that Christ died for man; therefore, every person of every race possesses full dignity and is worthy of respect and Christian love.

Article IV.

Salvation

Salvation involves the redemption of the whole man, and is offered freely to all who accept Jesus Christ as Lord and Saviour, who by His own blood obtained eternal redemption for the believer. In its broadest sense salvation includes regeneration, justification, sanctification, and glorification. There is no salvation apart from personal faith in Jesus Christ as Lord.
    A. Regeneration, or the new birth, is a work of God's grace whereby believers become new creatures in Christ Jesus. It is a change of heart wrought by the Holy Spirit through conviction of sin, to which the sinner responds in repentance toward God and faith in the Lord Jesus Christ. Repentance and faith are inseparable experiences of

grace. Repentance is a genuine turning from sin toward God. Faith is the acceptance of Jesus Christ and commitment of the entire personality to Him as Lord and Saviour.

B. Justification is God's gracious and full acquittal upon principles of His righteousness of all sinners who repent and believe in Christ. Justification brings the believer unto a relationship of peace and favor with God.

C. Sanctification is the experience, beginning in regeneration, by which the believer is set apart to God's purposes, and is enabled to progress toward moral and spiritual maturity through the presence and power of the Holy Spirit dwelling in him. Growth in grace should continue throughout the regenerate person's life.

Glorification is the culmination of salvation and is the final blessed and abiding state of the redeemed.

Article V.

God's Purpose of Grace

Election is the gracious purpose of God, according to which He regenerates, justifies, sanctifies, and glorifies sinners. It is consistent with the free agency of man, and comprehends all the means in connection with the end. It is the glorious display of God's sovereign goodness, and is infinitely wise, holy, and unchangeable. It excludes boasting and promotes humility.

All true believers endure to the end. Those whom God has accepted in Christ, and sanctified by His Spirit, will never fall away from the state of grace, but shall persevere to the end. Believers may fall into sin through neglect and temptation, whereby they grieve the Spirit, impair their graces and comforts, and bring reproach on the cause of Christ and temporal judgments on themselves; yet they shall be kept by the power of God through faith unto salvation.

Article VI.

The Church

A New Testament church of the Lord Jesus Christ is an autonomous local congregation of baptized believers, associated by covenant in the faith and fellowship of the gospel; observing the two ordinances of Christ, governed by His laws, exercising the gifts, rights, and privileges invested in them by His Word, and seeking to extend the gospel to the ends of the earth. Each congregation operates under the Lordship of Christ through democratic processes. In such a congregation each member is responsible and accountable to Christ as Lord. Its scriptural officers are pastors and deacons. While both men and women are gifted for service in the church, the office of pastor is limited to men as qualified by Scripture.

The New Testament speaks also of the church as the Body of Christ which includes all of the redeemed of all the ages, believers from every tribe, and tongue, and people, and nation.

Article VII.

Baptism and the Lord's Supper

Christian baptism is the immersion of a believer in water in the name of the Father, the Son, and the Holy Spirit. It is an act of obedience symbolizing the believer's faith in a crucified, buried, and risen Saviour, the believer's death to sin, the burial of the old life, and the resurrection to walk in newness of life in Christ Jesus. It is a testimony to his faith in the final resurrection of the dead. Being a church ordinance, it is prerequisite to the privileges of church membership and to the Lord's Supper.

The Lord's Supper is a symbolic act of obedience whereby members of the church, through partaking of the bread and the fruit of the vine, memorialize the death of the Redeemer and anticipate His second coming.

Article VIII.

The Lord's Day

The first day of the week is the Lord's Day. It is a Christian institution for regular observance. It commemorates the resurrection of Christ from the dead and should include exercises of worship and spiritual devotion, both public and private. Activities on the Lord's Day should be commensurate with the Christian's conscience under the Lordship of Jesus Christ.

Article IX.

The Kingdom

The Kingdom of God includes both His general sovereignty over the universe and His particular kingship over men who willfully acknowledge Him as King. Particularly the Kingdom is the realm of salvation into which men enter by trustful, childlike commitment to Jesus Christ. Christians ought to pray and to labor that the Kingdom may come and God's will be done on earth. The full consummation of the Kingdom awaits the return of Jesus Christ and the end of this age.

Article X.

Last Things

God, in His own time and in His own way, will bring the world to its appropriate end. According to His promise, Jesus Christ will return personally and visibly in glory to the earth; the dead will be raised; and Christ will judge all men in righteousness. The unrighteous will be consigned to Hell, the place of everlasting punishment. The righteous in their resurrected and glorified bodies will receive their reward and will dwell forever in Heaven with the Lord.

Article XI.

Evangelism and Missions

It is the duty and privilege of every follower of Christ and of every church of the Lord Jesus Christ to endeavor to make disciples of all nations. The new birth of man's spirit by God's Holy Spirit means the birth of love for others. Missionary effort on the part of all rests thus upon a spiritual necessity of the regenerate life, and is expressly and repeatedly commanded in the teachings of Christ. The Lord Jesus Christ has commanded the preaching of the gospel to all nations. It is the duty of every child of God to seek constantly to win the lost to Christ by verbal witness undergirded by a Christian lifestyle, and by other methods in harmony with the gospel of Christ.

Article XII.

Education

Christianity is the faith of enlightenment and intelligence. In Jesus Christ abide all the treasures of wisdom and knowledge. All sound learning is, therefore, a part of our Christian heritage. The new birth opens all human faculties and creates a thirst for knowledge. Moreover, the cause of education in the Kingdom of Christ is co-ordinate with the causes of missions and general benevolence, and should receive along with these the liberal support of the churches. An adequate system of Christian education is necessary to a complete spiritual program for Christ's people.

In Christian education there should be a proper balance between academic freedom and academic responsibility. Freedom in any orderly relationship of human life is always limited and never absolute. The freedom of a teacher in a Christian school, college, or seminary is limited by the pre-eminence of Jesus Christ, by the authoritative nature of the Scriptures, and by the distinct purpose for which the school exists

Article XIII.

Stewardship

God is the source of all blessings, temporal and spiritual; all that we have and are we owe to Him. Christians have a spiritual debtorship to the whole world, a holy trusteeship in the gospel, and a binding stewardship in their possessions. They are therefore under obligation to serve Him with their time, talents, and material possessions; and should recognize all these as entrusted to them to use for the glory of God and for helping others. According to the Scriptures, Christians should contribute of their means cheerfully, regularly, systematically, proportionately, and liberally for the advancement of the Redeemer's cause on earth.

Article XIV.

Cooperation

Christ's people should, as occasion requires, organize such associations and conventions as may best secure cooperation for the great objects of the Kingdom of God. Such organizations have no authority over one another or over the churches. They are voluntary and advisory bodies designed to elicit, combine, and direct the energies of our people in the most effective manner. Members of New

Testament churches should cooperate with one another in carrying forward the missionary, educational, and benevolent ministries for the extension of Christ's Kingdom. Christian unity in the New Testament sense is spiritual harmony and voluntary cooperation for common ends by various groups of Christ's people. Cooperation is desirable between the various Christian denominations, when the end to be attained is itself justified, and when such cooperation involves no violation of conscience or compromise of loyalty to Christ and His Word as revealed in the New Testament.

Article XV.

The Christian and the Social Order

All Christians are under obligation to seek to make the will of Christ supreme in our own lives and in human society. Means and methods used for the improvement of society and the establishment of righteousness among men can be truly and permanently helpful only when they are rooted in the regeneration of the individual by the saving grace of God in Jesus Christ. In the spirit of Christ, Christians should oppose racism, every form of greed, selfishness, and vice, and all forms of sexual immorality, including adultery, homosexuality, and pornography. We should work to provide for the orphaned, the needy, the abused, the aged, the helpless, and the sick. We should speak on behalf of the unborn and contend for the sanctity of all human life from conception to natural death. Every Christian should seek to bring industry, government, and society as a whole under the sway of the principles of righteousness, truth, and brotherly love. In order to promote these ends Christians should be ready to work with all men of good will in any good cause, always being careful to act in the spirit of love without compromising their loyalty to Christ and His truth.

Article XVI.

Peace and War

It is the duty of Christians to seek peace with all men on principles of righteousness. In accordance with the spirit and teachings of Christ they should do all in their power to put an end to war.

The true remedy for the war spirit is the gospel of our Lord. The supreme need of the world is the acceptance of His teachings in all the affairs of men and nations, and the practical application of His law of love. Christian people throughout the world should pray for the reign of the Prince of Peace.

Article XVII.

Religious Liberty

God alone is Lord of the conscience, and He has left it free from the doctrines and commandments of men which are contrary to His Word or not contained in it. Church and state should be separate. The state owes to every church protection and full freedom in the pursuit of its spiritual ends. In providing for such freedom no ecclesiastical group or denomination should be favored by the state more than others. Civil government being ordained of God, it is the duty of Christians to render loyal obedience thereto in all things not contrary to the revealed will of God. The church should not resort to the civil power to carry on its work. The gospel of Christ contemplates spiritual means alone for the pursuit of its ends. The state has no right to impose penalties for religious opinions of any kind. The state has no right to impose taxes for the support of any form of religion. A free church in a free state is the Christian ideal, and this implies the right of free and unhindered access to God on the part of all men, and the right to form and propagate opinions in the sphere of religion without interference by the civil power

Article XVIII.

The Family

God has ordained the family as the foundational institution of human society. It is composed of persons related to one another by marriage, blood, or adoption.

Marriage is the uniting of one man and one woman in covenant commitment for a lifetime. It is God's unique gift to reveal the union between Christ and His church and to provide for the man and the woman in marriage the framework for intimate companionship, the channel of sexual expression according to biblical standards, and the means for procreation of the human race.

The husband and wife are of equal worth before God, since both are created in God's image. The marriage relationship models the way God relates to His people. A husband is to love his wife as Christ loved the church. He has the God-given responsibility to provide for, to protect, and to lead his family. A wife is to submit herself graciously to the servant leadership of her husband even as the church willingly submits to the headship of Christ. She, being in the image of God as is her husband and thus equal to him, has the God-given responsibility to respect her husband and to serve as his helper in managing the household and nurturing the next generation.

Children, from the moment of conception, are a blessing and heritage from the Lord. Parents are to demonstrate to their children God's pattern for marriage. Parents are to teach their children spiritual and moral values and to lead them, through consistent lifestyle example and loving discipline, to make choices based on biblical truth. Children are to honor and obey their parents.

Appendix 3

Executive Summary of Open Letter to al-Baghdadi

(Source: *HuffPost*, September 25, 2014, https://www.huffingtonpost.com/2014/09/24/muslim-scholars-islamic-state_n_5878038.html)

1. It is forbidden in Islam to issue fatwas without all the necessary learning requirements. Even then fatwas must follow Islamic legal theory as defined in the Classical texts. It is also forbidden to cite a portion of a verse from the Qur'an—or part of a verse—to derive a ruling without looking at everything that the Qur'an and Hadith teach related to that matter. In other words, there are strict subjective and objective prerequisites for fatwas, and one cannot "cherry-pick" Qur'anic verses for legal arguments without considering the entire Qur'an and Hadith.

2. It is forbidden in Islam to issue legal rulings about anything without mastery of the Arabic language.

3. It is forbidden in Islam to oversimplify Shari'ah matters and ignore established Islamic sciences.

4. It is permissible in Islam [for scholars] to differ on any matter, except those fundamentals of religion that all Muslims must know.

5. It is forbidden in Islam to ignore the reality of contemporary times when deriving legal rulings.

6. It is forbidden in Islam to kill the innocent.

7. It is forbidden in Islam to kill emissaries, ambassadors, and diplomats; hence it is forbidden to kill journalists and aid workers.

8. Jihad in Islam is defensive war. It is not permissible without the right cause, the right purpose and without the right rules of conduct.
9. It is forbidden in Islam to declare people non-Muslim unless he (or she) openly declares disbelief.
10. It is forbidden in Islam to harm or mistreat—in any way—Christians or any 'People of the Scripture'.
11. It is obligatory to consider Yazidis as People of the Scripture.
12. The re-introduction of slavery is forbidden in Islam. It was abolished by universal consensus.
13. It is forbidden in Islam to force people to convert.
14. It is forbidden in Islam to deny women their rights.
15. It is forbidden in Islam to deny children their rights.
16. It is forbidden in Islam to enact legal punishments (hudud) without following the correct procedures that ensure justice and mercy.
17. It is forbidden in Islam to torture people.
18. It is forbidden in Islam to disfigure the dead.
19. It is forbidden in Islam to attribute evil acts to God.
20. It is forbidden in Islam to destroy the graves and shrines of Prophets and Companions.
21. Armed insurrection is forbidden in Islam for any reason other than clear disbelief by the ruler and not allowing people to pray.
22. It is forbidden in Islam to declare a caliphate without consensus from all Muslims.
23. Loyalty to one's nation is permissible in Islam.
24. After the death of the Prophet, Islam does not require anyone to emigrate anywhere.

Bibliography

Abdel Haleem, M. A. S., trans. *The Qur'an: A New Translation*. Oxford: Oxford University Press, 2004.
Abdullah II. "The Amman Message." November 2004. https://ammanmessage.com.
———. "A Common Word." September 2007. https://www.acommonword.com.
Abou El Fadl, Khaled. "Conceptualizing Shari'a in the Modern State." *Villanova Law Review* 56, no. 5 (2012) 803–17.
———. *Speaking in God's Name: Islamic Law, Authority, and Women*. Oxford: Oxford University Press, 2001.
Afsaruddin, Asma. *Jihad: What Everyone Needs to Know*. Oxford: Oxford University Press, 2022.
———. "Views of Jihad throughout History." *Wiley Online Library*. 2006. https://onlinelibrary.wiley.com/doi/10.1111/j.1749-8171.2006.00015.x.
Ahmed, Shahab. *What Is Islam? The Importance of Being Islamic*. Princeton, NJ: Princeton University Press, 2016.
Alexander, Scott. "The Prophet Muhammad and the Qur'an." Classroom lecture, Catholic Theological Union, Chicago, IL, December 2014.
Ali, Amir. "What Is Jihad? Islamic Holy War? Muslims Killing Jews and Christians?" December 2014. http://www.aboutjihad.com/jihad/jihad_explained.php.
Allen, Chris. *Islamophobia*. London: Ashgate, 2010.
Alnatour, Omar. "Muslims Are Not Terrorists: A Factual Look at Terrorism and Islam." *Huffington Post*, December 9, 2016. https://www.huffpost.com/entry/muslims-are-not-terrorist_b_8718000.
Altemeyer, B. *The Authoritarians*. Winnipeg: University of Manitoba Press, 2006.
———. *Right-Wing Authoritarianism*. Winnipeg: University of Manitoba Press, 1981.
Amayreh, Khalid. "Against Israel against God." *Aljazeera*, Sept. 2, 2003. https://www.aljazeera.com/news/2003/9/2/against-israel-against-god.
American Psychological Association. "Anger." http://www.apa.org/topics/anger/index.aspx.
American Psychological Association. "The Social Psychology of Religion, Prejudice and Intergroup Processes." 2015. http://www.apa.org/news/press/releases/2015/05/religion-prejudice.aspx.

Amstutz, Mark R. *Evangelicals and American Foreign Policy*. New York: Oxford University Press, 2014.
Andringa, Els, et al. "Point of View and Viewer Empathy in Film." In *New Perspectives on Narrative Perspective*, edited by Willie van Peer and Seymour Chatman, 83–99. Albany: State University of New York Press, 2001.
Ankerberg, John, and John Weldon. *The Facts on Islam*. Eugene, OR: Harvest House, 2008.
Antepli, Abdullah. "The Last Sermon of the Prophet Muhammad." *Huffington Post*, April 4, 2012. https://www.huffingtonpost.com/imam-abdullah-antepli/the-last-sermon-of- prophe_b_1252185.html.
Arab News. "How the Prophet Brought About Positive Change." October 4, 2013. http://www.arabnews.com/news/466639.
Aydin, Cemil. *The Idea of the Muslim World: A Global Intellectual History*. Cambridge, MA: Harvard University Press, 2017.
Azami, M. M. *Studies in Hadith Methodology and Literature*. Oak Brook, IL: American Trust, 1992.
Baptist Faith and Message. http://www.sbc.net/bfm2000/bfm2000.asp.
Barker, Gregory A., and Stephen E. Gregg. *Jesus beyond Christianity: The Classic Texts*. Oxford: Oxford University Press, 2010.
Bassiouni, M. Cherif. *The Shari'a and Islamic Criminal Justice in Time of War and Peace*. New York: Cambridge University Press, 2014.
Beinart, Peter. "Lindsey Graham's 'Religious War.'" *The Atlantic*, November 2, 2017. https://www.theatlantic.com/politics/archive/2017/11/terrorist-attack-lindsey-graham/544763/.
Beutel, Alejandro J. "Data on Post-9/11 Terrorism in the United States." Washington, DC: Muslim Public Affairs Council, 2011. http://www.mpac.org/assets/docs/publications/MPAC-Post-911-Terrorism-Data.pdf.
bin Ladin, Usama. "Full Transcript of bin Ladin's Speech." https://www.aljazeera.com/archive/2004/11/200849163336457223.html.
Blakeslee, Sandra. "Cells That Read Minds." *New York Times*, January 10, 2006, F1, F4.
Brenner, Mara. "Phases of Reflective Conversation." *Center for Development and Disability*. 2011. http://cdd.unm.edu/ecln/HVT/common/pdfs/2011_2.pdf.
Brown, Jonathan A. C. *Muhammad: A Very Short Introduction*. Oxford: Oxford University Press, 2011.
Center for Security Policy. "Shariah Law and American State Courts: An Assessment of State Appellate Court Cases." August 30, 2012. https://www.centerforsecuritypolicy.org/2012/08/30/shariah-law-and-american-state-courts/.
Chancellor, James, and Jeffery Wasserman. "The Religions of the Middle East: Islam and Judaism." In *Missiology: An Introduction to the Foundations, History, and Strategies of World Missions*, edited by John Mark Terry, Ebbie Smith, and Justice Anderson, 379–92. Nashville, TN: Broadman & Holman, 1998.
Chandler, Charles R., and Yung-mei Tsai. "Social Factors Influencing Immigration Attitudes: An Analysis of Data from the General Social Survey." *Social Science Journal* 38, no. 2 (2001) 177–88.
Christie, Jeanne. "The Value of the Narrative: The Story We Tell Becomes Our Narrative." *Psychology Today*, November 15, 2010. https://www.psychologytoday.com/us/blog/whats-your-script/201011/the-value-the-narrative.

Creech, Mark. "There, I Said It: Islam Is the Enemy." *One News Now*, 2015. https://onenewsnow.com/perspectives/guest-commentary/2015/11/25/there-i-said-it-islam-is-the-enemy.
Curtis, Heather D. *Holy Humanitarians: American Evangelicals and Global Aid*. Cambridge, MA: Harvard University Press, 2018.
Curzan, Anne. "Rhetoric: Positive, Negative, or Both?" Michigan Radio Newsroom, University of Michigan, Ann Arbor, MI, July 28, 2013.
Davis, Kenneth C. "America's True History of Religious Tolerance." *Smithsonian Magazine*, October 2010.
Denney, H. Ted, Jr. "Relationships between Religion and Prejudice: Implicit and Explicit Measures." Psychology thesis, Georgia State University, 2008.
Derrick, J. C. "ERLC Panel Denounces Anti-Muslim Policies." *WORLD*, December 10, 2015. https://world.wng.org/2015/12/eric_panel_denounces_anti_muslim_policies.
Dowd, Robert A. *Christianity, Islam, and Liberal Democracy*. Oxford: Oxford University Press, 2015.
Downey, Michael. *Understanding Christian Spirituality*. Mahwah, NJ: Paulist, 1997.
Dryer, Elizabeth A., and Mark S. Burrows. *Minding the Spirit: The Study of Christian Spirituality*. Baltimore, MD: Johns Hopkins University Press, 2005.
Dustmann, Christian, and Ian P. Preston. "Racial and Economic Factors in Attitudes to Immigration." *B.E. Journal of Economic Analysis & Policy* 7, no. 1 (2007) 1–41.
Dworkin, Ronald. *Law's Empire*. Cambridge, MA: Belknap Press of Harvard University Press, 1986.
Ekman, Paul. "Universal Emotions: What Is Fear?" April 1, 2016. https://www.paulekman.com/universal-emotions/what-is-fear/.
Endicott, Timothy A. O. "Putting Interpretation in Its Place." *Law and Philosophy* 13, no. 4 (1994) 451–79.
Espiritu, Belinda F. "Negative Media Portrayal of Islam." *WACC*, May 15, 2016. www.waccglobal.org/articles/negative-media-portrayal-of-islam.
"Fast Facts about the SBC." June 16, 2018. http://www.sbc.net/BecomingSouthernBaptist/FastFacts.asp.
Fatoohi, Louay. "One Night in a Cave That Changed History Forever." https://www.louayfatoohi.com/quran/one-night-in-a-cave-that-changed-history-forever/.
Fitzpatrick, Coeli, and Adam Hani Walker, eds. *Muhammad in History, Thought, and Culture: An Encyclopedia of the Prophet of God*. Oxford: ABC-CLIO, 2014.
Ford, Robert. "Acceptable and Unacceptable Immigrants: How Opposition to Immigration in Britain Is Affected by Migrants' Region of Origin." *Journal of Ethnic and Migration Studies* 37, no. 7 (2011) 1017–37.
Foundation for Ethnic Understanding. "Survey of U.S. Evangelical Christians & Muslims Shows Great Divide between Groups." March 27, 2009. https://ffeu.org/press-releases/ffeu-survey-of-u-s-evangelical-christians-muslims-shows-great-divide-between-groups/.
Freeland, Lori. "Why Christians Should Show Less Sympathy and More Empathy." *Crosswalk.com*, February 18, 2016. https://www.crosswalk.com/faith/spiritual-life/why-christians-should-show-less-sympathy-and-more-empathy.html.
Friedman, Thomas. "Thinking about Iraq." *New York Times*, January 22, 2003, A21.
Fries, Micah, and Keith Whitfield, eds. *Islam and North America: Loving Our Muslim Neighbors*. Nashville, TN: B&H Academic, 2018.

Gallup. "Islamophobia: Understanding Anti-Muslim Sentiment in the West." http://www.gallup.com/poll/157082/islamophobia-understanding-anti-muslim-sentiment-west.aspx.

Gallup. "Most Muslim Americans See No Justification for Violence." https://news.gallup.com/poll/148763/muslim-americans-no-justification-violence.aspx

Gallups, Carl. Southern Baptist Convention speech, June 6, 2016.

GhaneaBassini, Kambiz. *A History of Islam in America*. Cambridge: Cambridge University Press, 2010.

Glazier, Rebecca. "For God or Country? Comparing the Sources of Anti-American Muslim Attitudes." *Islam and Christian Muslim Relations Journal*, March 15, 2016, 153–74. http://www.tandfonline.com.proxy.library.nd.edu/doi/full/10.1080/09596410.2016.1142762?scr 011=top&needAccess=true.

Glenn, Patrick, H. *Legal Traditions of the World: Sustainable Diversity in Law*. Oxford: Oxford University Press, 2010.

Goddard, Hugh. *A History of Christian-Muslim Relations*. Chicago: New Amsterdam Books, 2000.

Greenwood, Shannon. "A Demographic of Muslim Americans." Pew Research Center for the People and the Press, August 29, 2011. www.people-press.org/2011/08/30/section-1-a-demographic-portrait-of-muslim-americans/.

Habeck, Mary. "Knowing the Enemy: Jihadist Ideology and the War on Terror." Seminar, February 15, 2006. http://web.mit.edu/ssp/seminars/wed_archives06spring/habeck.html.

Habib, Samara. "Islamophobia Is on the Rise in the US. But So Is Islam." *Public Radio International*, September 9, 2016. www.pri.org/stories/2016-09-09/muslims-america-are-keeping-and-growing-faith-even-though-haters-tell-them-not.

Hackman, J. Richard, and Neil Vidmar. "Effects of Size and Task Type on Group Performance and Member Reactions." *Sociometry* 33, no. 1 (Mar. 1970) 37–54.

Hainmueller, Jens, and Dominik Hangartner. "Who Gets a Swiss Passport? A Natural Experiment in Immigrant Discrimination." *American Political Science Review* 107, no. 1 (2013) 159–87.

Hainmueller, Jens, and Michael J. Hiscox. "Attitudes toward Highly Skilled and Low-Skilled Immigration: Evidence from a Survey Experiment." *American Political Science Review* 104, no. 1 (2010) 61–84.

Haji Adnan, Mohd Hamdan. "Mass Media and Reporting Islamic Affairs." *Media Asia* 16, no. 2 (1989) 63–70.

Hallowell, Beth. "Mixed Media: How the Media Covers 'Violent Extremism' and What You Can Do about It." American Friends Service Committee. 2016.

Hefner, Robert W., ed. *Shari'a Law and Modern Muslim Ethics*. Bloomington: Indiana University Press, 2016.

Henry, Patrick. Speech, Second Virginia Convention. St. John's Church, Richmond, VA, March 23, 1775.

Hobbs, Herschel H. *The Baptist Faith and Message*. Nashville, TN: Convention, 1971.

Hodge, David R., et al. "Correlates of Self-Rated Health among Muslims in the United States." *Families in Society Journal*, May 27, 2015.

Hoffman, Martin. *Empathy and Moral Development: Implications for Caring and Justice*. Cambridge: Cambridge University Press, 2000.

Hooper, Ibrahim. "Muslims and Christians: More in Common than You Think." *Islamicity*, April 14, 2016. https://www.islamicity.org/6404/muslim-and-christians-more-in-common-than-you-think/.

Hoover, Dennis R. "Is Evangelicalism Itching for a Civilization Fight? A Media Study." *Brandywine Review of Faith & International Affairs* 2, no. 1 (2004) 11–16.

Ibrahim, Ayman S. "Muslim Scholars vs. Isis: Is the Open Letter to the Islamic State Really Enough?" *First Things*, 2014. http://www.firstthings.com/web-exclusives/2014/10/is-the-muslim-scholars-open-letter-to-isis-really-enough.

Islam Awareness Homepage. "Types of Jihad." http://islamawareness.net/jihad/types_jihad.html.

Jasmin, Sayyid Muhammed. "The Marriage of Prophet Muhammed (PBUH) to Aisha (RA): Discrediting Accusations of Child Marriage and Pedophilia." *Al Jumuah*, August 28, 2021. https://www.aljumuah.com/the-marriage-of-prophet-muhammed-pbuh-to-aisha-ra-discrediting-accusations-of-child-marriage-and-pedophilia/.

Jeffress, Robert James. Sermon, First Baptist Church, Dallas, TX, August 23, 2010. https://www.youtube.com/watch?v=wfb9p3qSRqA.

Johnson, Jenna, and Abigail Hauslohner. "'I Think Islam Hates Us': A Timeline of Trump's Comments about Islam and Muslims." *Washington Post*, May 20, 2017.

Johnson, Scott, ed. *The Oxford Handbook of Late Antiquity*. Oxford: Oxford University Press, 2012.

Jones, Jim. "Baptist Pastor's Words Shock Muslim Leaders." Special to the Star-Telegram, 2016. https://www.islamawareness.net/Islamophobia/islamophobia_news0005.html.

Kabbani, Muhammad Hisham, and Seraj Hendricks. "Jihad: A Misunderstood Concept from Islam: What Jihad Is, and Is Not." http://www.islamicsupremecouncil.org/understanding-islam-/legal-rulings/5-jihad-a-misunderstood-concept-from-islam.html?start=9.

Kathir, Ibn. *Bidaya wa-al-Nihaya*. Volume 8.

Kearns, Erin M. "Why Do Some Terrorist Attacks Receive More Media Coverage than Others?" *Justice Quarterly* 36, no. 6 (2019) 985–1022.

Keen, Suzanne. *Empathy and the Novel*. Oxford: Oxford University Press, 2007.

Keen, Suzanne. "A Theory of Narrative Empathy." *Narrative* 14, no. 3 (2006) 207–36. https://muse.jhu.edu/article/201625.

Kelen, Betty. *Muhammad the Messenger of God*. Nashville, TN: Thomas Nelson, 1975.

Kinder, Donald R., and Cindy D. Kam. *Us against Them: Ethnocentric Foundations of America Opinion*. Chicago: University of Chicago Press, 2010.

Kurzman, Charles. "Muslim-American Terrorism Since 9/11: An Accounting." Triangle Center on Terrorism and Homeland Security, Chapel Hill, NC, 2011. http://sanford.duke.edu/centers/tcths/about/documents/kurzman_Muslim-American_Terrorism_Since_911_An_Accounting.pdf.

Langer, Gary. "Poll: Most Americans Say They're Christian." ABC News, July 18, 2017. http://abcnews.go.com/US/story?id=90356&page=1.

Lings, Martin. *Muhammad: His Life Based on the Earliest Sources*. New York: Inner Traditions International, 1983.

Marcum, John. "Trends and Changes in Mainline Denominations." Annual meeting of the Religious Research Association, Salt Lake City, UT, November 2002.

Markoe, Lauren. "Muslim Scholars Release Open Letter to Islamic States Meticulously Blasting Its Ideology." *Huffington Post*, September 25, 2014. https://www.huffingtonpost.com/2014/09/24/muslim-scholars-islamic-state_n_5878038.html.

Marmor, Andrei. *Interpretation and Legal Theory*. 2nd ed. Portland, OR: Hart, 2005.

Mattingly, Terry. "Wait a Minute! What Did Southern Baptists Say about Religious Liberty for Muslims?" *Get Religion*, June 16, 2016. https://www.getreligion.org/getreligion/2016/6/16/wait-a-minute-what-did-southern-baptists-say-about-religious-liberty-for-muslims.

McAlister, Melani. *The Kingdom of God Has No Borders: A Global History of American Evangelicals*. Oxford: Oxford University Press, 2018.

McBeth, Leon. *The Baptist Heritage: Four Centuries of Baptist Witness*. Nashville, TN: Broadman, 1987.

McCammon, Sarah. "Southern Baptists Split with Donald Trump on Refugee Resettlement." *NPR Politics*, June 16, 2016. https://www.npr.org//2016/06/16/482268688/southern-baptists-split-with-trump-on-refugee-resettlement.

McCormack, Michael. "Study Updates Stats on Health of Southern Baptist Churches." *Baptist Press*, November 15, 2004. http://www.bpnews.net/19542/study-updates-stats-on-health-of-southern-baptist-churches.

"Media Portrayals of Religion: Islam." *MediaSmarts*. http://mediasmarts.ca/diversity-media/religion.media-portrayals-religion-islam, accessed March 26, 2018.

Miller, David. *God at Work*. Oxford: Oxford University Press, 2007.

Miller, Steven V. "Economic Anxiety or Ethnocentrism? An Evaluation of Attitudes towards Immigration in the U.S. from 1992 to 2017." *Social Science Journal*, 2020.

Mohamed, Besheer. "A New Estimate of the U.S. Muslim Population." Pew Research, January 6, 2016. http://www.pewresearch.org/fact-tank/2016/01/06/a-new-estimate-of-the-u-s-muslim-population/.

Mohler, R. Albert, Jr. "Don't Just Support Missions. Do Missions." November 1, 2018. https://www.imb.org/2018/11/01/support-do-missions-albert-mohler/.

Montefiore, Simon Sebag. *Jerusalem: The Biography*. New York: Vintage Books, 2012.

Moten, Abdul Rashid, and Noraini M. Noor, eds. *Terrorism, Democracy: The West & the Muslim World*. Singapore: Thomson Learning, 2007.

Mufti, Kamil. "Core Values of Islam." *IslamReligion.com*, May 27, 2013. https://www.islamreligion.com/articles/10256/core-values-of-islam/.

Nacos, Brigitte L., Yaeli Block-Elkon, and Robert Y. Shapiro. *Selling Fear: Counterterrorism, the Media, and Public Opinion*. Chicago: University of Chicago Press, 2011.

Nargul, Veysel. "What Are the Purposes of Wars That Prophet Muhammad (PBUH) Fought?" *Questions on Islam*, September 19, 2018. https://questionsonislam.com/article/what-are-purposes-wars-prophet-muhammad-pbuh-fought.

Nell, Victor. *Lost in a Book: The Psychology of Reading for Pleasure*. New Haven, CT: Yale University Press, 1988.

Obama, Barack. United Nations General Assembly speech, September 2014.

Ochs, Peter. *Religion without Violence: The Practice and Philosophy of Scriptural Reasoning*. Eugene, OR: Cascade Books, 2019.

Ogan, Christine. "The Rise of Anti-Muslim Prejudice: Media and Islamophobia in Europe and the United States." *International Communication Gazette* 76, no. 1 (February 2014) 27–43.

Omar, A. Rashied. *Islam beyond Violent Extremism*. Durban: Afrika Impressions Media, 2017.

Osmer, Richard R. *Practical Theology: An Introduction*. Grand Rapids, MI: Eerdmans, 2008.
Oxford Dictionary of Islam. http://www.oxfordislamicstudies.com/article/opr/t125/e1577.
Park, Haeyoun, and Larry Buchavan. "Refugees Entering the U.S. Already Face a Rigorous Vetting Process." *New York Times*, January 29, 2017. https://www.nytimes.com/interactive/2017/01/29/us/refugee-vetting-process.html.
"Pastor to Southern Baptist Convention: Stop Push for Muslim Refugees." *WND*, June 17, 2006. http://www.wnd.com/2016/06/pastor-to-southern-baptist-convention-stop-push-for-muslim-refugees/.
Pew Research Center. "Demographic Portrait of Muslim Americans." July 26, 2017. http://www.pewforum.org/2017/0/26/demographic-portrait-of-muslim-americans/.
Pew Research Center. "Demographics and Political Views of News Audiences." September 27, 2012. http://www.people-press.org/2012/09/27/section-4-demographics-and-political-views-of-news-audiences/.
Pew Research Center. "The Future of World Religions: Population Growth Projections, 2010–2050." http://www.pewforum.org/2015/04/02/religious-projections-2010-2050/.
Pew Research Center. "How the Faithful Voted: A Preliminary 2016 Analysis." https://www.pewresearch.org/short-reads/2016/11/09/how-the-faithful-voted-a-preliminary-2016-analysis/.
Pew Research Center. "Muslim Americans: No Signs of Growth in Alienation or Support for Extremism." https://www.pewresearch.org/politics/2011/08/30/section-1-a-demographic-portrait-of-muslim-americans/.
Pew Research Center, "In Nations with Significant Muslim Populations, Much Disdain for ISIS." https://www.pewresearch.org/short-reads/2015/11/17/in-nations-with-significant-muslim-populations-much-disdain-for-isis/.
Pew Research Center. "Political Ideology among Members of the Southern Baptist Convention by Political Party." http://www.pewforum.org/religious-landscape-study/compare/political-ideology/by/party-affiliation/among/religious-denomination/southern-baptist-convention/.
Parshall, Phil. *New Paths in Muslim Evangelism: Evangelical Approaches to Contextualization*. Grand Rapids, MI: Baker House, 1984.
Piper, John. "Love Your Neighbor as Yourself, Part I." *Desiring God*, April 30, 1995. https://www.desiringgod.org/messages/love-your-neighbor-as-yourself-part-1.
Pratt, D., and R. Woodlock, eds. *Fear of Muslims? International Perspectives on Islamophobia*. Switzerland: Springer International, 2016.
Pratt, Richard H. "The Advantages of Mingling Indians with Whites." In *Official Report of the Nineteenth Annual Conference of Charities and Correction* (1892), 46–59. Reprinted in *Americanizing the American Indians: Writings by the "Friends of the Indian," 1880–1900*, edited by Francis Paul Prucha, 260–71. Cambridge, MA: Harvard University Press, 1973.
Quraishi-Landes, Asifa. "Five Myths about Sharia." *Washington Post*, June 24, 2016. https://www.washingtonpost.com/opinions/five-myths-about-sharia/2016/06/24/7e3efb7a-31ef-11e6-8758-d58e76e11b12_story.html.
Quinn, Robert. *Deep Change*. San Francisco: Jossey-Bass, 1996.

Raz, Joseph. "The Relevance of Coherence." *Boston University Law Review* 72, no. 2 (1992) 273–321.

Rizvi, Sayyid Muhammad. "The Concept of Polygamy and the Prophet's Marriages." September 21, 2018. https://www.al-islam.org/articles/concept-polygamy-and-prophets-marriages-sayyid-muhammad-rizvi.

———. "Peace and Jihad in Islam." http://www.al-islam.org/articles/peace-and-jihad-islam-sayyid-muhammad-rizvi.

Rogers, Fred McFeely. https://www.misterrogers.org/articles/he-helped-us-with-our-relationships-with-others/.

Rokeach, Milton. *The Nature of Human Values*. New York: Free Press, 1973.

Rooney, Francis. *The Global Vatican*. Lanham, MD: Rowman & Littlefield, 2013.

Royal Aal al-Bayt Institute for Islamic Thought. "A Common Word between Us and You." Jordan, 2009.

Runnymede Trust Commission on British Muslims and Islamophobia. *Islamophobia: A Challenge for Us All*. London: Runnymede Trust, 1997.

Rytkonen, Aaro. "Interreligious Encounters & Cultural Immersions." Al Amana Centre website, https://alamanacentre.org/what-we-provide/, accessed October 16, 2018.

Saalih al-Munajjid, Muhammad. "Meaning of the Word Islam." 2007. https://islamqa.info/en/10446.

Sachs, Susan. "Baptist Pastor Attacks Islam, Inciting Cries of Intolerance." *New York Times*, June 15, 2002.

Sadooq, Sheikh. *Uyun Akhbar Al Reza*. Vol. 1. Lulu Press, 2014.

Said, Edward W. *Covering Islam: How the Media and the Experts Determine How We See the Rest of the World*. New York: Knopf, 1996.

Saleem, Muniba. "Spreading Islamophobia: Consequences of Negative Media Representations." *Huffington Post*, April 24, 2017. www.huffingtonpost.com/entry/spreading-islamophobia-consequences-of-negative-media-representations_us_58fe682de4b06b9cb91963fb.

Scarboro Missions. "Principles and Guidelines for Interfaith Dialogue." https://www.scarboromissions.ca/interfaith-dialogue/principles-and-guidlines-for-interfaith-dialogue.

Schimmel, Annemarie. *And Muhammad Is His Messenger: The Veneration of the Prophet in Islamic Piety*. Chapel Hill: University of North Carolina Press, 1985.

Schneider, Ralf. "Toward a Cognitive Theory of Literary Character: The Dynamics of Mental-Model Construction." *Style* 35 (2001) 607–42.

Schoeler, Gregor. *The Biography of Muhammad: Nature and Authenticity*. Translated by Uwe Vagelpohl. New York: Routledge, 2011.

Schwartz, Shalom H. "Basic Human Values: An Overview." *Online Readings in Psychology and Culture*, 2012. https://scholarworks.gvsu.edu/cgi/viewcontent.cgi?article=1116&context=orpc.

Seltzer, Leon F. "What Your Anger May Be Hiding." *Psychology Today*, July 11, 2008. https://www.psychologytoday.com/us/blog/evolution-the-self/200807/what-your-anger-may-be-hiding.

Shellnut, Kate. "Most White Evangelicals Don't Believe Muslims Belong in America." *Christianity Today*, July 2017. https://www.christianitytoday.com/news/2017/july/pew-how-white-evangelicals-view-us-muslims-islam.html.

Siddique, Sharon. "Conceptualizing Patterns and Civilizing Processes." *International Sociology* 16 (2001).

Singer, Tania, et al. "Empathy for Pain Involves the Affective but Not Sensory Components of Pain." *Science* 303 (2004) 1157–62.
Stanley, Charles F. *Every Day in His Presence: 365 Devotions*. Nashville, TN: Thomas Nelson, 2014.
———. "The Side Effects of Fear." *InTouch Ministries*, August 7, 2015. https://www.intouch.org/read/magazine/daily-devotions/the-side-effects-of-fear.
Stosny, Steven. "The Primacy of Anger Problems." *Psychology Today*, January 18, 2009. https://www.psychologytoday.com/us/blog/evil-deeds/200901/the-primacy-anger-problems.
Stossel, John, and N. Jaquez. "The 'Fear Industrial Complex.'" *ABC News*, April 28, 2007. http://abcnews.go.com/m/story?id=2898636.
Strode, Tom. "Protestants Remain Majority Group in Congress." *Baptist Press*. https://www.baptistpress.com/resource-libraryy/news/protestants-remain-majority-group-in-congress/.
Symes, Copinger. "Is Osama bin Laden's Fatwa Urging Jihad against Americans Dated 23 February 1998 Justified by Islamic Law?" *Defense Studies* 3 (2003) 44–65.
Terry, John Mark, Ebbie Smith, and Justice Anderson, eds. *Missiology: An Introduction to the Foundations, History, and Strategies of World Missions*. Nashville, TN: Broadman & Holman, 1998.
Townsley, Jeremy. "Marx, Weber and Durkheim on Religion." PhD dissertation, 2004. http://www.jeramyt.org/papers/sociology-of-religion.html.
Tsausides, Theo. "7 Things You Need to Know about Fear." *Psychology Today*, November 19, 2015. https://www.psychologytoday.com/us/blog/smashing-the-brainblocks/201511/7-things-you-need-know-about-fear.
Uddin, Asma T. *The Politics of Vulnerability*. New York: Simon & Schuster, 2021.
Vitali, Ali. "In His Words: Donald Trump on the Muslim Ban, Deportations." *NBC News*, June 27, 2016. https://www.nbcnews.com/politics/2016-election/his-words-donald-trump-muslim-ban-deportations-n599901.
Weaver, Aaron D. "Baptist in the 111th Congress." *Intersection of Religion and Politics*. http://www.thebigdaddyweave.com/baptists-in-the-111th-congress.
Weber, Max. *The Sociology of Religion*. Translated by Ephraim Fischoff. Boston: Beacon, 1963.
Welch, Bobby. Report to the SBC Executive Committee, September 20, 2004.
"What Causes Fear?" April 1, 2016. https://www.effective-mind-control.com/what-causes-fear.html.
Williams, Jennifer. "White American Men Are a Bigger Domestic Terrorist Threat than Muslim Foreigners." *Vox*, October 2, 2017. https://www.vox.com/world/2017/10/2/16396612/las-vegas-mass-shooting-terrorism-islam.
Withrow, Brandon. "Is There a Christian Double Standard on Religious Violence?" *Daily Beast*, March 5, 2017. https://www.thedailybeast.com/is-there-a-christian-double-standard-on-religious-violence.
Wolfe, Michael. "Muslim Business Entrepreneurs and the American Economy." *Huffington Post*, March 28, 2016. www.huffingtonpost.com/michael-wolfe/muslim- biz-entrepreneurs-_b_9548540.html.
Yan, Holly. Fierce Backlash over Trump's Plan to Ban Muslims." *CNN*, December 9, 2015. http://www.cnn.com/2015/12/08/us/muslims-in-america-shattering-misperception/.

www.ingramcontent.com/pod-product-compliance
Lightning Source LLC
Chambersburg PA
CBHW062019220426
43662CB00010B/1400